INTO A
LIGHT BOTH
BRILLIANT
AND UNSEEN

INTO A LIGHT BOTH BRILLIANT AND UNSEEN

Conversations with Contemporary Black Poets

Interviews conducted and edited by Malin Pereira

The University of Georgia Press | Athens and London

A Sarah Mills Hodge Fund Publication

This publication is made possible in part through a grant from the Hodge Foundation in memory of its founder, Sarah Mills Hodge, who devoted her life to the relief and education of African Americans in Savannah, Georgia.

"Rita Dove" is a revised version of "An Interview with Rita Dove," originally published in *Contemporary Literature* 40.2 (Summer 1999). © 1999 by the Board of Regents of the University of Wisconsin System. Reproduced courtesy of the University of Wisconsin Press.

"Cyrus Cassells" is a revised version of "An Interview with Cyrus Cassells," originally published in *Contemporary Literature* 44.3 (Fall 2003). © 2003 by the Board of Regents of the University of Wisconsin System. Reproduced courtesy of the University of Wisconsin Press.

© 2010 by the University of Georgia Press
Athens, Georgia 30602
www.ugapress.org
Based on cover design by Cynthia Tringali
Set in Garamond PremierPro by Copperline Book Services, Inc.

Printed digitally in the United States of America

Library of Congress Cataloging-in-Publication Data
Pereira, Malin.
    Into a light both brilliant and unseen : conversations with contemporary Black poets / interviews conducted and edited by Malin Pereira.
        p. cm.
    Includes bibliographical references.
    ISBN-13: 978-0-8203-3107-2 (cloth : alk. paper)
    ISBN-10: 0-8203-3107-4 (cloth : alk. paper)
    ISBN-13: 978-0-8203-3713-5 (pbk. : alk. paper)
    ISBN-10: 0-8203-3713-7 (pbk. : alk. paper)
        1. American poetry — African American authors — History and criticism.
    2. American poetry — 21st century — History and criticism.   3. African
    Americans — Intellectual life — 20th century.   4. African American poets —
    Interviews.   I. Title.
    PS310.N4P46   2010
    811'.509896073 — dc22   2010018452

British Library Cataloging-in-Publication Data available

Contents

ACKNOWLEDGMENTS

A community of scholars, poets, and friends has helped this book become a reality. Jeff Leak was a constant support and open ear, ever ready with helpful suggestions. Deborah Bosley proved herself an able travel agent and companion for the Cave Canem tenth anniversary celebration in New York. Cyrus Cassells made certain I was invited to the party, and Cornelius Eady gave me almost two hours of his time there. Wanda Coleman trusted me based on an incendiary and exhilarating moment at Davidson College. Thylias Moss stuck with me through our mutual challenges over more than a year. Joanne Gabbin was a ready support and advocate, as was Henry Louis Gates Jr. Rita Dove and Elizabeth Alexander welcomed me into their homes and family lives, however briefly, and kept up with me afterward. Harryette Mullen was responsive, efficient, and on task! Yusef Komunyakaa shared with me two intense hours in his office in the beautiful Lillian Vernon Creative Writers House at NYU. John Gruesser and Daniel Shealy listened and sagely counseled throughout the decade it took to do this work, and Tony Jackson helped me realize that this would be an ideal project for me. Shanna Benjamin, Herman Beavers, Jennifer Ryan, Ivy Wilson, Lynn Keller, and Meta Jones offered me opportune and exciting conversations at important junctures. Many thanks to my editors at the University of Georgia Press — Andrew Berzanskis and Erika Stevens — who found great readers for the project at the proposal and manuscript stages, readers who helped this book become what it needed to be. Spokenword poet, actor, and black-theater producer Quentin Talley has enriched Charlotte — and me — more than he could know. The Sangati community nurtures me every week. Elizabeth Mills, as both a poetry scholar and an English department chair, has been a fellow traveler and good friend on our shared road, and helped create opportunities for me to meet poets such as Coleman. Meredith Green and Lesley Brown are "friend[s] of my mind."

At UNC Charlotte, the staff in the Africana Studies and English departments, most especially Elsie Byrd, David Landrum, Jennie Mussington, Monica Alston, and Angie Williams, provided administrative backup as well as satisfying conversations across several years of this work. My dean,

Nancy Gutierrez, understood the necessity of my continuing scholarship despite my role as a department chair; more importantly, she backed it financially. The interviews with Alexander, Cassells, Moss, Mullen, Eady, and Komunyakaa were each supported in various ways by UNC Charlotte and the College of Liberal Arts and Sciences; the interview with Coleman and the transcription of Alexander's interview were supported by the UNC General Administration Undergraduate Research Initiative. Students Jennifer Larsen, Jennifer Rivers, and Julie Mayes each logged in hours of time transcribing, copying, getting books and articles, and keeping me organized. Julie Mayes's assistance with editing made the final year highly productive, and this book's completion possible. I am deeply appreciative of her commitment to this project. Many of my students over these years have been coresearchers in the classroom with me as I engaged these poets and their work. Thanks to Mary Frances Jiménez, Ilona Cesan, Cedric Tillman, Miesha Rice, Veronica Jones, Demetrius Noble, Solomon Franklin, Heidi Bergman, Jennifer Williams, Danielle Weber, Tiffany Morin, Fran Voltz, Lauren Benjamin, Tamara Turner, Abdul Green, Rachel Brown, and Clarita Kornegay for their open minds and insightful contributions.

My family, as always, is both a part of the work and apart from the work, in all the ways that make life satisfying and complicated. My husband, Ernest, and sons Cameron, Blake, and Julian, all have enriched this book while also tugging me away from it repeatedly. My father and stepmother, Milton and Jewell Goodman; my mother, Marta McElroy Goodman; and my brother, Grant Goodman, have patiently and with genuine interest listened to me talk about this project for years.

None of this would have been possible or worth doing without the creative and intellectual riches of African American poetry, a home in which I have been made to feel a welcome guest.

Into a
Light both
Brilliant
and Unseen

WALKING INTO THE LIGHT

Contemporary Black Poetry, Traditions, and the Individual Talent

1. Walking (1963)

after the painting by Charles Alston

You tell me, knees are important, you kiss
your elders' knees in utmost reverence.

The knees in this painting are what send the people forward.

Once progress felt real and inevitable,
as sure as the taste of licorice or lemons.
The painting was made after marching
in Birmingham, walking

into a light both brilliant and unseen.
— from "Fugue," in Elizabeth Alexander's
    Antebellum Dream Book

This collection of eight substantial conversations with black poets, all born after World War II and comprising the generation following the Black Arts Movement of the 1960s and 1970s, offers readers — scholars, students, and a public interested in poetry — insight into the wide span of cultural and aesthetic concerns in black poetry today. The book's title, from Elizabeth Alexander's poem "Walking," marks the collection's generational focus: this is the first book of interviews published featuring the post–Black Arts Movement generation of contemporary poets. Concentrating on poets born between 1945 and 1965 whose poetry came into prominence during the 1980s and 1990s, this collection includes many of the most compelling and diverse voices of this generation: Wanda Coleman, Yusef Komunyakaa, Rita Dove, Thylias Moss, Harryette Mullen, Cornelius Eady, Cyrus Cassells, and Elizabeth Alexander. All of these poets are included because of their significant number of publications (at least four books of poetry), distinctive voices, range of cultural and aesthetic perspectives, awards of merit, and influence on emerging poets in younger generations.

One emerging poet, Kevin Young, remarked in his 1999 review of Komunyakaa's *Thieves of Paradise* that this generation often is "lost in the wake of the Black Arts sea change of the 1960s. Though that decade's black aesthetic (along with the Harlem renaissance of the 1920s) helped make these poets possible, their work does not fit the aesthetic's often strict parameters" (par. 1). Although, in the decade since he wrote this, many of these poets have been discovered both by literary critics and by a public increasingly interested in contemporary African American poetry, his identification of theirs as a distinct generation moving beyond the Black Arts Movement remains important to both literary history and our understanding of poetry today.

The work produced by these poets demonstrates a wide diversity of themes, aesthetics, and influences. As Young describes it, this generation has combined matters of "form and funk, . . . classicism and contemporary concerns" (par. 1). Far from the proscriptive manifestos of the previous generation's Black Arts Movement (approximately 1964–75), the generation of African American poets publishing in the 1980s and 1990s overtly constructs itself as highly inclusive of a range of voices, perspectives, and techniques. Unlike Amiri Baraka's claim in "Home" that he becomes blacker and blacker, positioning race as a determinative home or essence, the main voices of this generation imagine a plurality of homes and ideas about the relationship between blackness and poetry.

Rita Dove, for example, one of the generation's first poets to confront Black Arts Movement dominance, employs in her poetry birds, snails, ships, and other such tropes of movement to enable a less constrictive and more fluid understanding of the black poet. Likewise, Cyrus Cassells sets his poems across several continents and cultures, combining dictions and themes from European tradition, popular culture, world history, and specifically African American experience. Cornelius Eady and Elizabeth Alexander demonstrate how the mobility of the modern black subject has contributed to enlarging what Alexander terms the "stately mansion" of black identity, both individually and collectively. Eady's and Alexander's works reject narrow definitions of blackness — either imposed by white popular imagination or promulgated by black ideologies of African American identity — and counterpoint them with explorations of a wide-ranging and complex interiority that retains blackness as an inseparable component.

All the poets likewise abjure narrow definitions of black poetics. Two institutions of the period, Cave Canem (a summer poets' workshop begun in 1996 by Toi Derricotte and Cornelius Eady) and Furious Flower (conferences organized in 1994 and 2004 by Joanne Gabbin), emphasize inclusivity and diversity of aesthetics and techniques. Cave Canem, tellingly, calls itself "a home for black poetry"—not *the* home—thereby acknowledging and promoting a multiplicity of sites and poetics. Interviewed during Cave Canem's tenth anniversary celebration, Eady expressly asserts that one of his and Derricotte's goals in selecting faculty has been to feature diverse voices and poetics.

Not coincidently, the 1980s and 1990s have seen a rewriting of our understanding of the Black Arts Movement and the African American poetic tradition. Critics such as Aldon Lynn Nielsen have excavated an experimentalist, postmodern thread heretofore insufficiently examined, countering notions of the aesthetic uniformity of poetry written during the 1960s and 1970s. Harryette Mullen has called for more attention to the graphic (written and print) elements in the African American poetic tradition, arguing against the dominance of criticism that emphasizes the oral tradition. Individual studies of the preceding generation's poets Audre Lorde, Lucille Clifton, and Clarence Major have articulated their work as occurring concomitantly, yet not always thematically or aesthetically aligned with, Black Arts doctrines. Oftentimes, such revisionist, expansionist definitions of periods and traditions are sparked by their relationship to the literature that follows, for when critics cannot identify a connection between their contemporary literature and the tradition from which it is purportedly produced, they must reconsider the accuracy of the prevailing characterizations of that tradition. Thus poets in this generation have taken it upon themselves to contribute to our critical understanding of their forebears, commenting on Melvin B. Tolson, Gwendolyn Brooks, Amiri Baraka, and Robert Hayden, among others. In so doing, they trace for us the threads of the tradition that lead to their work.

Some of these poets refuse or resist the influence of the African American literary or poetic tradition altogether, Wanda Coleman most prominently. As she explains in her interview, academic constructions of the black literary tradition were nascent in her early childhood and not widely promulgated on the West Coast during her early adult years. Profoundly skeptical about critical schemas of tradition and influence that can be deployed as political tools to enfranchise some writers and ignore others,

Coleman's experience of coming of age as a poet outside of a strong sense of a black poetic tradition provides an instructive and important alternative to our received notions about the interrelations of race, tradition, and poetics. Coleman's and Eady's works draw upon black musical traditions and aesthetics more than from the black literary canon.

The literary precursors Coleman claims for herself are all white poets; she, along with most of the other poets herein, would acknowledge the usefulness of Ralph Ellison's distinction between literary ancestors (those who influence an author's writing) and literary relatives (those with whom a writer might be grouped due to perceived common circumstances such as race, region, or time period). Rather than re-inscribing the "aesthetic apartheid" Mullen attacks in her essay "Poetry and Identity," this project seeks to place African American poets and their poetry within both black-identified literary traditions and the larger national and world canons in which they situate themselves. Both Alexander and Coleman have poems dedicated to Sylvia Plath, for example, of whom they speak with deep respect in their interviews. Coleman, Dove, Mullen, Komunyakaa, and Cassells each, at times, draw upon white American, European, or global texts, authors, and inheritances: Coleman writing back to predominantly white American anthologies; Dove, Coleman, Mullen, and most recently Komunyakaa taking on the sonnet; and Cassells, in one collection, looking back to the tradition of the troubadours and, in another, honoring his patrilineage in Federico Garcia Lorca. This cosmopolitanism, as I have argued elsewhere, is an ongoing thread in the African American literary tradition, one that only with this generation is becoming more pronounced and perhaps better understood. Kevin Young, in his review of *Thieves of Paradise*, calls these writers "Third Stream," marking "their stance after the second black renaissance of the century as well as their relationship to the mainstream, a term Clarence Major defines in his *Juba to Jive* dictionary as 'a type of music . . . that reflects to a very noticeable degree both European and black technical experience'" (par. 1).

This book grew out of my previous book, *Rita Dove's Cosmopolitanism*. Fully understanding her work required extensive reading in her contemporaries, reading that showed me a generation of poets engaged in the very conversations I myself had been trying to demonstrate in my scholarship throughout my career. What captured me about this generation of poets is that they are quite consciously working out of the largest possible sense of

poetic tradition, one that is founded in African American cultural specific-
ity and literary traditions, yet at the same time quite at home with larger
American, European, and/or world cultures and literary traditions. In this
generation of poets, I found the third stream.

As I continued my research, I discovered that most of these poets' work
was virtually unknown. That has changed for several of them since I began
this project, but when I did the first interview, with Dove in 1998, with the
exception of Komunyakaa most of these poets were not receiving critical
attention, and Dove scholarship was only in its early stages. Poetry in gen-
eral seemed to have been shunted aside to make room for more attention to
narrative, but especially in African American literature, very few scholars
were working in poetry (a trend that I fear is continuing). I gave many
papers at conferences where I was the only person in the room who had
read the poet's work that was the subject of my paper. I began to view this
generation of poets as a treasure to be widely shared, and an important link
in the tradition that needed to be articulated. Once I had interviewed the
second and third poets, Cassells in 2001 and Alexander in 2005, I decided
that in-depth interviews of this generation needed to be pursued as a book
project.

Across the interviews, portraits emerged of how these writers have re-
solved the question first voiced by Dunbar and revoiced by many: how can
a writer be a poet and a black poet? The range of replies is fascinating and
important, as lyric poetry has often been perceived in the African American
literary tradition as a vehicle for articulations of black identity. Ultimately,
the expressions of black identity found in these pages may surpass their in-
tellectual or literary merits. The unexpected dimension of this project for
me was how personally revealing the conversations became (and not just
for the poet). As we delved further into the poetry, we always found our-
selves — what in the poet's life had prompted the poem or what in my life
had responded to the reading of the poem. The poets shared some of their
most personal hopes and fears, as well as musings on their relationships or
key events in their lives. I found myself talking with the poets about my
South African husband, motherhood, being a white woman teaching black
literature. I was astonished and deeply moved that the poets trusted me
enough to share their personal truths; I am humbled by the goodwill ex-
tended to me. Their candor offers readers eight compelling identities in the
process of navigating shifting boundaries of race, gender, class, national-

ity, and sexuality amid the ubiquitous experiences of love, loss, family, and community at the turn between the twentieth and twenty-first centuries.

The interviews are ordered by the poets' years of birth, beginning with Wanda Coleman and ending with Elizabeth Alexander. Read in order, the interviews reveal how issues such as the perceived dominance of the Black Arts Movement change across the generation. Each interview is preceded by a brief biocritical introduction, placing the poets and their work in relevant biographical, literary, cultural, and political contexts. Lists of the poet's primary works and secondary sources are included at the end of each introduction for further reading. I elected not to follow a prescribed set of common questions, preferring instead to let the unique concerns of each poet's work and career direct my questioning; at the same time, the reader will find recurring topics across the conversations.

In the course of these interviews, some patterns began to emerge, patterns that help us begin to sketch the poetic landscape of the 1980s and 1990s, in which these poets became prominent. One key feature is the national/international dimension that I've already mentioned: several poets are writing themselves into American and world literary canons to an extent far greater than preceding generations. Part of this is due to globalization and what Inderpal Grewal terms "transnational connectivities" driving literature and other cultural productions. Most of these poets, especially Coleman, Dove, Cassells, Komunyakaa, and Alexander, have been exposed to global contexts and see themselves and their poetry as part of a world conversation. National boundaries have become for the most part diminished, or at least readily traversable, and the racial boundaries in American literature have yielded to some extent to a comparativist model of increased inclusiveness, in which critical studies and course syllabi have significantly diversified. While of course African American poets have always been part of the larger literary and cultural world, national and global literary canons have all too often excluded both African American poets and their engagement with the broader canon. Today, Ellison's world-and-jug metaphor, in which there is the white world "out there" and a jug of supposedly "black experience," has been to some extent dissolved.

At the same time, the poetry of these two decades continues to pay attention to racism, stereotyping, and the politics of race. Every poet in this collection at various moments in his or her poetry examines — albeit some more often than others — the brutalities of racism and the injustices it perpetuates. This chasm in the poetic landscape has, if anything, been subject to greater scrutiny than in previous generations, perhaps in part due to key changes brought on by the Black Arts Movement, which emphasized writing to a black audience and gaining control over black publishing. This generation of poets can count upon multiple audiences, some of which are relatively well informed in racial politics; they also have access to or controlling interest in magazines, journals, and/or book publishers with the desire to publish black poets, and thus can feel free to write about racism without fear of losing their publishers.

One connecting stream in this era is the recurring attention in the poetry to key moments in history. Most of these poets have written poems or poetic sequences tied to significant events, figures, or periods from African American history. Importantly, these stand alongside pieces representing the transnationalism I identified earlier. Such historical nodes provide opportunities for the poets to reimagine their own relationships to the U.S. and its ideologies, and often serve a transitional function in their processes of self-definition as African American poets.

Also, representations of the black body and sexuality in this period have broken down barriers to expression that hindered earlier generations. A general consensus in early and mid-twentieth century writing to resist stereotypes of blacks as hypersexual jezebels and rapists of white women by maintaining decorum in black representations of the body and sexuality has been overturned in favor of an outspoken honesty about the body, sex, and sexual identities. To a person, these poets mine the poetic materials of their bodies and sexual experiences with unprecedented frankness. Of course, the entire culture has relaxed in relation to concerns about sexual expression as well; significantly, this generation has been willing to shed centuries of sexual stereotyping to move beyond what James Weldon Johnson in 1922 called (quoting Synge's remarks about Irish drama) "symbols from without" to articulate "symbols from within" (38).

One of the most striking themes in the work of this diverse generation of poets is the idea of *home*. This generation never cohered into a group or a movement, never rallied around an aesthetic or an agenda. Each of them had to find, make, or constitute a *home* for themselves, in all the dimensions of that word: a place in the post–Black Arts Movement poetic tradition, a place in the U.S. and the world post–civil rights and post–Black Power, a place for their identities as people and poets. Coleman and Komunyakaa often return to one *homeplace* (to use bell hooks's term, which connotes a space for black identity) for the setting of their poems — for Coleman it is Los Angeles, for Komunyakaa it is Bogalusa — yet also step in and out of transnational aesthetic connections. Mullen and Moss tie their poetry to theoretical abstractions, texts, and experimental aesthetics, Mullen in language and Moss, in her most recent work, in a conceptual matrix transcending any one medium. Coleman, Komunyakaa, and Eady write poetry that often emerges from a jazz and blues aesthetic home. Alexander and Eady migrate among a few, select homeplaces, including a metaphoric homeplace of blackness, while Dove and Cassells nomadically traverse the world as home, touching down upon occasion in temporary homes. Komunyakaa's most recent work is reminiscent of the later poetry of William Butler Yeats or William Carlos Williams, seeking a universal, transcendent home in literature, art, and archetypal patterns.

The epic voice, to tell a tale of the tribe, must write from a specific place. The lyric, although often atemporal and timeless, likewise produces a perspective; the place in lyric poetry is often not a literal one yet is implied by the ground from which the voice speaks. Each of these poets, by necessity, had to imagine a place from which his or her voice could speak, a home in which lyric identity — and for some, an epic griot role — could be forged. The homes produced in their work have provided the space for a wide variety of aesthetics and voices to emerge in today's younger generation. One cannot understand black poetry today and how it emerged without understanding this generation, born between 1945 and 1965, who came of age as poets in the 1980s and 1990s. My hope is that this collection of conversations honors their key role in expanding the realm of the possible in black poetry, and beyond.

WANDA COLEMAN

Wanda Coleman's productivity rivals that of Yusef Komunyakaa, with fifteen books published to date. Her career is singular among the poets of this generation in that she has accomplished it without a college education and despite innumerable financial and personal hardships. Coleman's body of work from 1977 to today tells the tale of a black woman becoming an accomplished poet without appreciable societal, institutional, or peer support. Coleman's forthright, sometimes abrasive personality has cost her, as reactions to her highly negative review of Maya Angelou's *A Song Flung Up to Heaven* for the *Los Angeles Times Book Review* in 2002 (on April 14) attest. Yet her work since the 1990s has demonstrated a mastery and sophistication that demands our attention and respect: *Mercurochrome*, the bronze medal finalist for the 2001 National Book Award, shows the poet she has made herself become.

Coleman was born in 1946 in the Watts community of Los Angeles. Her childhood was intellectually rich in the literature and ideas of the Western tradition as it was known in the 1950s, but her parents struggled financially and experienced many racist incidents. Due to her upbringing, Coleman feels very connected to Los Angeles, and today she is sometimes called Los Angeles's poet laureate. A precocious reader, she began writing during her teenage years growing up in South Central, but was unable to pursue a college education. She knew she would be a writer and took a few college courses. She joined white American deep image poet Diane Wakoski's poetry workshop in 1971. An early marriage to civil rights worker Charlie Jerome Coleman in 1964, when she was eighteen, produced two children: Anthony, in 1965, who died of complications of HIV in 1997, and Luanda, in 1967. The couple lived hand to mouth, scraping by with intermittent jobs and welfare, and struggling for survival. They divorced in 1971. Coleman married her second husband, Stephen Grant, in 1976. Her marriage with Grant ended in 1980, after the birth of her third child, Ian, in 1979. She married her third husband, poet-artist Austin Straus, in

1981. Coleman and Straus cohosted a Pacifica Radio literature program for Southern California, *The Poetry Connexion*, from 1981 to 1996. During this time, they interviewed numerous poets; Coleman describes this fifteen-year period as providing her with an intensive education in poetry because she had to prepare for the interviews by researching a wide range of poets and their work.

Coleman's poetry addresses and is fueled by black music, urban reality, poverty, racism, sexism, and a breathtaking desire to write herself into the poetic tradition. Her earlier work often focused on subjects such as the black female body, sexuality, friendship, and motherhood. Many poems evidence a gritty, urban aesthetic in which the personae of the poems or characters in stories contend with racism, poverty, and the hazards and truths of street life. With *Hand Dance* in 1993, Coleman's poetry began to evidence serious interest in challenging the literary canon, and consequently, her work garnered greater attention in national literary circles. She began writing jazz sonnets, many of which are collected in *American Sonnets* (1994). Coleman achieved significant notice with *Bathwater Wine* (1998), in which she continues her wholly original reinvention of the sonnet; it won the 1999 Lenore Marshall Prize from the Academy of American Poets. One of Coleman's most accomplished volumes, *Mercurochrome* (2001), continues her series of sonnets up to 100, and introduces a new project, "Retro Rogue Anthology," a section in which she takes on the literary canon by writing back to mostly white anthologies.

Coleman's early poetry descends from a lineage of open-form poets such as Charles Olson and strongly resembles Wakoski's in its narratively shaped landscape of images. Wakoski's trademarks — anger, repetition, and feelings of loss and betrayal — also find parallels in Coleman's poetry. She makes use of spontaneous utterance, social protest, the poet as apparent speaker (rather than more distant personae), and naturalistic depiction. Most interesting to watch unfold in Coleman's poetry is a move toward form across her body of work. Her sonnets demonstrate an increasing attention to form in her work, as do her "Retro Rogue" poems. She sees these works as black interventions in the Western literary tradition. Given her traditional education in the classics, such a return to the tradition-bound side of modernism (T. S. Eliot and the early poetry of Robert Lowell, Sylvia Plath, and Adrienne Rich) appears understandable, but it is worth noting that she moves in the opposite direction of Lowell, Plath, and Rich, from antiformalism to formal innovation. Social protest dominates all her work alongside these aesthetic and formal concerns.

Literary criticism on Coleman has been slight, with an early article on her work by Tony Magistrale in the 1980s, sustained discussion in one book chapter, and a few interviews. Kristin Cormer offers an important reading of how Coleman's early poetry creates a new Western space in order for her to speak; placing her work in the context of literature from the American West helps articulate her differences from other black poets. Coleman's jazz poetic, a very important lens for viewing her oeuvre, is the subject of one chapter in *Post-Jazz Poetics: A Social History*, by Jennifer D. Ryan. While the West and jazz are key influences on Coleman's poetic, her sonnets and "Retro Rogue" poems also deserve extended critical attention as interventions in the dominant tradition.

Although Coleman's work has attracted a popular following, she consistently has felt shut out of most of the institutionalized poetry world. Across her thirty-year career, she has won a Djerassi residency and fellowships with the NEA (1981–82) and Guggenheim (1984) foundations. As her 1984–97 letters to E. Ethelbert Miller, published in *Callaloo* and reprinted in *The Riot Inside Me* (2005), explain, she feels as if "I watch and I watch on the sidelines," working without recognition or remuneration on par with her talent and publications.

I interviewed Coleman via email after meeting her at Davidson College in the spring of 2006 when she gave a public reading. These e-mail exchanges took place from October 5, 2006, to December 28, 2006. I sent her each question, one at a time, and we sometimes added comments to questions and answers as they went back and forth. It had a conversational feel despite being in an e-mail format, and it afforded some useful distance when she got mad at me a couple of times.

Selected Works by Wanda Coleman

POETRY

Art in the Court of the Blue Fag, Black Sparrow Press, 1977.
Mad Dog Black Lady, Black Sparrow Press, 1979.
Imagoes, Black Sparrow Press, 1983.
Heavy Daughter Blues: Poems & Stories, Black Sparrow Press, 1987.
The Dicksboro Hotel & Other Travels, Ambrosia, 1989.

African Sleeping Sickness: Stories & Poems, Black Sparrow Press, 1990.
Hand Dance, Black Sparrow Press, 1993.
American Sonnets (chapbook), Woodland Pattern/Light and Dark Press,
   1994.
Bathwater Wine, Black Sparrow Press, 1998.
Mercurochrome: New Poems, Black Sparrow Press, 2001.
Ostinato Vamps, University of Pittsburgh Press, 2003.
Wanda Coleman — Greatest Hits: 1966–2003 (chapbook), Pudding
   House Press, 2004

OTHER

24 Hours in the Life of Los Angeles (with Jeff Spurrier, photo essay),
   Alfred Van Der Marck Editions, 1984.
A War of Eyes & Other Stories (short stories), Black Sparrow Press, 1988.
Native in a Strange Land: Trials and Tremors (nonfiction), Black
   Sparrow Press, 1996.
Mambo Hips & Make Believe (novel), Black Sparrow Press, 1999.
The Riot Inside Me: More Trials and Tremors (nonfiction), David R.
   Godine, 2005.
Jazz & Twelve O'Clock Tales: New Stories, David R. Godine, 2008.

MALIN PEREIRA: I'd like to hear about your sense of your development as
a poet. To me, it seems that you have moved from representing your lived
experience — and that of a community in Los Angeles — in an almost
stream of consciousness mode, toward more of a focus upon poetic craft
and an interest in the poetic canon, starting in *Hand Dance* (the poem
"Ethnographs," for example), then *Bathwater Wine* and *Mercurochrome*.
But you tell me how you see it!

WANDA COLEMAN: A keen observation, yes. This was uncalculated,
and has happened as I have absorbed hundreds of hours of intense reading,
analysis, and discussion about poetry for an entire lifetime, fifty-five years.
"Ethnographs" is truly a marker. Very astute of you. I'm impressed and
pleased that you have noticed. Talking about that fine distinction between
"wanting to be a poet," "becoming a poet," and "being a poet"—

MP: Tell me about wanting to be a poet.

WC: I discuss the impact of my culturally rich upbringing in the essay
"Dancer on a Blade," [in *The Riot Inside Me*], so I'll focus on an overlying

love of reading in this answer. One of my early writing difficulties was in revising or repairing flawed text. When I looked back at old poems, I could not figure out how to crack the text and make them work. I was too good at what I did, if done badly. This was true of scripts and stories as well. Standard *Writer's Digest* advice to the novice did not cover the territory I was entering. Workshop mentors, encountered later, did not have either the grasp or the patience to appreciate my clumsy gropings. There was a direct contradiction between what I looked like on the surface and my true nature. I was the chronic daydreamer, introverted and shy, struggling to transcend my shortcomings. I escaped as often as I could into books. I intuitively have read (focusing only on the sensibilities I enjoyed, dismissing the rest, along with most of the racists), with only the vaguest of guidance, virtually the entire Western canon according to certain men. Given that most of my life occurred in the latter third of the twentieth century, I focused on what was accessible at home, in the public libraries and bookstores of the day, available in Southern California. So I feel little hesitation about wading in when, in contemporary situations, I find myself confronted by exclusionary talk of "the classics," and "the great books." As I read so voraciously, escape evolved into learning how to write, the revision and perfecting of text.

At some unknown point in my tenacious search, I solved my problem. This took place unnoticed, somewhere in that decade 1981–91 between *Imagoes* and *African Sleeping Sickness*. I was unaware of the extent to which I had evolved until I began occasionally teaching university classes (1989–99) and talking about the "flawed" work of other writers, suddenly, almost compulsively my favorite subject. This applied to all genres. I could not look at a written text without breaking it down into its craft elements. When I assigned written work to students I did the assignment also. I was amazed at what I could see in another writer's work.

I was not always hip to sophisticated word games, and impatient with them, at first. I even "dissed" them on the radio, with words tantamount to "acquired bourgeois taste and a luxury for us worker-warriors," thinking of, for example, *Finnegan's Wake*. But the critique was beyond subjective, it was biased. I didn't have the hours needed "to play games," as much as I might otherwise admire and enjoy them. I suspect my read on Joyce's *Finnegan* might be different today, nearly thirty-two years later.

Nevertheless, I developed an instinct for telling precisely when a writer's logic failed, he or she had become tired or disinterested, was faking it, had hurried the ending, or had truncated a good story for considerations outside the artistic, et cetera. Sitting on grantsmanship panels, I discovered that I could read the writer despite "blind" judging, in which the name of the writer was unknown. I could read through it to discern native-born American writers from foreign born. I could read gender, degree of education, and often region, not only by the content, but by form!

As I went on to discover: there seemed to be no form or kind of writing in English, including translations into English, that I could not analyze to the point of being able to recreate the process used by the same writer! This was far beyond mere mimicry! Having developed such a remarkable eye, over decades of intense private study, egged on by my burning dissatisfactions with the world, I then turned that critical eye on myself. It was painful at first, but then it became amusing, then "the play" turned serious when I took a renewed look at other writers between book manuscripts.

MP: What about the stage, actually becoming a poet?

WC: Suddenly, I could make all those old drafts of poems-that-did-not-work work. I could sing six out of one, as if a raging flautist. I felt possessed, although I knew that was only an expression of self-doubts. Poetry was more fun than ever. Now, I thought I was brilliant. Poems began to come in streams and waves, in ways Antonin Artaud, Bob Kaufman, Stuart Perkoff, and Anne Sexton would have envied. But I knew that if I waved my brassiere, bragging about writerly prowess and dexterity, no one (including my poet-artist husband, Austin Straus) would give me credit for having the brains to accomplish any such feat on my own, outside of academe, and without the sanctioned frou-frou (mentors, sponsors, awards). One might say I was stewing over the difference between "being an intellectual" and "showing off one's intellect."

Early on, I was driven by the all-consuming urge to put myself in the world. To have others see my point of view, read and appreciate my stories. Why wasn't it represented as I knew it to be? As the years rolled on, I found my answer. But, too, I began to feel that *that* was never going to *be allowed* to occur. I felt doomed to the outside of the narrow mainstream of American literature. I was hurt over the misreadings of and lack of enthusiasm (and response to) my first book, *Mad Dog Black Lady.* With each subsequent book, I hoped for a breakthrough. It did not and has not happened.

In the meantime, coinciding with the desire to show off my intellect were several writing projects that began making themselves felt in my psyche. One for "jazz sonnets" had occurred to me in the late 1970s when I began to earnestly pursue fellowships and grants. I applied twice to the National Endowment for the Arts for support for "jazz sonnets," but did not make the cut. I stated "poems" on the 1981 application, and was rewarded (but at the end of the Carter administration's NEA). Upon rereading much of similar grants and fellowship criteria, it appeared that perhaps these philanthropic organizations gave preferences to more conservative poets and writers, those who had specific ideas about their writing, or who had specifically stated projects, perhaps even had theories. I was not about to dismount the high egalitarian horse I was riding; however, I chided myself on being completely disorganized in that regard, with many ideas yet to coalesce.

At that time, I was intuiting the sonnets project. I would not have actually known a jazz sonnet if it had conked me on the noggin. Focus in my work had been as much on form (*The Maximus Poems* by Charles Olson) as on content (under the spell of deep-imagist poet Diane Wakoski). But my content always received the most of any outside attention, positive or (largely) negative (like under the Reichian scrutiny of a Clayton Eshleman).

Too, I was an excellent performer and found my non-Black poetry lovers and peers all too quick to dismiss serious African-American writing as "oral," and to further denigrate us by their failure to draw distinctions between us in technical and regional terms. There was never any discussion about degrees of excellence. A Mari Evans or Langston Hughes was equated to a Phillis Wheatley or James Weldon Johnson without the serious critique each poet merited. I resented it when my work was embraced for what I felt were the wrong reasons, especially when I was being reduced to stereotype, regardless of who was doing the diminishing. Often, I was disappointed by many of the critical Black voices emerging in the trail of the Black Arts Movement, my generational peers, especially when they lamely criticized me for not aping the ancestors or confining myself to an already tired iambic pentameter (a form I occasionally play with, if anyone notices), long the staple of the pulpit, which would continue on to evolve into the numbing signature of hip-hop "poetry."

"If it's Black and can hold a pencil, it's an African-American literary writer," I used to say quite acidly. I might then point out that our spe-cious Negro Great Books literary canon, post LeRoi Jones/Amiri Baraka, seems overly generous and stuffed with popular genre writers, whereas the Western literary canon it consciously apes ignores authors of crime, inspirational, romance, "uplift," and science fiction books. There may be some, but I cannot think of a single nonphilosopher religious leader, sci-ence fiction or mystery writer in the top five hundred — needless to com-ment on the dearth of mid-twentieth-century women, Black, and "other" Americans.

MP: And then the stage, being a poet?

WC: As the years whizzed by I found myself cohosting Saturday inter-views with poets from all over the nation with my third husband, Austin Straus. We were Pacifica Radio's literary program for Southern California, *The Poetry Connexion* (1981–96). To prepare for the biweekly evening show required reading a vast amount of poetry, biographical material, and tomes about the craft of poetry, and talking to poets about thought processes, technique, etc. It was tantamount to continued informal education de jure, as I absorbed hours of information about poetry over fourteen years. Often, in privacy, between shows, my husband and I would joke about some of the poets we thought were terrible, and made cruel fun of several of the locals. I once proposed that we do a mock anthology of poems purportedly writ-ten by such poets, in their style but with fake funny names. I believed I had the ability to do so. I even drafted a couple. My husband loved the idea, and while we often laughed ourselves silly with oft-bawdy extemporaneous lines, we never executed our mean-spirited idea.

Then, in 1991, the year after I spent six weeks, split over two years (1989 and 1990), in the Djerassi Resident Artists Program, I encountered at a Santa Barbara, California, museum exhibit Ethnography, a stunning painting by David Alfaro Siqueiros. It had as great an impact on me as Salvador Dalí's *Christ of St. John of the Cross* did at thirteen. I could not forget Siqueiros's vision, and lived restlessly with it in my mind for weeks. "Ethnographs" (written on November 28, 1991) was inspired by that deso-late spiritual dialogue that took place in the wake of viewing Ethnography. In it I attempt to eschew editorializing and strive to accomplish evocative "volume." Craft issues are again paramount, as they were in the beginning, but now I approach my text armed with a wealth of study. My poems now flow according to new impulses with uncharacteristic ease. I am in a new zone, and when I write it is virtually automatic, and I call it "zoning."

MP: What about the early seeds of your development? How did your childhood and young adulthood create a poet in you?

WC: If I did a mini-chronology of my early growth it would go something like this:

Ages 5–13: Falls in love with poetry at school. Unguided reading and study, at home, except for Mother who is partial to Paul Laurence Dunbar. Published first poem in community newspaper. I'm aware of *Beatitude* and The Hells Angels. I read the complete works of William Shakespeare and the King James version.

14–17: Writing seriously and often, fledgling work, not bad but extremely imitative of Lord Byron, Edgar Allan Poe, Robert Louis Stevenson, and the like. No voice. An amorphous sense of self in relationship to the world, except for gender and skin shade darkness. At home my parents are reading Richard Wright, James Baldwin, anything else Black they can get their Lincoln Republican hands on, Somerset Maugham and Henry Miller. A collector of comic books, I've found old copies of pulp magazines like *Black Mask* and have started gravitating toward novelists like James M. Cain and Jim Thompson and the stories of Saki (H. H. Munro) and Guy de Maupassant. I discover the French existentialists, then Edward Albee, Sherwood Anderson, Samuel Beckett, Eugene O'Neill, Arthur Miller, Tennessee Williams. I read the philosophers, favoring Baruch Spinoza, Friedrich Nietzsche, and Bertrand Russell. I read the Egyptian funerary book *The Book of the Dead*.

18–22: Malcolm X comes to Los Angeles. Political awareness comes with my first marriage, to a white civil rights worker, in the pages of the autobiography of Marcus Garvey, followed by Frantz Fanon, and a deluge of Black poetry and poets in the wake of the Watts Riots (August 1965). I'm introduced to the work of LeRoi Jones, the Last Poets, the Watts Prophets, everyone from Wheatley and Hughes to the emerging generation that includes Sonia Sanchez, Ted Joans, Etheridge Knight, Larry Neal, et al. Form is exploding. American English is becoming more fluid. Everyone's reading Carlos Castaneda, Lawrence Durrell, Hermann Hesse, and D. H. Lawrence. By now I'm facing a dismal prospect: I secretly think that a good deal of the Black poetry I am encountering, when compared to other writing, is largely "dreck." But this work is being lauded and published, it seems, everywhere — while I'm nursing three thousand rejection slips.

Voice matters to me, and even as I embrace what seems to be a trend, I want my arms around it in a particular way. I want to somehow individuate myself from those who will become known as the Black Arts poets. Between twenty-two and twenty-eight, I focus on getting "blackness" into my text, considering my breakthrough complete in November 1974. I am also beginning to be published locally, with work accepted in literary and "little" magazines across the nation. I continue my struggle toward my larger goal in public workshops in Watts, Hollywood, and Venice Beach. By 1977, I have published nearly a hundred new poems.

MP: Which poems or volumes of yours would you identify as showing special poetic growth in your development?

WC: Between March and June of 1985, I tentatively experimented with the evocative powers of language in a short series of poems called "Auguries." On December 20, 1986, my various tangents intersected. "American Sonnet" emerged thirteen years after conception of the ill-articulated "jazz sonnet." I recognized it immediately. I was excited, but it took a while for me to understand where I was going creatively. I opted to take the risk and follow the impulse. The second one did not show up until December 10, 1988, the third on December 4, 1990 (after *African Sleeping Sickness* appeared). After June of 1991, they came unbidden with increased and demanding frequency. Dividing my work time, I wisely applied the few days I had at Djerassi. I used eight of them to catch up on reading, while I adjusted to the shock of life outside the urban for the first time since childhood sojourns "down home." In the second three-week period, I mined my psyche to produce over a hundred pages of spanking text that became the core of *Hand Dance*.

The second sonnet had been an answer poem. In it I am dialoguing with Robert Mezey, to whom the poem is dedicated. It followed his appearance on *The Poetry Connexion*, during which he read a favorite poem. I took that poem, "inversed it," and addressed the author (forgotten as of this writing) as well as Mezey.

Sonnet 10 seized me after rereading some Robert Lowell, likewise sonnets 12 and 13, after Robert Duncan and Sergio Macias. I got angry after a well-known Black feminist writer lifted a line out of one of my poems for a book title. Sonnet 23 emerged like a shot in April 1994. I deliberately mimicked Anna Akhmatova, a poet [the Black feminist] writer chose to acknowledge, if conveniently ignoring me — her so-called "sistuhwomon." It was therapy of a sort. But quickly, the impulse went beyond such pettiness to continue its genuinely artistic course. I virtually could not read anything without a poem of one kind or another emerging even as I read, as fast as I read. Given that I had so little writing time, this seemed like a blessing at first. (I was under considerable stress in my personal life. In January 1991 my father died after a twelve-year decline. In January 1994 my oldest son announced he was HIV positive.)

I could not seem to curb or stem this must-write impulse. It seemed to have spent itself by fall of 1997, as I prepared the manuscript for *Bathwater Wine*. One night, two years later, in August 1999, I decided to conduct an experiment on myself. Casually letting my eyes roam tomes on one of our bedroom bookcases, I selected Mark Strand's *The Contemporary American Poets: American Poetry since 1940*. The resulting "play" was uproarious joy. It was as if I had been turned loose in a designer fashion showroom and was trying on every available dress to discover they were all my size! When the fantastic experiment was over, I was exhausted but thrilled. The sonnets had continued to come, as did the fugues, and, it seemed, I had reached some kind of marvelous plateau. I assembled those, and like poems from other sources, and titled it "Retro Rogue Anthology" (*Mercurochrome*, 2001). Now it was time to descend to more reasonable writing climes.

MP: How so you see the sonnet form? What poetic contribution/innovation do you see your sonnets as making? Sonnet 100 is particularly incredible — is it perhaps the apex of your sonnet achievement?

WC: I am ever pursuing new outlets for my "familiar" material or content . . . ways of keeping it interesting for myself. My sonnets are primarily jazz sonnets, minimalist (14, 15, 16 lines), often surreal and ironic. My idea was to take a conventional form and "play," "bust," and "shape-shift" it according to the basic dictates of the musical concept. I wanted to have my form and explode it too. I think that my poetic contribution has been to refresh the sonnet, renew appreciation for it, and to assist in bringing it back into vogue, if Billy Collins and Gerald Stern are any indication (both having borrowed my title, "American Sonnets," if not giving me credit for the notion). I have read/studied the complete works of Shakespeare at three different times of life, on my own, intensely, over the space of three to four days (my last reading, at Djerassi, in 1989). Additionally, I have encountered individual works, usually the plays and sonnets, in the classroom and on stage, as well as on television. I even wrote a "modernization" of *Julius Caesar*, in high school, making the First Man of Rome victim of a Mob hit or some such. My husband often sings one or two of his favorite Shakespearean sonnets, for which he has made up brief tunes. It seemed fitting that the jewel in my sonnet crown be written in homage to and after The Bard.

MP: *Mercurochrome* — in my framing of your development — is your most developed and crafted volume. Do you agree?

WC: I agree on one hand and disagree (somewhat) on the other. Choosing a favorite among my books is like choosing one child over another. Much of the work in my volumes overlaps. Too, each book has its own dynamic. Unlike those artists and poets who dole out good work, interspersing it among the bad and mediocre, withholding the best work for a calculated and presumed afterlife, I have always selected the best of what I have produced at the time of manuscript preparation.

In the earlier volumes *Mad Dog Black Lady* and *Imagoes*, the poems span a decade or more. In *African Sleeping Sickness*, they span nearly a generation because I reedited *Mad Dog* as part of the manuscript. I restructured several of the original poems, changing line breaks and deleting some repetition. I replaced three of the original selections with three others from the same period. That book was combined with newer poems at the suggestion of my publisher, John Martin, who confessed he had cut corners on *Mad Dog* to save money and then wanted to "do right" by me eleven years later. I went along with this, but worried that I was reprinting the poems too soon. I worried about turning off the few faithful readers I had.

Until *Bathwater Wine*, I personally thought the mixed genre *Heavy Daughter Blues* (1987) was my tour de force, the three full stories, the so-called flash fiction, mini-stories or vignettes marvelously suspended between poems to create a bluesy and gritty aesthetic whole. It contains "Essay on Language" (composed June 27, 1986), precursor to four of the fugues. As a whole, *Heavy Daughter Blues* is the favorite of my books, from cover to content. Yet, I am inclined to think that three later books taken in toto comprise the manifestation of my aesthetic and craft mastery: *American Sonnets*, *Bathwater Wine*, and *Mercurochrome*. Too, taken together, they contain all one hundred jazz sonnets, initially conceived as a separate, perhaps later annotated, manuscript.

As important to me as "Retro Rogue Anthology" and the sonnets are the five fugues I've managed to compose. "The Ron Narrative Reconstructions" (composed January 5, 1995), the second and most playful of these fugues, and "Salvation Wax" (composed October 4, 1995), the third and most important, appear in *Bathwater Wine*. The last, "Amnesia Fugue," appears in *Mercurochrome* and is my second favorite. In these fugues I am doing what was wished for in *Hand Dance*, as suggested in the form of the poems "ethiopian in the fuel supplies," "Essay on Language (2)," "Vet," and "Cancer"— poems in which I explore the "shattered narrative."

Wanda Coleman — Greatest Hits (Pudding House) and *Ostinato Vamps* (Pitt Poetry Series) may seem lesser efforts. But the transitional *Greatest Hits* chapbook allowed me to let off aesthetic steam, provide Wanda Coleman scholars with new insights, yet introduce myself to new readers. My difficulty with *Ostinato Vamps* is attributable to its size, 113 pages. Considerably larger than my chapbooks, it is less than half the length of my Black Sparrow books. I was more at ease with the extremes of manuscript preparation. I was particularly adept at wrestling with three-hundred-odd pages. The advantage in so many pages was that I had more layout options in the making of each section (or movement), and in juxtaposing poems to create a meta-language (something I've recently discussed in "Poetic Dynamics and the Meta-Lingo of the Manuscript," in *Ordering the Storm: How to Put Together a Book of Poems*, edited by Susan Grimm). I also had a firmer sense of the book as objet d'art.

Ostinato Vamps came after the retirement of Black Sparrow Press, and favorably, I hoped, represented the end of one period for me and the beginning of another. Virtually all the poems were written within a three-year period. I had not completely regenerated after *Mercurochrome*, and did not have the available selection of poems, or the distance from those poems that I usually had when working on a new collection. Said distance makes me less subjective. However, on the plus side, instead of a publisher-in-the-rough, such as was John Martin of Black Sparrow Press, who was primarily a Charles Bukowski worshipper and collector (of Persian rugs, rare books, and edgy writers), at the University of Pittsburgh Press I found myself working with consummate professionals for the first time (this can also be said of David R. Godine). I was very skittish about this, worried that perhaps my generation-long inexperience would show. Too, it felt strange working with people I had never met, and who did not know me outside the work itself.

Plus, sadly, due to the acceleration of sweeping digital technology, bringing about the demise of the print world of the twentieth century, there most likely would be no more quality hardbacks. I had treasured the exquisite Black Sparrow hardbacks. They partly made my sacrifice of little money and few royalties worthwhile. There is nothing like opening the pages of a beautifully designed hardback of one's hard-written work. John Martin's wife, Barbara, did the honors. It was the way Black Sparrow books were printed that had attracted me to the press. I wanted my books designed like their books. Each time one of my Black Sparrow books appeared, I relived the major thrill of my childhood, prowling the library stacks, high on the ambrosia of leather bindings and fine papers.

Nevertheless, *Ostinato Vamps* resonates with my characteristic fire. Part 3 is particularly incendiary, starting with "Night Widow Fugue" (composed September 5, 1997), an homage to unmarried/unloved Black women of all ages. It is wed to "Sorceress of Muntu" (composed May 1973), the first of the fugues drafted, but unfinished until revision in August 1997. I had intended to use it as the title poem of a separate manuscript; however, the poems it apparently "needed" failed to materialize. I had tried placing it in other manuscripts, but it overwhelmed them. In *Ostinato Vamps* it is not only a perfect fit, but an exquisite climax. It equals "Amnesia" as my second favorite of the fugues.

All that said, essentially you are correct. *Mercurochrome* is my "most developed and crafted volume."

MP: Could you talk to me about the distinct shape/structure of *Mercurochrome* in relation to the volume's themes? To me, it's in *Mercurochrome* where those two aspects of a poetry volume most work in concert together, as compared to your earlier work.

WC: Actually, I discuss and illustrate what I'm doing, my technique, quite thoroughly in the "theoretical" essay titled "On Theloniousism" (published August 1988 in *Caliban*). Reading this particular essay may sorely tax the linear thinker, and most likely offend anyone who thinks they've figured out what African Americans are all about. In it I playfully lay out "the kind of poetic sensibility yet to achieve recognition as one which does with language what Thelonious Monk did with music — as if the two were successfully divorced." I define this as the Jazz Principle: "rhythm refreshed, beyond style and lyricism, ascends . . . to its rightful throne along with content and form and copulates with both. That which starts with homage and/or satire, takes on its own independence."

"Speaking of furnished rooms, suppose Classical/traditional writing and/or music were compared to an apartment (compartmentalization). The Classical apartment is very lovely. You can paint it. You can move things around in it. You can buy new furniture and lay down new floors. It is still the same apartment.

"A Jazz apartment has modular/movable walls. It is an environment allowing for the predictable to coexist with the unpredictable; ape the Classical then suddenly break loose into variation to the point of unrecognizability; i.e., new, alien, and always renewable as the occupant (artist/creator) desires — limited only by the occupant's pocketbook/imagination." And perhaps stamina (hahaha).

Then later I write: "Simply put, Theloniousism is the Jazz Principle applied to verse." (And prose, as demonstrated.) This is the technique I've perfected and applied in both the writing of the poems that comprise *Mercurochrome*, but also in the preparation of the manuscript.

Theloniousism is a word I came across during my readings of controversial and militant new Black literature in the mid-1960s. There was loads of it in gazettes, small magazines, underground newspapers, and pamphlets handed out at political rallies. I no longer remember who the author was, or what the brutha posited in his particular essay. But in that word, I saw an opportunity to express what I had been attempting to achieve for a generation. My train of thought had been agitated by an editor who had rejected my poems as "jazz poetry." I was shocked and dismayed at the time (circa 1973). I could not see what he apparently saw. I thought it was merely poetry. I did not know that I was writing jazz poetry. What else was I expressing? I wrestled with this notion for years. It required considerable self-diagnosis before I embraced it, then defined it according to my private explorations and study. A good portion of the musical aspect of the beginnings of that exploration, in retrospect, is discussed in "My Blues Love Affair" essay, the rest covered in "Dancer on a Blade," in *The Riot Inside Me*.

In *Mercurochrome* I did not have to think about it. The poems virtually wrote themselves. I was driven to, as magnificently as I could, artistically release the killer demons that rode me: the death of my eldest son, familial conflicts, a literary career that failed to materialize, the various numerous disappointments and unfulfilled promises that defined my existence. I did so. I had perfected the chops. All I had to do was write.

MP: I think the "Retro Rogue Anthology" in *Mercurochrome* is simply brilliant, writing back to the nearly all-white anthologies that exclude black poets (among others). One of the subtleties of the section is how the poems have elements of both poetic appreciation and also correction. Could you talk about how you approached those poems, what your goals were, beyond what you have already indicated (perhaps by referring to one or two specific poems)?

WC: As I approached each poem in the Mark Strand anthology, my takes on those particular poems were written quickly, occurring as I read, one to three drafts, each with minor edits. In tandem, count fifty-odd years of examining the subtleties of racism and analyzing the horrific impact; how it has ferociously defined me, my relationships with everyone and to everything. In terms of content, my observations are profoundly ingrained — to the extent that, to repeat, I don't have to think about it. It was an exercise in virtuosity, like laying down the trombone and picking up the violin, then laying down the violin to stride to and straddle the piano on my way to the drums. This statement is not intended as braggadocio. It is my actuality. *It comes automatically.*

As an example, compare Mark Strand's aphoristic "Keeping Things Whole" with my equally aphoristic "Keeping Things Honest." I do not think that this kind of flavorless, spare, abstract poem is abstruse, either to grasp or to write, provided one is interested in so doing. This kind of poem smacks of the influence of great Chinese poetry on its adolescent Euro-American counterpart. For fun, I simply superimposed my "very black" perceptions over the culturally "neutral" event as announced, expanding, turning and/or reversing it — *jazzing it up.* I felt so comfortable doing it, maintaining the essential spareness, that I added an extra line as my signature because I thought it made for better balance of the final stanza. Any writer who refuses to anchor spare text by using "information" leaves themselves open to this kind of play. Yet it is tempting. I've taken that risk occasionally. Strand has said: "poems must exist not only in the language but beyond it" [*The Weather of Words*]. That sounds great, and upon first read I would be inclined to agree; but since a poem is made with and of language how is that possible? Strand does not say. Certainly, "Keeping Things Whole" does not live up to that criterion. In my answer poem, I have addressed that issue directly and definitively.

Not all of the poems are homages or takeoffs. A few are distillations of a poet's oeuvre or book, as with the John Berryman poem, "Dream Song 811." Some are answer poems, responses to the feelings another writer's poem arouses. The poem after Lisa Fineberg ("The Big Moment"), a former poetry seminar student, is such an instance. Accessing the original in this case does not matter. Her fledgling poem about early romantic disappointment set off corresponding emotions inside me, so I tapped material specific to my second failed marriage to write a poem similar in tone and style, but using my private allusions (content). Some of the poems in "Retro Rogue" double as letters to the poet, the subtext the degree to which I was moved or inspired by their original effort, as with the Jane Hirshfield poem ([to which I replied with] "By the Light of the Word"). When it is not obvious (or important to me), I opt to let the reader decide how I feel about the poem or poet acknowledged. When I respect the poet, and they are living, I occasionally send them my answer poem at the time of its writing.

To repeat: It could have been anyone's anthology. It happened to be Strand's. And the example above is only one of many poems. My primary goal was writerly (to test my poetic skills while at play). It was a much-needed break from my usual Sturm und Drang. In short and in sum, appreciation and/or correction occurred inevitably and unavoidably as part of my creative bent.

MP: As you suggested earlier, one of your trademarks is publishing poetic series that cut across your volumes. Are you intending to subvert conventional boundaries of poetic collections? Could you tell me about how some of these series developed?

WC: Subversion of conventional boundaries on my part was half-conscious, if quite deliberate when I started out. It evolved. By the time I got to *Mercurochrome*, impetus had become impromptu. I did not pattern this after anyone.

The ideas for the series poems come spontaneously, largely driven by my constant drive to deepen the dialogue on American racism. I am never bored by the subject. I am constantly searching for new ways to illustrate the damage or to exorcise the demon. Too, I have always been fascinated by the process that, in effect, allows society to "blame the slave for slavery." In "Auguries," I wanted to lay out and refract my inner turmoil in delicate or lacelike fashion, hence the surreal one-line stanzas and random couplets. Oft playing the concrete against a pared-down reportage, I shaped my language to make meaning opaque and translucent, wanting the reader to be left with disquiet on one hand, wonderment on the other, and to occasionally say "yeahhhhh."

In tandem with my attempt to deepen said dialogue, I also wanted to deepen my journey into language. It was not enough to be rhetorical, morally or sociopolitically correct — if, at the same time, I had to be who I was. I wanted to master the power that I had so admired in the poets who had gone before me, those who suffered inner torments, dealt with the great questions of existence and engaged in introspection. I began to attempt this tenuously between April and September of 1976 with a second series of fifteen poems titled "Signatures." Dissatisfied with them, I abandoned them rather quickly. Nine of them were published after being revised as individual poems and given new titles. A couple were looted for epigrams, one woven into another text. [The poem that was initially named] "Signatures (15)" appears untitled, except for a black square to denote it, in *African Sleeping Sickness*.

"Art in the Court of the Blue Fag" was the second of these series. It had little to do with discussing homosexuality, so perhaps the title may be off-putting to that extent. But I was looking for a new image for Hollywood, aiming to write poems about it, and attempting to avoid the clichéd images (bitch goddess, etc.). I lived and worked in the Hollywood area for twenty years after leaving South Central. On my daily routine, I frequently passed a costume shop. Its sign resembled a 1930s theater marquee, and was crowned by a huge bright blue mask with giant bee-stung lips in a permanent pout. It could be seen in traffic for blocks. I must have roared past that sign hundreds of times. On one drive, I actually stopped the car, got out and studied it. It was neither male nor female, but seemed a rather imperial unity containing both. The Blue Fag became my nickname for it, and I its fag hag. I never entered the shop to ask about it. But given the severe pressures I was under at the time, that mask began to symbolize the whole horrific shebang of urban survival as I was barely managing it.

MP: Which of the series poems stand out to you as most important or meaningful?

WC: The dream poems are my favorites of the series. When I say I am a dreamer, it is to be taken literally. They are actual dreams. Often, my dream lives are more actual than reality — I dream in full vivid color and always have. When I am ill with the flu, it can seem as if I exist in two worlds at once. As a child, I was able to maintain a mental catalogue of all my dreams in which I kept them filed in date order. I often entertained my younger brothers by telling them my dreams, a few influenced by movies and television. But most were my excursions into another, oft corresponding, realm. I could go into my catalogue, thumb through my dreams, and select one to dream again, and dream it as many times as I wanted. I often had dreams within dreams. I thought everyone could do this (if they wanted); that it was great to be able to have so much fun and so many exciting adventures while one was asleep.

I engaged in this up until about age eleven or twelve, losing interest in my catalogue altogether as my attention was diverted by boys and the goings on at Gompers Junior High. Until my longtime friend, poet Sylvia Rosen, began to study dreaming and redreaming with the Senoi Indians (mid-to-late-1970s), later writing and lecturing about it, I had not considered using them as material for poems. I had never written them down, and given my difficult lifestyle, could not see myself keeping a dream journal. Then two things began to happen: my second marriage began to fail and I began to experience what are called "prison dreams" (because in them, one has escaped). Casual telephone conversations with Sylvia began to bear fruit.

The first dream poem is in *Hand Dance* ("The Dream," composed November 21, 1980) and loosely establishes the form I will use for those that follow: the dream as dreamed, presented in lyrical prose or gussied-up reportage, usually ending with the literal or metaphorical waking. The numbers that appear after the [dream poems] are dates, not the order in which they were written, and not necessarily the date on which they were dreamed, hence the second poem is "Dream 13." Thus, the poems are numbered according to the day, month, or year, keeping to my arbitrary rule that no title have more than four digits. Once I realized that I was going to continue the series, I paid more attention to what I was doing ("Dream 522" was written on May 23, 1984, having occurred during the preceding night, and so forth).

MP: Is perhaps *Ostinato Vamps* the end of this practice, a new sense on your part of what a poetry volume is? (For example: slim, highly focused theme, minimalist.)

WC: It is not a new sense of what a poetry volume is, but an old one. Remember, I metaphorically grew up in Black Sparrow Press, and, in a sense, was (unwittingly?) provided with contentious mentors (if more for their benefit, as a body to fill a seat) and the opportunity to stretch artistically, whether my publisher understood and appreciated that stretch or not. I thought of myself as the Black stepchild. I am uncertain, because actual communication with Martin, in my case, was minimal until the late 1990s. It was a very odd situation. But since I could not find an enthusiastic publisher elsewhere, or find an agent to represent me, I stayed. After *Imagoes*, I was left alone to do whatever I wanted, Martin occasionally prodding me in one direction (toward the novel) or another (from the void).

This unique happenstance had its effect on my writing development as I scrambled not only to "break through" to the literary heights, but to impress my strangely illusive and unimpressionable benefactor — (although, in the early days, Martin used to gasp over the phone: "No one has ever said that! Do you realize that you're the first person to ever say that?" My response was: "Of course.")

Even the appearance of my books was dictated by the lapses and failures of Martin's other writers to come through or complete manuscripts they were working on. My manuscript was used to fill the gap. My books were never regularly scheduled and did not come out the same time of year. I never knew when or if I was going to have a book, even once I was given a contract. I had mixed feelings about being Black Sparrow's Cinderella, miffed that I was given so little consideration, yet so thoroughly committed that I had to accept "seconds." As the years progressed, I went from Cinderella to feeling like Frankenstein's monster. The publisher who created me did not understand me and wanted to be rid of me because I had become dangerous. To the positive, my uncomfortable tenure at Black Sparrow enabled my explorations and experiments. If *Ostinato Vamps* is the end of this, it won't be because of any decision on my part. I have always wanted a "slim, highly focused theme, minimalist" volume, and, in addition to that, to have it printed on fine vanilla paper with blue ink and blue marbling! I imagined my "Auguries," should I pick up and continue the series, as that kind of book.

MP: One way I'm seeing your more recent work is that *Hand Dance* battles the canon, and *Bathwater Wine* writes you into it, with all the "after so and so" poems.

WC: Bravo. Thank you. That's quite a compliment. I hadn't even given it much conscious thought, in that direction. The battle was taking place on the ground, rather than in the halls of academe. As said, my living circumstances have been *extremely* difficult and I have spent my life, thus far, in a 360-degree squirrel to maintain existence yet seize quality writing time. Lolling around on divans with delusions of literary grandeur has never been my style. I am a worker and a doer. I have merely attempted to keep myself open to the process as I have studied it and have allowed it to move through me. At some point, as obliquely expounded upon in "On Theloniousism," I quit worrying the poem and allowed it to worry me.

MP: You've mentioned how you started writing the sonnets, but could you talk about whether these two differing ways of interacting with the canon reflect a change of emphasis/strategy on your part?

WC: I would love to kiss my fingers and say, "Yeah — Baby! Dig dat strat-te-gee," but that would not be the truth. I wanted to (eventually) earn my way into the canon (or priesthood) by achieving the highest degree of craft excellence I could attain. In *Hand Dance*, as the title partly suggests, I was pushing my limits/showcasing my "style of styles." I had hoped it would bring me the literary success I had craved since childhood forages in the public library, swooning over *Poetry* magazine. In the five years between *Hand Dance* (which contains sonnets 3–11) and *Bathwater Wine* (sonnets 26–86), it finally sank in that my presumed acceptance into anyone's literary canon was a destructive and expensive notion. If I were to carry on, I had to let go of it. I needed to place maximum focus on craft alone. *Bathwater Wine* was the result of that decision.

As mentioned above, the majority of the sonnets were strictly intuited, the first having "appeared," after a thirteen-year gestation, an old idea that had taken its time to mature in my mental recesses. Any emphasis was primarily an outgrowth of the circumstances surrounding the deaths of my father in January 1991 and my eldest son six years later, also in January. All of that "stuff" had begun to find ways through me. Around these losses, I was deluged with images and occurrences from my past. *Hand Dance, American Sonnets* (twenty-six of the original twenty-nine), sonnets 27–76, and the somewhat autobiographical *Native in a Strange Land* appeared in the interval. Hmmm. I've never paid this any attention, but, as I'm finding out in the process of answering your question, only one *American Sonnet* was written in 1996, and they did not reappear until its revision in March 1997. That was sonnet 77! There was a one-year gap between sonnets 86 (composed September 29, 1997) and 87 (composed October 21, 1998). Malaise? Distractions? Grief? I spent a year working with a friend on a screenplay about the speculative life of poet and slave trader Arthur Rimbaud, after he left France for Africa. It was never produced. That may account for the lapse.

To the extent that there was any strategy on my part, it was focused inwardly on my craft abilities and their development. They came about strictly as the result of my accomplishments or failures. I aspired to greatness without assuming I would achieve it, fingers crossed. At the same time, I coveted recognition for whatever I managed to achieve, having been raised in a social milieu where that was the promise if not always the actuality — especially for exceptional or outstanding Blacks. The silence continued with each book, up to *Bathwater Wine*. As said, publisher John Martin was not a font of information, and whenever he passed anything along it was usually cryptic. At the twenty-sixth year mark, I took a count. I had averaged exactly one letter a year from someone stating they liked my work. And I was lucky that the handwriting or typing was legible. One of those letters was from poet Carl Rakosi, offering to help me, but misreading my persona. It was an offer I was unable to accept; however, that and a characterization of me as "a fine poet," by M. L. Rosenthal (expert on Pound and Yeats who recognized Fearing and O'Hara), in a mid-1980s letter to my husband, his ex-student, kept me sufficiently encouraged. Otherwise, praise for my "pyrotechnics" was rare in literary quarters of any color. My analysis and disappointment led me to conclude that I had crossed into uncharted territory. My mixed feelings about this worked their ways into the poems.

MP: Are you interested in initiating a dialogue? Why (or why not?)

WC: I thought I had done exactly that twenty-seven years ago. I was at once deeply interested in literal dialogues on multiple levels, and excited by the notion. This impulse has long since passed, rousted and routed by cynicism and a grudging pragmatism. Also muted by the actuality of intellectual theft. Given my age and state of exhaustion, I now think it is best that I place my focus elsewhere. The dialogue has long entered the page (best place for it), will take place there to any extent, will remain there for anyone interested.

MP: Could you also talk about this in relation to the poems "Intruder" and "Dinosaur Sonnet" from your collection *Bathwater Wine*?

WC: Well, in using the title "Intruder" I am embracing a Black stereotype and reversing it. In so doing, I express exactly how I think I have been maltreated. The literary world is as cutthroat as any corporate turf, or the pitch dens of Hollywood. "Intruder" voices my complex anger and frustration as precisely as I can put it, yet remain poetic, making light of any who have romantic delusions about poets and poetry while being anti-romantic. Too, it is a slap at those who overly worship the Spanish bards, even as I use Latinate phrasing and tone to demonstrate that I also admire them.

"Dinosaur Sonnet" is a belated response to one of my husband's professors at Cal State Los Angeles. The man had invited his MA students and others into his home following a reading in which I was featured, knowing that at least two individuals present were well published and had budding reputations. In the middle of benign conversation, he declared that Wordsworth was the last great poet and that there was nothing written worth reading after World War II. While everyone else was still sucking in The Shock, I called him a dinosaur, set my plate down and told my husband we were leaving. My poetic response became a cumulative one, as I factored in other encounters with like narrow minds, virtually all white males, straight and gay, and no matter their politics or literary agenda. The poem skewers a dated academic patriarchy with its own language; one that ever struggles (like Mortimer Adler) to turn back the clock, to keep Blacks, women, the poor, and "the experimental" silent.

MP: One of the "after" poems is "Sonnet 77," "after Barbara Presnell," who is on the faculty at my university. One thing I find admirable about that is your interest in an emerging poet, not just canonical biggies. Could you talk about how you are responding to Barbara's poetry in that poem?

WC: "Art feeds art," is what I tell students. If I recall, Barbara's book or manuscript was an entry in a competition I was judging, probably for the North Carolina Arts Council. There may have been two other judges as well, Sherman Alexie and a fiction writer. Going through my poetry index card file, I am able to discern that her poems had significant impact, informed and/or refreshed me. As I recall, in reading her poems, I was struck by the manner in which she allowed grief into her text. (I'm not certain, but I think there may be a stanza spacing mistake in 77, I've just noticed.) Once Presnell had reminded me how, I "copped her licks" and released into sonnet 77 some of the grief that attended the deaths of my father and eldest son. Sonnet 77 was first drafted in June 1996 and revised in March 1997. The sonnets pick up after that and continue two years later, until crowned with the last fourteen.

In the instance of Sonnet 77, "licks" does not refer to Presnell's material or the content of her text, and not necessarily to her form (although I usually retain enough of another poet's form signatures necessary to establish the appropriate nod). Rather, it is what I garnered in her process that attracted me at that moment (what it set off inside me). The material I use is always my own, since I have a considerable amount of it and am constantly undergoing self-reevaluations. The dialogue is not with the canon. My dialogue is much larger and transcends my writing focus.

I believe I have, in my relentless stirrings to perfect a poetic technique, effectively identified the creative process that is at the core of African-American existence, survival, and thought — beyond W. E. B. DuBois and other Black thinkers, if aided by a handful. It is the true and only "Black aesthetic" the young bucks in academe keep redefining every five years or so, perchance to get unearned attention from the establishment by dismissing a previous generation. At the core of this core is an unparalleled and inexhaustible excellence. It is the stuff that has influenced generations of European and American painters. It is the stuff our music legends are made of, from Robert Johnson to John Coltrane to Billie Holiday to Nina Simone to Jimi Hendrix to George Clinton to Tupac Shakur. In my lectures I often touch upon Black music in that regard (taking up where LeRoi Jones/Amiri Baraka left off in *Blues People*). In the essay "My Blues Love Affair" [in *The Riot Inside Me*], I approach the same turf as expounded upon in "On Theloniousism," but biographically. In it I state: "The blues was essentially Black, however. It stained anything it touched" (20). In tandem with this, I have often embellished a saying that lovingly castigated the psychology of American Blacks. To paraphrase: "Not a single part of the pig is inedible. We use every damned part ..." To that I added the logical conclusion: "... including the oink."

MP: You've referenced music several times. Your blues poems always employ a refrain and the traditional AAB blues structure — do you see yourself writing in a tradition of blues poetry, such as that of Hughes and others?

WC: Frankly, I did not care all that much for the blues poems of Langston Hughes. They perform well, when someone with an ear takes them on, but they are rather flat on the page. They rely too much on posture, less on substance. I was much more impressed with the musicality of James Weldon Johnson. I thought that it might be possible to do much more with the root form, in terms of treading that very fine line between the lyric and the lyrical — even crossing over and coming back. Plus, I wanted to retain the gritty aspect of stomp-down blues lyrics. I did not want to civilize it for white consumption, as Hughes did. I wanted the pure evil. This notion is first fully realized in the seminal "Blues Song Sung in Room of Torrid Goodbyes" (composed August 15, 1975, published in *Imagoes*). Ironically, my version of the [blues] form starts [in publishing terms] in *Mad Dog*

Black Lady with a poem actually written later: "A Lyric" (composed February 5, 1976), in which the content is acidly and nastily antilyrical. It then picks up again in *Imagoes* with "Blue" (composed April 1, 1979), in which I go for the essence of the blues over the form itself. But by the start of the 1990s, I've more or less ceded to form in the more rigidly structured "The Laying Down Blues," and "Starved for Affection Blues." I had actually begun to sing-talk these poems when I performed them, making up intermittent music on the spot. The effect or "conjure" is often magical, as a 2005 performance for the dance department of an Ohio university proved. I actually attended some movement sessions for writers, and the instructor developed a dance, of sorts, to fit my presence: "Morning Widow's Song," *Bathwater Wine*. I then presented it onstage the next night. I gauged the degree of my success by a twenty-year-old in gold chains and baggies who sought me out afterwards. He told me he did not want to like my performance, but enjoyed it in spite of himself.

MP: Who would you count among your black literary influences?

WC: I was raised in a small Los Angeles community that consisted in part, but not all, of Blacks who had migrated from the midwestern and southern United States after World War I and World War II. Their origins were almost exclusively rural (farming). These hard-working, largely Christian people felt entitled to enter into white society and culture because they had earned the right to do so. Their constant aim was to prove themselves worthy of an ever-illusive equality and parity. In the raising of their children, they passed on this sense of entitlement, reinforced by the American ideals and mores of their day and the larger society. I was raised with all the expectations of my white generational peers. At no time was I ever given a sense of inferiority. My parents psychologically reinforced my developing identity by constantly repeating key phrases that remain with me yet — a crude but effective hypnosis: "You are as good as anyone. . ." Add to that: "regardless of race, creed, or color." I had extended this to include gender long before reaching puberty.

Consider the gulf that exists between me and many of the younger Black writers I now encounter, and others — particularly those who have studied Black literature. Consider that in the Southwest, during my critically formative years, there were no Big Black Literary honchos in the region making pronouncements about what should and should not be read. There were no fleets of Black academics bucking to win prizes, galvanizing like-minded ninnies to buy their leavings, or impress their colleagues with arbitrary aesthetics (much of it intellectual pisswah) set out for less-educated others to ingest like hogs to slop. The Southwest, as I lived it, was truly open and wild intellectually, fertile and inviting territory for exploration and experimentation. In that sense, I was absolutely and uncannily free to partake of whatever came within access. Therefore, H. L. Mencken and Ayn Rand were greater influences on me than the less accessible Ralph Ellison and the less interesting Langston Hughes. When I play with, or off of, poets and writers encountered after my formative years (1951–74, marking 1974 as my breakthrough year), it is usually just that — play, with or against. Homage from me for fellow African American writers is weighted heavily, carefully placed within context, and announces itself loudly.

Accessing Black literature was very difficult in the ghettos and Black communities of the Southwest. I had encountered *Beatitude* as a twelve-year-old — the beatniks, their poets and novelists and finger-snapping prosody, long before reaching back to read Ellison's 1947 classic, *The Invisible Man*, which I do not personally regard as an "Ur text." In 1958, African American literature was considered contraband when brought onto the grounds of South Park Elementary School, which I attended, and confiscated by authorities. Otherwise, African American literature was confined to a small section of the anthropology shelves in public libraries, along with Mexican and American Indian tribal literature, was absent from or hard to find in bookstores that did not specialize in it, and had to be begged for or borrowed from friends. Because of my parents' attempts to keep up with contemporary literature as best they could, I had access to novels by Richard Wright and James Baldwin. Members of Our Authors Study Clubs were invited to address classrooms during Negro History *week*. Around 1964, under mysterious and unusual circumstances, I was lent a manuscript or folio of poetry by LeRoi Jones (Amiri Baraka) to study. I was also shown a copy of the seminal literary journal *Yungen*, edited by Jones. Black literature did not become prolific in my part of the Southwest until after the Watts Riots in August 1965, when I would start to consume whatever was available by volumes. Virtually all that is identifiably, accessibly "black" in my poetry and prose comes from Black music, not from Black writers.

MP: Do the jazz greats of the past and other musicians that you know personally influence or inspire you to write some of your poetry?

WC: Yes, fortunately. I usually write to it. Music has always been a wonderful presence in my life, live and recorded. My tastes are eclectic with the caveat of quality.

There was always a piano at home and a series of heavy-chested, wall-shaking, high-spirited colored lady piano teachers. Mahalia Jackson was God. I studied with Mr. DiPinto, a wealthy Italian violinist who had immigrated to the U.S. during World War II. I thought I would grow up to become a concert violinist (that dream was aborted by motor-skill damage after "African sleeping sickness" at age ten). My father had a tremendous baritone, and sang Robeson-style solos at every opportunity. My mother sang and accompanied herself on piano. I am old enough to remember when the boogie-woogie became a dance craze and my parents' friends came by the house to demonstrate the music and dance steps. Tenor saxophonist and flutist Buddy Collette was in my father's Eagle Scout troop. He used to show us (me and my brother) how to blow reveille and taps on the bugle. I spent many hours listening to music in the public library, particularly Franz Liszt and Camille Saint-Saëns. I had a crush on Johnny Ace. In the mid-1960s you could find me and my schoolmate Sandy in Hollywood in Music City's listening booths exploring the new sounds. Billie Holiday was God.

I got to see Marvin Gaye, Rosie Hamlin ("Angel Baby"), The Platters, and The Coasters when they came to Gompers Junior High School, 1958–61 (dancer Donald O'Connor was a frequent guest performer, too). Chuck Man was everyone's favorite DJ at our school, listened to devoutly over the new portable transistor radios. When he went off-air in the payola scandals, it jolted the Black community. Mr. Avery Smith, my guardian during my difficult transition from junior high to high school, was a frustrated clarinetist. I pounded out the frustrations I could not yet articulate on the piano. My first husband, an itinerant folksinger and guitarist, took me to my first live blues performances, to see such greats as John Lee Hooker, Josh White, Taj Mahal, and many others. We double-dated with Jayne Cortez and Horace Tapscott. We spent time helping retired jazz and pop singer Jerri Reed run her Black youth talent showcase in South Central Los Angeles, 1964–66. Odetta was God.

When the Chambers Brothers debuted "Time Has Come" at a MacArthur Park love-in, I danced a-go-go with them onstage. We were introduced to jazz legend Ornette Coleman while climbing some bleachers at the John Anson Ford Amphitheater. He was considering doing a concert there and was talking to the organizer. I discovered jazz organist Jimmy Smith, and Otis Redding, on travels to San Francisco, and Janis Joplin while walking the halls of the first experimental coed dorm, at Stanford University, when I was there briefly with a theater troupe. We gloried to the folk of Pete Seeger; Peter, Paul, and Mary; and Jan and Jean. We asked Phil Ochs for his autograph. We learned about the Moog synthesizer and that it would change the nature of music. A year later, we met a man who claimed to play the first electronic violin. During the late 1960s I attended Len Chandler and John Braheny's Songwriter's Workshop, usually in the company of Bonnie White (daughter of singer Kitty White, one-time coach of Elvis Presley). Morgana King was God.

Soon Motown and James Brown governed ways of life, house party to house party on the "Black hand side." On the "White hand side" we had followed the throngs to see *A Hard Day's Night*, and were devoted until *The Yellow Submarine. Revolver* revived my interest, and *Sergeant Pepper* kept it alive. Following our divorce, I found an LP titled *Black Sabbath*, then later developed a taste for The Rolling Stones and Alice Cooper. There were nights of hanging out at The Bridge with Judee Sill. I discovered Jimi Hendrix and "Purple Haze" at the same intersection. As the 1970s went from funk to disco, I interviewed Black music personalities of the 1960s for the underground press, including Sticks Hooper, Smokey Robinson, Mary Wells, Jerry Butler, and reggae newcomer Bob Marley with his Wailers. I met an enthusiastic Don Cherry, I met a reluctant Ron Carter. Before Bolic Studios burned to the ground, I was invited into the round and empty bed of Ike and Tina Turner to test the sound quality of its recording equipment. Nina Simone was God.

Chuck Man became my longtime lover and steeped me in Garland Green, Bobby Blue Bland, Solomon Burke, and B. B. King. I discovered Al Green on my own. As it so happened, I was at the Saint Patrick's Day Riots, 1975, when New Wave debuted in Los Angeles. There were three punk rock groups on the bill: The Go-Go's, The Plugz, and X. I had met John Doe and Exene in passing at the Wednesday night Venice poetry workshops at Beyond Baroque. My second husband declared, "Music is my religion," and although he was a consummate violinist, I never heard him play a note. His papa Harold was one of a trio of Black men who played banjo for a twenty-year stint at Disneyland's Frontierland. We got deeply into Fleetwood Mac, Led Zeppelin, and Patti Smith (live at the Fleetwood, in Hermosa Beach).

His favorite instrument was the air guitar, although his musician stepdads brought us tangential to the circles of guitarist Ray Pizzi, bassists Frank Butler, Leroy Vinnegar, and Red Callender. I did a Venice Beach gig with Alice Coltrane. Over the decades, I would perform with Horace Tapscott several times, and once with Richard ("Louie Louie") Berry. Jazz guitarist Thomas Tedesco would become a friend and accompanist. Betty Carter was God.

I soon entered the sphere of Jello Biafra, Henry Rollins, and Lydia Lunch. But by the late 1970s, performance poet Max Schwartz had tapped me on the shoulder and reminded me that jazz is supreme. He introduced me to the flesh-and-blood Nina Simone. (I make heartsick sojourns down to the Parisian Room to catch Big Mama Thornton, Ahmad Jamal, and Big Joe Turner.) Jazz pianist Dorothy Donegan, jazz singer Joe Williams, and a new man come into my life shortly thereafter, and together he and I follow them club to club. Husband three, Austin Straus, prefers classical music and jazz, from Mahler and Mozart to Chet Baker and Billie Holiday. In the early-to-mid-1980s, we vamped at the jazz bars and grills. In the late 1980s, I discovered the LP stash of a former Blue Note salesman at a local record shop, and went into spasms revisiting Miles, Coltrane, Gillespie, Parker, and company. Later I will start channeling Tito Puente and the mambo. Circa 1993, photographer Susan Carpendale introduced us to the ailing Eddie "Clean Head" Vincent as she finished a documentary on him, and we made two of his farewell performances. Along the way, we had started hanging out with jazz singer and poet Lynn Carey (daughter of actor Macdonald Carey), bumping aesthetics with jazz historian Leonard Feather, then jazz soloist Dwight Trible. We walked out on a Miles Davis concert in Beverly Hills when I noticed his fingering did not match the audio. We walked out on Bobby McFerrin when he insisted on singing "The Itsy Bitsy Spider" and "The Mickey Mouse Club Song." Poet Kamau Daaood declared: "Music, music, all is music!" Etta James was God.

MP: The *Heavy Daughter Blues* title poem is "for Yusef Komunyakaa." Do you see him as a precursor?

WC: Are you kidding? You've touched an exquisite wound on my ego. I have a major "bug up the bongalong" about Komunyakaa. We're roughly the same age. By 1977, I had published *Art in the Court of the Blue Fag*, and a hundred and fifty poems in literary journals and little magazines, and was entrenched in a burgeoning Southern California literary scene. His

Dedications and Other Darkhorses also appeared in 1977, and *Lost in the Bonewheel Factory* in 1979, the same year *Mad Dog Black Lady* appeared.

I first met Komunyakaa when he invited me down to UC Irvine to do a reading for the class he was teaching. It was in the late 1970s, around 1978. He paid me a hundred dollars. He came off as a cold but intelligent customer with a monstrous curiosity and marginal civility. I perceived that he had the smarts to appreciate the enormity and uniqueness of what I was accomplishing. Perhaps he was merely shocked (and pissed) to find a similar power and sensibility in a slightly older woman of his own race. He was not very forthcoming. If I remember correctly, he was married to, or living with, an Australian or aboriginal woman. I was married to my second husband, had two children in puberty, and was working two jobs. There was mention of him going to France. Prior to the reading, perhaps afterwards, we talked craft. He sported a kofi in those days. During the class session he listened more intensely to my answers (arms crossed) than any of his students.

My assessment of him was that he was a diligent worker, a strategist and cagey by nature. I was not familiar with his work at the time. He asked me pointed questions about my technique. (Remember, I was less than five years out from my breakthrough, still groping for my tongue, the language in which to discuss poetry.) It noticeably upset him when I stated that the poems came without my having to think about or dwell on them (I explain this in detail in workshops and seminars, and it relates to my having been a scriptwriter and its intense demands). Komunyakaa looked at me and choked, complaining about how much work it was for him to write a poem, all the while giving off vibes that he thought what I had said was preposterous and flip. When I went home that afternoon, I knew it would not be the last I had heard of him. I began to survey the cultural terrain, watching for and charting his progress.

Sure enough, when *Mad Dog Black Lady* was published in 1979, Y. K. reviewed it for *Callaloo* a year or two later. In so doing, he called me "a presumed genius." I have never forgiven him for that nasty and unnecessary crack. Particularly since he had the nerve to "cop my licks," as soon as he could, parlaying my *knowing* into his stellar literary career while, comparatively, I have remained in obscurity. (Later I found it extremely troubling when I discovered that one of his lovers was the book review editor at *Callaloo*, which, coincidentally?, has not reviewed any of my books since.)

Without sufficiently understanding how our backgrounds differed, this imperious taskmaster also criticized me for not "honoring" such "ancestors" as Bob Kaufman and Langston Hughes. After considerable seething on my part, the poem "Heavy Daughter Blues" emerged as my answer to that criticism (composed December 21, 1983), in which I take off on Kaufman's "Heavy Water Blues."

MP: His early poetry parallels your early work, such as his *Lost in the Bonewheel Factory* — a similar bleakness. There's also a jazz aesthetic parallel. Is he a model or peer for you?

WC: To the contrary. I was the peer model for him. He "threw down" or challenged me in his poem "Looking a Mad Dog in the Eyes." In the poem, he tells me all I need to know: that he regards me as a rival, and that he intends to best me on all literary fronts. In terms of our similar bleakness, that relates to the fact that, at that time, we both regarded ourselves as soldiers or veterans of war. He was, if taken at his word, literally in Nam. I had done so metaphorically since 1974, publicly calling myself by such labels as "page," "woman warrior," and "manwoman/womanman"— my meanings coyly oozing the socioeconomics of racism (I thought). I was also going around cheekily calling myself "a veteran of ghetto wars," sincerely attempting to back up the phrase by articulating those circumstances in poems and stories. As for the jazz aesthetic parallel, his most likely comes via the seminal Black musical traditions of the Old South, in which he was born and raised.

As the years progressed, I was surprised when invited to submit poems to his jazz anthology (such as "At the Jazz Club He Comes on a Ghost," from *Imagoes*). Too, a few years ago, he referred a student to me (who became a Yale Younger Poet series author shortly thereafter). I took these two instances as evidence that I, too, was still being looked at, if askance, by Komunyakaa. Academic push come to literary shove, he had to give me attention, if minimally.

We chanced to meet again, in New York City, when I was awarded the 1999 Lenore Marshall Prize. He was singularly unimpressive as a presenter, contrary to what one young Black female acolyte recently described online in gushingly purple terms. Over dinner that night, I found an opening and gently prodded him about our long-ago meeting at UC Irvine. He deftly sidestepped any implications.

As it now stands, it is impossible for me to be unbiased when asked to speak about the man or his work. I have attempted to turn this negative into a positive by putting it into my poetry. One of the more recent poems, "The Warning in a Mad Dog's Eyes," is dedicated to Komunyakaa's associate Sascha Feinstein, and closes *Wanda Coleman — Greatest Hits: 1966–2003*.

Despite my resentments about him, I have gone on record as enthusiastic about his work (if he fails to return the favor). Over the years, I have frequently recommended him to students, and anyone interested in Black poetry. I still do. I feel perfectly comfortable so doing, as I privately nurse my smoldering ego. You see, my satisfaction, in this war between us, is derived from his knowing that I will always exceed his poetic grasp, no matter how many prizes he wins — I can write circles around him and have.

MP: What exactly in Komunyakaa's poetry do you admire and why?

WC: I don't admire Komunyakaa. I do appreciate his poetry — his intense risky content over his rather conservative tight form. The contradiction inherent in this, his desire for creative freedom, trapped within the confines of religiously pared lines driven by a fierce point of view and an ear to the earthy rhythms that define a people-culture.

MP: I was struck by your Amiri Baraka poem, sonnet 34 in *Bathwater Wine*. How do you see Baraka? As a poetic rebel? Warped? He's disabled at the end of the poem, and the Tiffany slippers are not a positive image.

WC: LeRoi Jones was one of the most gifted and important American writers to emerge after World War II. He never got his proper due (or his deserved prizes) because of the bigoted circumstances of the literary day. Amiri Baraka is a mean-spirited cult leader, egotist, and rhetorician who has attempted to corral, circumscribe, or silence any Black creative entity he cannot take credit for having influenced. Ironically, his reputation looms so large that many want to honor and praise him (like the misguided governor of New Jersey [James E. McGreevey, who appointed him poet laureate for the state of New Jersey in 2002, only to eliminate the position in 2003, following intense public criticism after Baraka read his poem "Somebody Blew Up America" at a poetry festival]), without understanding that he is metaphorically beyond their literal reach. Giving him all due respect as one of the progenitors of the Black Arts Movement, I see Amiri Baraka as having committed "revolutionary suicide" (in the words of H. P. Newton), by abandoning his best artistic approach, or genius, which he expressed while writing as LeRoi Jones. He has never bested those earlier works and, since the 1970s, has resurrected himself to become a walking spewing ranter of questionable verse. His attempts to "cop the licks" of other, younger Black writers (including myself) have backfired. For example, it is no coincidence that his controversial 9/11 poem, "Somebody Blew Up America" echoes a rhetorical stanza from my polemic "The First Day of Spring 1985," from *African Sleeping Sickness*. It is a poem he had heard me read:

COLEMAN: who remembers Mary Smokes?
who remembers Wounded Knee?
who remembers The Night of the Long Knives?
Kent State? Jackson State? Attica?
The Greensboro Five?
Geronimo?

BARAKA: Who knew the World Trade Center was gonna get bombed?
Who told 4000 Israeli workers at the Twin Towers
To stay home that day?
Why did Sharon stay away?

Fortunately or unfortunately, the literary jury is still out when it comes to my complex feelings about Jones/Baraka. Despite my contempt for his cock-of-the-walk behavior, I still admire his early work as Jones (particularly the exquisite and excruciating *Dutchman*), and his valuable contribution in the fight against racism. Other than as mentioned above, I have had spotty contact with the man, some of it unpleasant, some of it pleasant. Yet I feel shafted by and repulsed by him. My last reading with Baraka took place during this interview, three weeks ago (October 2006) in New Orleans, when we did a benefit reading for a post-Katrina volunteer organization. Ever polite, he conducted himself as a gentleman, and emitted elder-statesman vibes. When we went to dinner that evening (with a young man who happened to be the nephew of playwright and novelist, Pearl Cleage), it was left to me to pick up the check. Rather than see him as a poetic rebel, I see him as a poetic Janus: the rebel (Jones) and the reactionary (Baraka). Along with Langston Hughes, Amiri Baraka is responsible for fostering some of the worst writing ever produced by younger generations of African Americans. That is a tragic part of his legacy.

MP: Who among contemporary black poets might you see as truly innovative or excellent?

WC: Since Small Press Traffic's April 2000 conference, *Expanding the*

Repertoire: Continuity and Change in African-American Writing, the poetic landscape for African Americans has broadened considerably. Some of the poets I have come to enjoy reading over the years, for various reasons, include Ai [deceased], Etheridge Knight (deceased), Nate Mackey, Marilyn Nelson, Wanda Robinson, A. B. Spellman, Michael Afaa Weaver, and Michael Warr.

As you know, one can be excellent, perhaps in the extreme, without being innovative. Sometimes, the price of being avant-garde is being misunderstood, overlooked, and confined to the cultural margins (often because the average reader, regardless of race, creed, or color, is passive and wants to be uplifted or entertained). In my interview in *Quercus Review*, I mention a number of fresh African American voices who offer greater diversity when it comes to the complex dynamics of form and content on the "Black hand side." All consider themselves excellent, but I would imagine that less than a half dozen consider themselves innovative — C. S. Giscombe, Terrance Hayes, Tim Siebles, and Harryette Mullen, perhaps. I find that among those I specifically mention, Reginald Shepherd [deceased] (*Angel Interrupted*), a sibling at University of Pittsburgh Press, is unquestionably innovative. Among several, across diversities, I helped jumpstart the literary career of Patricia Smith (*Life According to Motown*) and influenced the work of Chicano writer Jimmy Santiago Baca when he found *Mad Dog Black Lady* in a prison library. Others I did not mention include Giovanni Singleton, Paul Beatty, Renee Gladman, and Will Alexander, who seem to cultivate and enjoy being considered innovators. Nathaniel Mackey thrives on it. Ishmael Reed and Thylias Moss have been certified "geniuses," which, in our culture, automatically presumes the innovative.

MP: One of your poems that caught my eye is "The African beneath the American"—why Plath?

WC: Why not Plath? The poem is in *Ostinato Vamps*, and in it I take a rhetorical stance drawing my declarative line, evermore, in the literary sand. I encountered her work in the late 1960s, early 1970s, and count her among my many influences (especially *Ariel* and *The Bell Jar*).

MP: What does Plath represent to you?

WC: In the poem, I evoke Plath's spirit. I conjure. Plath represents the throttled potential of American feminism. She is the bittersweet nurturing darkness that defies a brutal burning light. The searing emotional content snatches the reader into her text, becomes visceral, a power few poets command. At my best, my writings have that same quality. I did consider adding Plath to "Retro Rogue Gallery." But at that time, such an act felt too much like sacrilege.

MP: I also love your poem "Thirteen Ways of Looking at a Bluesbird" from *Bathwater Wine*. Could you talk about how the poem is rewriting Wallace Stevens, white modernism, poetry, and racial stereotypes?

WC: I couldn't summarize it better. The process is identical to that demonstrated in my answer earlier in this interview. Whereas Strand angles for success, Stevens succeeds wonderfully in "Thirteen Ways of Looking at a Blackbird." In "Bluesbird" I am vaulting Stevens forward, and, exactly as with the Strand poem, overlaying my issues, concerns, perspectives. Again, this type of surreal and minimalist poem relies on the sensibility of the reader as heavily as it relies on connotation and denotation. Stevens's extension of the image taps into associated folklore (for its information) since the blackbird is often considered a bad omen (Poe's *The Raven*), and its soaring often represents the flight of the soul. In my poem, Emmett Till becomes the blackbird, hence the soul of America's struggle to resolve its race issue.

The most demanding stanzas were numbers four and thirteen. I solved the last one first, playing on the word *snow*, one of its slang definitions, "to deceive." As Stevens chose a symbol for change/death, I chose to represent one of the psychosocial deaths America has offered to Blacks in lieu of true freedom; I also went for double meanings.

In order to make my stanza work, I had to juxtapose the stale ideal contained in the first sentence against the more intriguing, teasing second sentence, then search my experience for its counterpart. I puzzled down the list of my demographics, focusing on single mom. I still couldn't make it work. Then I reread my stanza two and recalled Sojourner Truth's "Ain't I a Woman?" quote. Stanza four immediately fell into place, my Stevens poem finished.

MP: Thanks so much for your time in doing this interview.

WC: Malin, I enjoyed your challenging interview. It has been a struggle to keep my head clear and to remain cogent. Thank you for being level-headed and even-handed in your approach. One previous interview of me I forgot to mention (just as well) occurred in the farewell issue of *Chiron Review*, May 2004 I think. I'm not certain. Except that the adolescent, pugnacious interviewer had also written a resentment-and-jealousy-stained review of one of my books. When the editor/publisher asked me to assign someone to interview me, I trembled at the idea of being accused of the kind of smarmy favoritism and self-promotion that dogs so many American poets. Therefore I deliberately picked that reviewer. I figured he was such a contentious blabbermouth that he would go to fisticuffs declaring that I had not influenced him one iota in his assessment of me and my work. Dandy in lieu of the real thing, an intellect. That said, Doctor, bravo and thank you for your intelligent approach to my thorniness! Best to you in this coming year!

[2006]

YUSEF KOMUNYAKAA

Yusef Komunyakaa is perhaps the poet of greatest stature in this generation, with a substantial body of work and a highly acclaimed presence in several poetic arenas, including jazz poetry, Vietnam War poetry, and African American poetry. His fourteen books of poetry evidence a prolific poet whose writing continues unabated in his sixties; additionally, he has coedited two anthologies of jazz poetry, published a book of his interviews and essays, and collaborated on a verse play rendering of the epic tale *Gilgamesh*. He currently is a professor in the Creative Writing Program at New York University.

Komunyakaa was born James Willie Brown Jr. on April 29, 1947, in Bogalusa, Louisiana, a place that remains central to his imagination. He later took the name of his grandfather, who came to the U.S. from Trinidad as a stowaway. Komunyakaa served in Vietnam as a correspondent and managing editor of the military newspaper the *Southern Cross*. He was awarded the Bronze Star. Returning to the States, he earned a BA from the University of Colorado in 1975, an MA from Colorado State University in 1978, and an MFA from the University of California, Irvine in 1980. He has been on the faculties of the University of New Orleans, Indiana University at Bloomington, and Princeton University. He was married to Mandy Sayers, an Australian fiction writer, from 1985 to 1995, and was subsequently in a relationship with Reetika Vazirani, a poet, who killed herself and their son in the summer of 2003.

Komunyakaa's poetry exposes brutal truths and poignant human weaknesses. The settings of his early poems are typically unforgiving and harsh. In this world, one fights for survival either directly and physically or as a trickster, manipulating situations. The rich, rhythmic voice of the poems and the use of archetypal imagery, combined with intense formal restraint, create an elegant beauty amid pain and trauma. Across his oeuvre, Komunyakaa draws upon personal meditations and family stories, racial issues and American civil rights history, vernacular and pop culture lore, jazz and blues, epic tales, and the history of Western civilization. His broad range of subjects and themes has only increased, with his most recent work including a sequence of sonnets on the history of war, a series of poems investigating blacks as represented in the global history of arts and culture, and an extended dramatic monologue with autobiographical implications. His formal technique has proven most adaptive, ranging from tercets, quatrains, and sonnets, to one-stanza poems, in various voices and personae. Always, his highly crafted poems feature tight control of imagery, diction, and line lengths.

Komunyakaa's poetry situates itself in relation to several strands in the poetic tradition. His use of personae and tight formalism separate him from much of postmodern American poetry, which often makes use of open form and a poet-speaker. His continuing focus on the sound of the poem as spoken ties him to organic modernists such as William Carlos Williams. His is a poetic focused on a highly crafted product, however, not the process of creation. His poems are often ideal for New Critical poetic explication. As such, Komunyakaa can be seen as affiliated with early T. S. Eliot and Ezra Pound, and the New Criticism much of postmodern poetry rejects; he might also be spoken of with midcentury modernist poets such as Gwendolyn Brooks and Robert Hayden. Komunyakaa's poems often (but not always) emanate from a specifically black perspective, drawing upon racial and cultural materials, themes, and elements of social protest. At the same time, his poems make it clear that perspective is quite broad and is, in fact, global and timeless. His most recent work steps in and out of racial frames as it wishes, without leaving race behind. Some critics find his poetry postmodern, perhaps due to the jazz perspective infused throughout his oeuvre; I myself find it more modernist in sensibility, especially the later poems' emphasis on a quest for meaning.

Critical reception of Komunyakaa's poetry has been very positive and at times effusive. His work is the subject of multiple interviews, several essays, a special issue of the journal *Callaloo*, and one largely descriptive study by Angela Salas. The majority of critical attention to his work has focused on its jazz elements, foundations in African American vernacular culture, or the poems of the Vietnam War in *Dien Cai Dau*. His contribution in each of these areas provides a defining pillar in its scholarly discourse: we cannot think about any of these fields of inquiry without thinking of his poetry. One unexplored area is his depiction of women, a topic that comes up in our interview. His work after 2003 is richly epic and global, while at the same time deeply personal; it calls for new critical frames beyond our current understanding of his work.

Komunyakaa has won numerous fellowships from organizations including the NEA, the Fine Arts Work Center in Provincetown, and the Louisiana Arts Council, and significant awards, including the Ruth Lilly Poetry Prize, the Pulitzer Prize for Poetry, the Kingsley Tufts Poetry Award, the Robert Creeley Poetry Award, and the William Faulkner Prize. He was elected a chancellor of the Academy of American Poets in 1999.

I interviewed Komunyakaa in October 2008, in his sparsely decorated office at the Lillian Vernon Creative Writers House at NYU.

Selected Works by Yusef Komunyakaa

POETRY

Dedications and Other Darkhorses, Rocky Mountain Creative Arts Journal, 1977.
Lost in the Bonewheel Factory, Lynx House Press, 1979.
Copacetic, Wesleyan University Press, 1981.
I Apologize for the Eyes in My Head, Wesleyan University Press, 1986.
Toys in a Field, Black River Press, 1987.
Dien Cai Dau, Wesleyan University Press, 1988.
February in Sydney, Matchbooks, 1989.
Magic City, Wesleyan University Press, 1992.
Neon Vernacular: New and Selected Poems, Wesleyan University Press, 1993.
Thieves of Paradise, Wesleyan University Press, 1998.
Talking Dirty to the Gods, Farrar, Straus, and Giroux, 2000.
Pleasure Dome: New & Collected Poems, 1975–1999, Wesleyan University Press, 2001.
Taboo: The Wishbone Trilogy, Farrar, Straus, and Giroux, 2004.
Warhorses, Farrar, Straus, and Giroux, 2008.
Gilgamesh: A Verse Play (with Chad Gracia), Wesleyan University Press, 2009.

OTHER

The Jazz Poetry Anthology (coedited with Sascha Feinstein), Indiana University Press, 1991.

The Second Set: The Jazz Poetry Anthology, Volume 2 (coedited with
Sascha Feinstein), Indiana University Press, 1998.
Blues Notes: Essays, Interviews, and Commentaries (edited by Radiclani
Clytus), University of Michigan Press, 2000.

MALIN PEREIRA: In both interviews and essays, you speak or write about
the power of rituals. I'm curious about your own writing rituals, down to
the level of how you begin. On paper, with pen or pencil? Do you write in
notebooks or journals?

YUSEF KOMUNYAKAA: I write in notebooks and on scraps of paper. I
write everything in longhand because the whole formation of the human
brain seems to have a lot to do with tactile relationships — the pressure
of the pen or pencil against the paper. When we think about the brain's
evolution, we have to admit that it has much to do with the dexterity of the
human hand. I wonder how technology is affecting that evolution. When
are our tools unnatural? I still keep a pad of paper beside my bed and often
I will jot down a line or a stanza; at times when I'm lucky, I may jot down
a whole verse poem. When I'm writing, I realize it has been influenced by
a certain kind of observation that's based on my growing up in Bogalusa,
Louisiana. I was first very observant of the rituals of animals, then parental
rituals, which led to an acute observation of other human beings. I knew
the ins and outs of my neighborhood. I knew Bogalusa. I believe that kind
of observation is linked to the writing process.

MP: How do you revise?

YK: I revise a whole lot. I read everything aloud. That is the first mo-
ment of revision, because the ear is a great editor. It keeps us true to the
music that belongs to each of us. So in that sense, I hope that there's an
excavation of a natural terrain. Language is our very first music, so the oral
tradition is very important to me. I do like to see the symbols and such. For
me, the poem is a composite of symbols and silences.

MP: When do you move it onto the computer? That seems a big shift.

YK: For a long time, I had a typewriter, and it seemed much easier. Now
I'll go through a number of drafts before I commit it to the computer,
because I really don't want the instrument — the machine — to get in the
way of the process.

MP: So it has to be to a certain point before it's safe, codified or set?

YK: Right. Once it's on the computer, it seems committed to its destiny.

That's problematic because the poem is usually still evolving. Even after the point when it's been published, I may find myself circling a word or a phrase that seems extraneous, not for the ideas in the poem as much as to the music in the poem.

MP: I'm thinking suddenly of Marianne Moore's poem "Poetry," which has one longer version and one far shorter version. Have you ever done anything like that?

YK: Not to that extent, no. I'm always afraid of polishing the heart out of the poem, so I don't want to be extreme about it. With Marianne Moore, I've gone back and forth between those two poems, because I think they're different poems. In many ways, I do like the brevity of the shorter one, but sometimes I wanted a more extended musing on such an important topic.

MP: I read a number of your interviews in preparation for this one. I enjoyed reading an interview done by Kyle Dargan in *Callaloo* in 2006 because it sounded like a lively exchange. One of the other interviews introduces you as being a postmodernist. I've just finished reading Edward Pavlić's *Crossroads Modernism*, and he cites you numerous times to illustrate African American modernism. I'm more convinced than ever that you're more of a modernist, although of course, we know modernism and postmodernism are difficult to divide. In particular, your long poem "Autobiography of My Alter Ego," which was just published in fall 2008 in your collection *Warhorses*, has a main character whom you described in your interview with Ernie Suarez in 1999 in modernist terms. You said, "He attempts to bring all the fractured parts of himself together to make himself whole again." This is very much like T. S. Eliot's quest in "The Waste Land." How much do you see yourself as a modernist?

YK: I don't know if I see myself in the light of either modernist or postmodernist forms. I do think that one is condemned to write in one's own time, historically and biologically. But sometimes it's that we're too eager to graft ourselves to some very abstract ideas and theoretical concepts, and if we aren't careful we'll soon find ourselves talking about post-post-human. Well, I have read Eliot very closely, especially "The Waste Land." I've argued with Eliot, especially when considering *The Inventions of the March Hare*. On the surface, his misogyny and bigotry are apparent, and he attempted to deny them for so long. Eliot is influenced by his surroundings. While we think of St. Louis as being in the Midwest, I think of Eliot as being from the South because of the industry of the river in St. Louis. With

Eliot, one can see that he agonizes about how he sounds when he talks. He goes to Harvard, and his voice changes.

MP: Listening to tapes of him, you'd think he was British.

YK: Quite right. I think the reason is that growing up in St. Louis, in that household, perhaps he sounded black from being around his black caretakers. That's the basis for a classic love-hate complex. The caretaker is a symbol of love, but later on becomes a symbol of derision.

MP: Have you read the article on "The Waste Land" that suggests it was based on his experience seeing minstrel shows?

YK: I know of it. But, it would be interesting to know who his caretakers were, how they influenced him. The minstrel show as a source of influence seems too deliberately literary, too staged, and too closely associated with the internal landscape of John Berryman's *Dream Songs*, with Henry as alter ego. I see the terrain of "The Waste Land" as highly personal. Perhaps it is a psychological purging, something driven by a terrifying necessity.

MP: He was a privileged person. There would have been caretakers. Perhaps there's a story there.

YK: Yes, I think so. Also Eliot was influenced by jazz, which was quite alive in St. Louis. In *The Inventions of the March Hare*, he talks about wandering into an alleyway in north Cambridge, and I think he's really talking about St. Louis but he doesn't want to say *St. Louis*. It sounds too common, too provincial.

MP: What about this alter ego in your poem? I wasn't thinking about all of the specifics of Eliot as much as how this alter ego echoes an Eliotic modernist quest: "Make my fragments whole."

YK: I often say we internalize everything, and that which we have internalized becomes a psychological overlay of how we experience the world and how we see the world. So in a sense, yes. It becomes how we view ourselves in the final analysis as well. How one makes oneself whole. James Baldwin attempts to make himself whole. He does that by being distant from America, by discovering a certain possibility while in France. In that way, he becomes even more intensely American. Eliot, with his speech and his top hat, attempted to be more British than the British are, but his work is very American.

MP: How do you mean that?

YK: Not so much his concerns, but I'm thinking about the language, the cadence, the sound of it.

MP: I was just reading in the paper about the Nobel Prize in Literature, and how the committee supposedly has a prejudice against Americans — at least according to the article I read. Our literature doesn't make the grade. Perhaps Eliot understood that and assimilated.

Let's talk a little bit about this new collection of yours, *Warhorses*. The flyleaf says — and this is continuing on the modernist quest idea — that you sound like a breathless and exhausted but desperate prophet in "Autobiography of My Alter Ego." So, in coming to this long poem, first I'm hearing *quest of a fragmented self*, and now I'm hearing *exhausted and desperate prophet*. These are modernist themes. Do you feel at this point in your work a responsibility to speak out about 9/11, the Iraq War, or the Bush Administration? This is a contemporary volume, but also expresses a larger concern about war.

YK: I don't necessarily feel a responsibility. The long poem "Autobiography of My Alter Ego" was started so long ago. The first section of the book is fourteen quasi-sonnets, although I've written twenty-five or so. My original idea is still intact. I intended the volume to imaginatively pursue warfare, its history, its intention. I think all wars are connected. We only have to briefly consider Homer, how he depicts the high and low moments of warfare. We only have to think of the depiction of Humbaba as the *other* in *Gilgamesh*. The so-called enemy still has to be reduced, degraded, or called an infidel. For me, how I look at warfare, the inhumanity visited upon each other, perhaps goes back to that moment I picked up James Baldwin's essays and began to read. He always queries humanity, showing how we constantly dehumanize ourselves by dehumanizing others.

MP: You're reminding me of your poem from your collection *Talking Dirty to the Gods*, "Slaves on Blades of Grass," and its line about dismantling one world to make the other appear whole. I think you're getting to the same essential truth.

The title poem "Warhorses" is a creative history of warfare and how it's tied to the horse and horsepower.

YK: I could hear the thundering hooves of horses in my head. The history of the horse is also the early history of modern warfare. It's all about speed and brute strength. I see the title poem as a performance. Susie Ibarra set music to the poem, and performed it at a small museum near here.

MP: Neat. One section in *Warhorses*, the first, "Love in the Time of War," links love and violence, which I think is a reoccurring theme throughout your body of work. How do you see the two connected?

YK: They live beside each other. I started thinking about what horrible things people do to each other, moving from moments of concentrated violence to love. It has been very difficult for me to understand that. How the brain can be fractured that way; I think that's what happens, the psyche is fractured. Today in our modern society, a moment of love is often only an illusion and it has more to do with possession than love. Perhaps it has always been that way.

MP: Like in *Beloved* — Toni Morrison plumbs the depths of that. Both love and war are often twisted and about possession. It's an odd thing, that the somatic response in the body to both crying and laughing is virtually indiscernible. If you're weeping or laughing, it's difficult for sensors to detect the difference. And sometimes people veer between the two.

YK: There was an interesting postcard from the time of Thomas Jefferson showing two images, a slave being whipped and a woman being courted. To have the two side by side created an immediate tension.

MP: In lynching scenes there's often a linking of sex and violence.

YK: People were sending each other postcards of lynchings. Also, people would take loved ones to these performances of violence. It is my understanding that some white southern schools were let out so students could attend such organized violence as public performance.

MP: You can see in the photographs the faces in the crowds, the jubilation on people's faces. What does this say about the human psyche?

I had read about "Autobiography of My Alter Ego" nine years ago as a work in progress, and was excited to see it finally in print. After reading a couple of pages, I realized he was white! I went back to the beginning and started reading again. He's a Vietnam vet, and he's into music; I see the parallels to your own life.

YK: He's really a composite of many people.

MP: He's a very racially aware white guy.

YK: I think that exists in a lot of Americans.

MP: From that era or that location?

YK That era and that location. I believe there's a great risk to admit that awareness.

I'm not talking about a risk that's external. It's that constant argument, that necessary negotiation that takes place deep in the psyche.

MP: A forged double consciousness, created, not inborn.

YK: Right. It takes a lot of work to be aware of what's there. Being aware of how one's own psyche has been formed. Early on, I don't even know if racism or racial awareness is taught. A great deal happens in body language. Racism isn't taught by a derogatory expression necessarily, especially for children. There's more to it. Their eyes, their ears, their bodies always observing—the whole being on notice.

MP: And they don't often listen to what adults say, anyway.

YK: Right, they are all eyes, all ears, intensely aware, and that has something to do with survival. We are complex organisms, so we are informed by the senses, perhaps even the sixth sense.

MP: How is he your alter ego?

YK: The speaker in the poem is a composite of numerous white American veterans I've known. Some are keenly aware of what's happening regarding race. And, in this sense, I suppose there's a discourse at the heart of the poem. I think the narrator is talking to someone; he could be talking to himself as well.

MP: Like a dramatic monologue?

YK: I think he's talking to someone. He's a bartender, and he's talking to someone seated before him. He may be talking to me.

MP: You open yourself up for those questions because of the title. I would have been marveling over your creation of this character, but you bring him so much closer to you when you use the word *autobiography*, and then you also use *alter ego* in case we weren't taking you seriously enough. Those are tempting words. There's also this element of self-reflection on your part to create an alter ego/character/persona. Is this a function of where you're at right now in your career?

YK: It's an interesting place for a dialogue to exist. Maybe that's what creating an alter ego is all about — there's a dialogue. First, in the context of oneself, in order for it to then exist outside of oneself. Otherwise, why would we do it?

MP: I'm thinking of Elizabeth Alexander's final line from her poem "Ars Poetica #100: I Believe"— "and are we not of interest to each other?" Your poem is a very sad poem near the end. When you start talking about hands, there's a whole motif about forgiveness. It comes to a crescendo by the father's passing, and then the final poem, which is just beautiful. It ends, "but don't forgive my hands." I also thought of Toni Morrison's *Jazz*: "look where my hands are now." What about forgiveness and what about hands?

YK: Forgiveness is necessary. Forgiving others is another way of making ourselves whole. I think Baldwin was very instructive in that sense. To forgive white people was necessary in order to not carry the burden of anger and anguish around. It's destructive to others, and to oneself more deeply.

The hands? I suppose it has a lot to do with growing up in Louisiana. I admired people who worked with their hands. My dad, my great-grandfather, ones I admire who were able to root out a living with a kind of honesty in work. Even Calvinistic. It's a kind of celebration. Something about that is concrete. Getting one's hands into soil. It's important for young people to be aware of that. I want to write an essay on work.

MP: The meaning of work? What is meaningful work? It would be a great essay.

I think there is a sense of ethos behind how you talk about hands. They represent something that is more to be trusted, or is about being responsible for your actions. Other stuff is more ephemeral, more ethereal. This is what is more concrete and tangible.

YK: I grew up that way in a rural southern environment. I grew up with people who respected the soil. One reason was because of course they were able to at least create out of the soil. Also, that becomes a living as well. Sometimes it was a necessity. It had a lot to do with some very pleasant moments, such as at age fifteen cutting pulpwood with my uncle. Being out in the woods at five o'clock in the morning just as the light begins to creep in. It's interesting, realizing everything is so alive. That was instructive for me. The whole rhythm of things was important to me, truly human.

MP: Those patterns. You make it sound almost magical. The smell of your mother or your mother's cooking are scents you could recognize anywhere. And the way you're talking about your upbringing, it's evoking the same connection. You could probably smell the pulpwood on your skin when you're out there at five o'clock. Those are primal sensory experiences that really shape you.

YK: Also, realizing the brain is such an engine for imagination. Being there and not being there, you can bring it all back. To bring it back through one's imagination. One of my earliest memories is of looking through one of those viewfinders and finding this huge world out there. To travel in my imagination and at the same time being connected to that landscape may have been the foundation of my writing.

MP: I was really struck by your epic of Gilgamesh. I found that a beautiful verse play. Gilgamesh is so poignantly depicted. He faces life and death and it makes him a man. I don't remember the epic of Gilgamesh being that interesting. What drew you to it?

YK: I read it some time ago, and I started trying to think of it as a play. "Where's the action?" one might say, but once I had written the first few lines I had the music. I knew I wouldn't use any contraptions. I knew there would be action but the language was the main thing. I wanted it to be contemporary but also not too contemporary. It's timeless, that's how I feel about the piece. I had to discover the language, though an element of that is already there in the original work.

MP: Do you think that it is a universal struggle or plot for a man to think he's a god, then go through traumas and figure out he's a man? A plot of finding oneself?

YK: Yes. It is that necessary moment of deep meditation. And Gilgamesh is alone in that cedar forest. Because of death, friendship has been severed through what happens.

MP: So, recognizing mortality is when you really become human?

YK: I don't know that one has to go through the rigors of that kind of meditation, but we all have that capacity. That's what makes Gilgamesh human. His mother fed him too much; the glut of her giving weakens him.

MP: I know that often the temptation of mothering is to give them everything. In one way, Gilgamesh is like the persona of "The Autobiography of My Alter Ego." Gilgamesh is also trying to take the fractured pieces of himself and make himself whole.

YK: For him, he has to deny something in order to make himself whole. He denies his constructed privilege of being a god.

MP: The moment he says all the prisoners should be released is where he finds his humanity.

YK: That's the moment he realizes he is in this world, a part of this world, and that he has the capacity to do good.

MP: I want to move on to one of your poems published in 2004 as part of *Taboo: The Wishbone Trilogy*. The collection is about how blacks have been treated or represented in art. The poem that caught my attention is "Chiaroscuro." It seems to be in conversation with a poem that follows it a few pages later, especially the epigraph to the poem "To Beauty," which is Otto Dix's quote: "painting things black will get you nowhere." The term *chiaroscuro* means "clear dark" in Italian. It's a style that uses light and dark for effect. This poem is central to this collection because of the way in which you are articulating a black aesthetic, but not in the sense of the Black Arts Movement. It is viewing art, history and culture through a black lens. In fact, I'm thinking back to your early volume *I Apologize for the Eyes in My Head*. You weren't apologizing back then, in fact you were deeply sardonic. But in this newest collection, you're doing it without pretending to have an apology. So could you talk about the aesthetic you are articulating in "Chiaroscuro" and also in "Taboo," and then step to the larger picture of what this means for *The Wishbone Trilogy*?

YK: I think of how *The Wishbone Trilogy* came about. I have lengthy discussions with my students and often it's about history and literature. I used to talk about history, and then I looked at the students and saw there's a blank.

Maybe it had a lot to do with growing up in Louisiana, where I didn't have any idea about this history at all. I began to look at certain authors, and the first two poems I memorized were Edgar Allan Poe's "Annabelle Lee" and James Weldon Johnson's "The Creation." That brought me into knowing that there were black writers out there, and it really clicked when I got to Baldwin and I began to read everything I possibly could. I never took a class in African American literature; however, I have done my homework. So it's almost like food for me, in many ways. Not just for my imagination as such, but for who I really was. Some of the people I grew up with, it's the essence of their existence. I'm writing an essay now called "The Colors in My Dreams." This essay starts off this way: "Dead Red's left eye is blue. His right eye was grey." I talk about this black man and how the complexity of color has always been a part of my life as well as my imagination. Those contradictions have also been there. So maybe those early moments have a lot to do with my persistent inquiry about what's out there.

A good example is this summer: I went to the little town of Łódź, Poland. I have been taken with the idea of Ira Aldridge, an African American Shakespearean actor. His career spanned the 1830s to the 1850s, and he was a significant actor. I didn't realize he had died in Poland. It was an interesting moment going there and seeing his picture on his gravestone. It's probably some kind of ceramic. Visiting and putting flowers on his grave was very important to me. These figures in history keep visiting me, and I'm quite taken with the fact that there are so many of them. The women and men came to life because of certain situations. The man or woman of the hour is always there. I'm particularly thinking about people like Frederick Douglass. The perfect person for the situation just seems to show up.

MP: These people pop up and change history.

YK: They do. Sometimes, they are also very quiet; they are glossed over. There's a certain excavation that takes place.

In chiaroscuro, there's both light and dark. One enhances the other. One makes the other possible.

MP: You wouldn't have light unless you had dark to contrast. It's a mutual definition.

I think of several of the writers I've read or talked to, and I think about the "Banneker" poem by Rita Dove, for example. Poets have to do their excavations of those characters. Elizabeth Alexander does a lot of them. You bring out the black figures that were in the margins, just like Rubens's paintings.

YK: We are so astounded by history sometimes because we assume there was all this opposition, when in fact I think people were crossing all kinds of boundaries.

MP: Oftentimes, when the poets I've spoken to have done these things, it goes back to Morrison's comments back in the Black Arts Movement about creating a usable past. By going back and excavating those figures, you create for a genealogy for yourself.

There have been people going across oceans participating in world cultures for centuries. One of the more bizarre experiences I have had was in Madrid. I'm in a museum and I go around the corner and there is a picture, and I swore it looked like George Washington's portrait, but it was a black man. I could tell by the way he was posed, the whole style, the person who did this had painted the George Washington portrait we all know. It turns out that it was done by the same portrait artist who painted Washington. It was of Washington's cook! I went to the gift shop to buy cards with this portrait on it. It was such an object of conversation when I came back.

YK: It also shows how connected we are, and that is the most important thing. It shows that we have all been connected — sometimes, in some intimate ways. That was a revelation to me, because that was a bridge for me that was so important in my imagination. When I was a teenager dreaming myself out of the woods, I was across the ocean. Many people dreamt themselves across the ocean, took ships and made their way.

MP: Elizabeth Alexander has an interest in the translator figure from the *Amistad* story — she names him Covey in *American Sublime*. He becomes a key figure for her. This relates to something that interests me — the cosmopolitan thread running through your work. So many of you in this generation have that cosmopolitan sensibility of movement around the globe, borrowing from whatever cultural materials are necessary to say what you have to say. I see this in your more recent works, the ones after 2000, and

I'm wondering if that cosmopolitanism in your work has deepened into this "universal" pattern — that we're all connected, these eternal archetypes. Do you see that in your work?

YK: If it's there, it has been there or at least the possibility of it has been there all along. I suppose I have embraced it in my work.

MP: You accepted it and went with it in your work.

YK: Yes, that kind of inquiry has been there since day one. In that sense, I have taken a license to pursue it deeper. *The Wishbone Trilogy* started off with the idea of three books, *Taboo, Lust,* and *Bread.* Those were the three titles I had. They are still the same, believe it or not. There's something provocative in those three titles.

MP: When you get down to one-word titles you're saying something as deep as you can say, these deep eternal truths. With *Taboo,* you're fingering the taboo in history and art that hasn't been articulated. You're highlighting the presence that's been made an absence. In some of your recent work, I'm reminded of late William Butler Yeats, late William Carlos Williams, that pursuit of the eternal answers. Like *Paterson,* and Yeats's stuff with the gyre, you're mapping a deep set of universal connections.

YK: It's all inquires, not answers. Questions, not answers.

MP: There's nothing static. That's where I'd pull back from comparing you to Eliot, who is searching for answers. He gravitates to a static system that is closed.

One of the things that has come up in your other interviews is your connection to Faulkner — no one is saying that, but you bring him up. I have thought for a few years that you do have some connections to Faulkner. Your poem "Salt" is Faulknerian. I was excited to see "Toby's Blues" in *Taboo.* In other interviews, you have said that you don't see yourself as a southern writer, you see yourself as an American writer. Would you entertain the idea of being a Faulknerian poet or having some parallels to Faulkner?

YK: We both internalize the landscape, so in that sense yes. But there are many overlays; that is just one overlay. Faulkner interests me because he had such a sense of place. He knows, even though he gives a fictitious name to a place (Mississippi) — he knows every nook and cranny of it. I found myself recently writing in this essay that I wasn't afraid of the night as a kid. One reason is because I knew everything around me. I knew the place well. That was my very first expertise. It was that I had my fingers on the pulse — all over the place. I feel like Faulkner knew his environment in a similar way.

MP: "Toby's Blues" is very useful to me. In my American literature survey classes, there's not time for a Faulkner novel. Yet, the short stories are too short and don't use the narrative techniques of the novels. Your poem gives me something to pair with "A Rose for Miss Emily." I want to talk about the racial issues, but the story doesn't yield up enough. It doesn't willfully go there.

YK: But it's there.

MP: Yes. My students always want to talk about the character Homer, and if he's gay. My students will be happy to have this poem. We all want to talk about these things, and you have lifted the fingerprints off the story, what Faulkner didn't put into words.

YK: In a certain sense. It's not hiding. He just wouldn't go there, but he was writing in another time. I'm surprised he went that far in that time and in Mississippi.

MP: It's difficult to explain Faulkner and Mark Twain to my students because they find them so lacking in the things they need them to be saying about today. I try to show them how far they went — that for their times they went really a long way. Faulkner dedicated his 1940 stories to Caroline Barr, and this is an astonishing degree of awareness. He never figured out his issues about white women, though. He had a lot of obsessions about his daughter and her virginity and those types of issues, and he never got further on those. But he knew the black people of his community intimately.

YK: And the caretaker of the land — the Native American. It's interesting he realized that necessity. Faulkner is a poet. His poems in that one little volume taught him something about prose. There is embedded in Faulkner's prose, influenced by his poems, those love poems.

MP: Reading Faulkner passages aloud in class is a beautiful thing. He, like you, is attuned to the way the prose sounds. You can imagine people speaking like this in a darkened room, telling these stories. It's so real and the sound is so accurate.

In some ways, he's the precursor to the alter ego figure in *Warhorses*. To some degree, for his time, Faulkner has some of that same self-awareness and self-reflexiveness. In the short stories, he shows he can think from two angles. There's one Faulkner short story about a man whose wife has just died, "Pantaloon in Black." He manages to relate both the white point of view of this man and the man's own point of view — and that's double consciousness.

YK: It is. That's definitely what W. E. B. DuBois is talking about. That necessity — the survival tactic. It's not even a tactic; it's a natural double consciousness.

MP: I'm wondering if with cosmopolitanism and global awareness we're becoming multiconscious.

YK: The civil rights movement has been so important to bringing us to where we are at this moment. There's been immense change within the context of America, and consequently that change has influenced the world now, and we might not even be aware of it. But it was necessary and it is still in progress. It is incomplete. Guess what the possibilities are. That our country has become multicultural has to do with the civil rights movement. When we think of people coming from Latin America, the Caribbean, Southeast Asia, it's all possible because of the civil rights movement.

MP: In part because of it we have women's rights, gay rights. One interesting experience I have had in the last few years was going to a Sylvia Plath conference in England. Several black women poets I have interviewed pay homage to Plath in their poetry — Wanda Coleman, Thylias Moss, and Elizabeth Alexander.

One of the scholars on my panel was a man from India, a member of the lowest caste. He is doing his scholarship on the writings of people of his caste. Basically, he's modeling it on what we have here in America from the civil rights movement and the Black Arts Movement. It's this self-empowerment, finding a useable past. All that has gotten us to this point, at least, in the field of African American studies. He saw a parallel between the two movements, and he's modeling the scholarship for his people on our history and the struggle of the civil rights movement and then the Black Arts Movement.

YK: That is very interesting.

MP: It's a global model.

YK: He saw the connection. When I was in Australia, I was speaking with some of the aboriginals who said the civil rights movement in America was very important to them.

MP: I've heard the same from people in South Africa and the scholars and writers there. What I like about this particular generation of poets I'm looking at is that they all pay homage to the civil rights movement. It's what made your writing possible.

YK: The civil rights movement is not a black movement. It is a collective of white and black voices all there together. So it's an American movement. I see photos of young people going down on the Freedom Rides. I have my students look at those photos. I ask them if they can picture themselves doing the same thing. Many of them freeze, because there's an act of real bravery there — people died — people who had been in service broke from the attitudes of their families, took that leap. Later on we repaired those fractures, or at least sometimes.

MP: It's reminiscent of the choices people made around the time of the Civil War, which side they would take in the war. Then, that's when you go against your upbringing to imagine a new possibility, which is a very difficult thing.

YK: It's very patriotic, at least as we would define it.

MP: It is patriotic and brave. That's the other part of it, that oftentimes, within this group of poets, writers very quickly back off from claiming they themselves have that same type of bravery. I'm thinking of Harryette Mullen. In one of her poems, she lauds the civil rights questers, but then the poem turns its point of view to what the civil rights people would think of her and her generation. It's not laudatory at all. We're comparatively a very pampered generation.

YK: Also, their being able to maintain a certain kind of dignity and presence. That's something I do admire.

MP: We've made so many strides in people being able to have the dignity that should be accorded them, but at the same time we have the problem that we're not willing to risk it for certain things. We're not willing to risk *everything*. Does that mean we won't do the hard things?

YK: I think we have a critical apparatus within the context of communities and what have you, and sometimes we have to be rather brave about our pronouncements. That's necessary. I think about what Baldwin would say now.

MP: Sometimes you have to be the one to say it, because we don't have Baldwin anymore. This is sort of coalescing for me now, that this is what's going on in *Warhorses*. You've made up your mind to say some things. You're not grandstanding — it's just that it's time. It's as if you are saying, "Maybe there are ways in which I need to be a war horse now about certain things — speaking up. There are all kinds of wars."

YK: Yes, that's true.

MP: Since this interview is supposed to be about poetry, I should ask you about poetry a little bit more. One of the issues with this "lost genera-tion" of yours is the question of, lost in what sense? What I think Kevin Young meant in part by that phrase is that there wasn't a manifesto like the manifestos during the Black Arts Movement. You didn't have a set of aesthetic principles, or even a mantra, such as "Harlem is a Mecca" during the Harlem Renaissance. As a group, you are a key generation in transition-ing between the Black Arts Movement and the current generation. In your individual poetic processes and bodies of work, you and your peers have enabled people who are now writing in this generation to dream their big-gest dreams. There's eight of you in my book — all eight give a wide spread of options for black poets today.

YK: That's all from the civil rights movement. Before that, we were writ-ing basically service literature and it had everything to do with defining blackness. For the most part, it was an external voice — it was what was out there. After the civil rights movement — not that anyone sat down and said it was time — but it was time to attempt an internal voice as well. Most of us were not condemned to be on this one track writing one kind of poem. But perhaps that started even before. It started with someone such as Robert Hayden, and yet he was systematically criticized by the Black Arts Movement. He had taken it upon himself to create his own direction. He would not submit to any dictation.

MP: He was brave and he was vilified for it in many ways. I know Rita Dove looks more to Tolson, although she respects Hayden. Tolson was one of the attackers of Hayden at that 1967 conference at Fisk.

YK: He had to be in the camp of those younger voices, maybe for reasons that he probably couldn't even articulate.

MP: You see, then, how your writing can be used by this next genera-tion in a genealogy? You have your genealogy — poets you look to such as Hayden, Baldwin, and other writers. If you could ask the next generation of poets what they would take from your writing as a part of their own genealogy, what would it be?

YK: To realize that, although you're taught it's taboo, you have to have a certain system of aesthetics.

MP: So a consistent voice or an operating framework?

YK: I think each of us has to be aware of who we are.

MP: Who are you reading among the younger generation? Or do you not want to pick out anybody?

YK: I don't want to single out any one person. There are some great poets out there, and they are constantly surprising me and everyone else.

MP: I feel very fortunate to be working in black poetry today because it's an embarrassment of riches.

YK: It's amazing what's out there.

MP: You have voiced some concern over experimental poetry. You have said: "It seems as if these poems come out of everything except experience. The poems come out of certain cultivated practices that have to do with reading the right books, consequently we can probably program computers to write those poems based on the intake of certain details from theory books and encyclopedias and what have you."

That's in your 2002 interview with Tod Marshall. I wonder if you're specifically talking about any African American experimental poets? In particular, I thought of Harryette Mullen with the reference to encyclopedias. Do you have any concern about the experimentalism of such black poets as Mullen or Nathaniel Mackey?

YK: Well, I'm not against experimentation, per se. I'm against experimentation that erases content.

MP: Linguistic play for play's sake?

YK: Exactly, that erases content. When I edited *The Best of American Poetry* [2003, with David Lehman], that introduction was partially about erasure. There have been these voices who have experimented for some time. For example, the playful voice of Ed Roberson in *When Thy King Is a Boy: Poems*, published in 1970. Experimentation has been there, but it is a very informed experimentation. It's not a question of what's in vogue at the moment.

MP: I did find in preparing for my interview with Mullen that many of her early interviews are about theory. I'm wondering if writers who fit these dominant theories in the larger poetic arena, in academia more specifically, get showcased or lauded or accepted because they fit these critical theories.

YK: It's interesting when content is not addressed. If it is not addressed from a poetic point of view in the poems, how can it be addressed in a critical critique?

MP: Here's a contrast that perhaps expresses your point: one of the best articles on your early poetry is one by Ed Pavlić. I require my graduate students to read this article before writing on Komunyakaa. They have to see what some of the basic themes are, first. But one of the best articles on Mullen is all about puns and word play and how to figure out her poems. I call it one of the best articles because it enables my students to understand what her poetry is doing. That critical article is about what the poetry is *doing*, while Pavlić's article is about what your work is *saying* and where it's coming from. Am I getting your point about the content versus the technique right?

YK: Yes. It's basically what I was talking about in the process of erasure. The content is erased; the only thing that is left to talk about is the mechanics or methodology ...

MP: And that's not enough for you. That's not why you write poetry.

YK: No, it's not enough. There are moments when I go in that direction. But it seems problematic to me.

MP: That's why I would call you a modernist and not a postmodernist. Modernism does embrace a quest for meaning, and it will accept plural meanings. But it doesn't just play with the quest. It is a quest with a purpose and a result.

One thing I wanted to ask you about is something I have been thinking about in your work for a long time, your depiction of women. There are lots of women in your poetry. I read them as highly archetypal. They are either sexualized temptresses or desexualized maternal figures. In one of your poems, "At the Screen Door," there is a figure behind a screen door. The male speaker gives the impression, "I'm coming home to the mother." Even if they aren't mothers, they are maternal figures. In some of your more recent work, I'm wondering if the two archetypes — temptress and maternal figure — are merging. How do you see the depiction of women in your poetry?

YK: In a way they are archetypal. I suppose a lot has to do with being raised primarily by women, especially grandmothers. How do I see women in my poetry? It's an interesting question.

MP: When I teach your poetry I find it very easy to have students use your poetry to do an archetypal reading because it's there. It ties to the mythic sensibilities you seem to be moving toward, although we've agreed that was there from the beginning.

YK: Women are always important to the physical landscapes.

MP: They always played these two roles in the quest. Temptress, mother, and the figure of the witch/crone are the three options you have when you do archetypal criticism and women. You haven't really thought about this, have you?

YK: No, not really.

MP: Part of me wonders if this comes from being a male poet writing about women archetypally because it's how it fits into a male quest.

YK: It's coming out of the landscape, too. In the landscape I grew up in, women did all types of jobs. They were not just homemakers. They were doing all kinds of things. I'm informed by those observations and experiences.

MP: In "At the Screen Door," he's walking toward the door and you know everything will be provided to him when he makes it to the door. In Toni Morrison's *Song of Solomon*, when Sweet takes in Milkman, he gets *everything*.

YK: There's a foundation, and a place to return to, but also, since it's a foundation, it's a place to take off from.

MP: That's the other side of it. That recurs in many stories.

I wanted to talk about one of your essays. You have a beautiful and very sober essay titled "Dark Waters" in a collection called *The Color of Nature: Culture, Identity, and the Natural World*. It gave me a label for the concept *environmental racism*. Since that essay was published in 2002, we've had Hurricane Katrina. It exposed a lot of environmental racism, among all the other kinds of racism. And then more recently, I read your poem "Requiem" in *Callaloo*.

YK: That's an ongoing poem. That's the first section of what I think of as a short book.

It's not all on the subject of Katrina. It's about New Orleans and what's been lost.

MP: Can you talk about Katrina and its impact on you, on New Orleans, and on Louisiana and even on America?

YK: It was sobering moment, because many of us were aware that underneath that underbelly there was the horror of racism. It's there, but something we don't talk about is very much there too: class. I'm getting ready to go back to New Orleans later this year. I'm going to Newman, a high school.

MP: I've been told New Orleans is still devastated.

YK: Yes. For me, New Orleans was always a place for turmoil and great beauty. It was a kind of push and pull. People I grew up with were very aware of the beauty of the place but also the underbelly. It has a turbulent history.

MP: You're reminding me of Sweet Home in Morrison's work *Beloved*. It is described as absolutely gorgeous and absolutely horrifying. I've heard reports recently that up to 40 percent of the New Orleans residents were illiterate. When FEMA came in with all the paperwork needed to get money for your house, because it's all literature based, people weren't able to avail themselves of the federal assistance they were entitled to receive. People elsewhere in America watching were most likely unable to believe what they were seeing, and were unable to comprehend that this could happen in America. No one realized what was going on in our own country.

YK: Exactly. One reason is because when out-of-town Americans visit New Orleans, they're interested in the French Quarter and Bourbon Street. Some New Orleans citizens have never even been there. There used to be twenty-four districts, and I've talked to people who were in there in the 1980s, and some of them had never been out of their neighborhood. Everything was right there in the context of the neighborhood. This has changed through the years.

MP: You think now you're going to do a book about this topic?

YK: It will be a short book. I'm fascinated with New Orleans, and it's a way of dealing with that topic. I want to write about its history. The hurricane is part of that. The hurricane itself did its own natural excavation.

MP: Do you think in some way you're memorializing New Orleans? You have the poems about the Twin Towers memorializing that event, and I wonder if excavating the history of New Orleans or at least getting it written down matters because it will never be the same.

YK: At one time I had a title for a book I wanted to write about New Orleans — *The Golden Octopus*. There used to be a fun house in New Orleans called The Golden Octopus — this was in the 1920s.

MP: You called this poem "Requiem," and I'm reminded of a colleague of mine who wrote a hip-hop requiem for New Orleans. *Requiem* seems an appropriate word for these types of work.

YK: I wrote it for *Oxford American* magazine. The editor wrote to me after Katrina and asked if I would consider writing something. I knew it would be one movement and that later, it would become something bigger.

MP: I have noticed that you bring up Native Americans on occasion.

At Cave Canem's anniversary a few years ago, I was at the panel you and Elizabeth Alexander were on. You brought up the issue of Native Americans and how they were represented in African American literature. You brought it up again today early in the interview. What brings out this awareness in you and how have you developed this awareness?

YK: It may have started with my maternal grandmother — I think of her as part Native American. There were so many other people who were also part Native American. It's always there. One piece I did about a year and a half ago, *Wakonda's Dream*, was the libretto for an opera originally done for Opera Omaha [composed by Anthony Davis]. I thought about it — what's going to happen, should I write about this or that — but I was asked to write it. Native Americans have always been in that landscape I know.

MP: So it's acknowledging them and making them visible.

YK: Yes, being aware of their presence. Also, growing up in Bogalusa, I could go into the woods. I always felt the presence of Native Americans in my early imagination.

MP: You've brought up *home* so many times in this interview. One of the themes I recognize in this generation of poets is the different way you all approach the idea of home. You and Coleman are the two older poets in this group, and you both seem to treat the idea of home similarly. Do you have thoughts about the idea of home and what this might mean to this generation of poets?

YK: For me, those early experiences are so important — those early observations. That's probably the reason why I always return to home. Those early observations have informed my imagination, and it is such an important overlay of the multiple overlays that exist within the context of one's psyche. I grew up with the idea that Bogalusa is a good place to be a long way away from — to grow up and leave. I never was able to totally erase those first impressions, and I wouldn't want to.

MP: You take your home with you wherever you've gone. The voice in the poem is still there. You still believe in things like point of view in a poem and voice, things that, compared to some of the experimental poetry today, look more traditional. That's the home being carried with you, the poetic persona you've developed over time. Coleman has something similar in her work, some versions of what you've done. With her, there is probably more of a class issue; she hasn't been able to travel all over the world like you have. She brought the poets of the world to her instead of going out to them. It's so interesting to see the idea of home, because it's so often denied in early African American history. There was the irony of being at Sweet Home but not being able to possess a home.

YK: In this essay I'm writing, there's a moment when I'm talking about early experiences. My first memory is of my great-grandfather and three of my great-uncles. They were all still living. They were tearing down this house that was beside my maternal grandmother's house. This house was on three acres of land, so there was a huge garden. They had built the house, he was a carpenter. That's my first memory.

MP: Did they build something new where it had been standing?

YK: Yes, they did. He was a brick mason as well as land owner.

MP: Having a home and building a home from the beginning was important. You've built a home that goes with you. And, when you talk about the home, you tie it to the identity that is your home. For me, metaphorically, what this generation has been is building a home for black poetry, like Cave Canem has done. That's a big home. We had such wonderful poetry early in the century, but this is a multiplex of options.

YK: That's what this moment is about, isn't it?

[2008]

RITA DOVE

Rita Dove's career has seemed more public than those of most others in this generation, as she served as U.S. poet laureate for two terms (1993–95), authored the weekly "Poet's Choice" column for the *Washington Post* from 2000 to 2002, and has played a national and international role as an ambassador of poetry. She has published ten books of poetry, a play, a song cycle, a collection of essays, a collection of short stories, and a novel. Much of her work moves beyond views of black poetry commonly promulgated during and after the Black Arts Movement. She is currently a professor of English at the University of Virginia.

Dove was born August 28, 1952, in Akron, Ohio, to a middle class family. Her father had a master's degree in chemistry but had to work as an elevator operator at Goodyear until jobs in the tire industry opened up to blacks. Her mother was a homemaker; Dove was the eldest of four children and an excellent student. Her childhood was one enriched by books, music (she studied cello from grade school through college), and language (she learned German when her father, influenced by the experience of World War II, suggested she should know the language of the enemy). Dove was a Presidential Scholar in 1970, visiting the White House. She earned a BA from Miami University of Ohio in 1973, graduating summa cum laude, and an MFA from the University of Iowa in 1977. Before graduate school, she spent a year at Universität Tübingen in West Germany, where she solidified her fluency in German. At Iowa, Dove's second language caused her to be assigned to assist a visiting novelist from Germany, Fred Viebahn, whom she married in 1979. They have one daughter, Aviva Dove-Viebahn. While the couple tried to live in Germany in 1979–80, Dove found the language environment was affecting her poetry, so in 1981 they moved to Tempe, Arizona, where she taught creative writing at Arizona State University until 1989. She won an NEH fellowship to serve as a writer in residence at the Tuskegee Institute in 1982. Dove left Arizona in 1989 to become a professor of English at the University of Virginia. The Dove-Viebahn family spends extensive time in Germany and also travels widely. During the past fifteen years, Dove has invested considerable time in musical and dance pursuits. Her husband gave her a custom-made viola da gamba (an archaic predecessor to the cello) in 1992, which she plays. She also sings and has taken up ballroom and Argentinean tango dancing. These interests have led her to several musical collaborations, one with John Williams. Dove has turned her energies most recently to editing the *The Penguin Book of Twentieth-Century American Poetry*.

Dove's work has taken on big questions of history, culture, identity, and archetypal patterns, as well as racial categorization. Her work asks how people build cultures and what cultural artifacts show about how people think. From her earliest work, *The Yellow House on the Corner*, to her most recent, *Sonata Mulattica*, Dove has explored racial and cultural mixing through tropes of incest, color, and the figure of the mulatto. Her poems are highly crafted and distilled, with an emphasis on formal control and technical mastery. She has said in interviews she thinks of poems as puzzles, which suggests the highly cerebral approach she brings to poetry.

As a formalist, Dove descends from modernist poets such as Marianne Moore, Elizabeth Bishop, and Gwendolyn Brooks. Her forte is the small, well-crafted lyric poem; even when she writes longer sequences that one might term *epic*, she views them as composed of individual lyric poems strung like beads on a necklace. She often constructs poetic personae, most notably in *Thomas and Beulah*, written from personae based on her maternal grandparents; *Mother Love*, which employs a range of personae based on the Demeter-Persephone myth; and, most recently, in *Sonata Mulaticca*, told from the multiple perspectives of personalities involved in the classical music world around the time of Beethoven's *Kreutzer Sonata*. She also writes poems from the perspective of an implied (or sometimes overt) poet-speaker. The sound of her poems is not based on the voice or spoken word but more on classical music, in which she was immersed as a cellist. Dove's postmodern sensibility lies mainly in her poems' indeterminancy: her poems do not resolve; instead, they revel in the abyss and the unknown, and refuse sentimentality.

Dove's work was slow to gain critical attention at first, as it eschewed easily identifiable "black" subjects or themes as shaped by dominant views of the Black Arts Movement, which puzzled some critics and scholars. Unlike Komunyakaa and Coleman, she seldom drew upon black music or vernacular culture. Yet, over time, critical attention has built into a groundswell of substantial scholarship, including three critical monographs, a collection of interviews, a special issue of *Callaloo*, and a body of essays and journal articles on her work. Criticism has ranged broadly across a range of topics, including her technique, her poetry's relation to world and national literary traditions, the incest motif, themes of gender and motherhood, ties to black culture and the African American literary tradition, and cosmopolitanism or cross-cultural themes. Dove's work has changed many readers' and scholars' received ideas about what a black female poet might care to write about, how she might go about writing poetry, and what she might say in her poems. She has opened doors wide for the younger generation of poets.

Her work has been recognized by a Pulitzer Prize for Poetry, the Academy of American Poets Younger Poet Award, the Heinz Award in the Arts, and the Duke Ellington Lifetime Achievement Award; she has also received Mellon and Rockefeller Foundation fellowships.

The interview with Dove is the first one completed for this book. It took place at her home outside Charlottesville, Virginia, in the spring of 1998. We drank tea and ate Girl Scout Cookies in her living room, surrounded by her collection of handmade black dolls and musical instruments.

Selected Works by Rita Dove

POETRY

Ten Poems (chapbook), Penumbra Press, 1977
The Only Dark Spot in the Sky (chapbook), Bookslinger, 1980
The Yellow House on the Corner, Carnegie Mellon University Press, 1980.
Mandolin (chapbook), Ohio Review, 1982.
Museum, Carnegie Mellon University Press, 1983.
Thomas and Beulah, Carnegie Mellon University Press, 1986.
The Other Side of the House (chapbook), VARIS Studios/Pyracantha Press, 1988.
Grace Notes, W. W. Norton & Co., 1989.
Lady Freedom among Us, Janus Press, 1993.
Selected Poems, Vintage Books, 1993.
Mother Love: Poems, W. W. Norton & Co., 1995.
On the Bus with Rosa Parks, W. W. Norton & Co., 1999.

American Smooth, W. W. Norton & Co., 2004.
Sonata Mulattica, W. W. Norton & Co., 2009.

OTHER

Fifth Sunday (short stories), University of Virginia Press, 1985.
Through the Ivory Gate (novel), Vintage Books, 1992.
The Darker Face of the Earth: A Verse Play in Fourteen Scenes, Story Line
    Press, 1994; rev. ed. Story Line Press, 1996.
The Poet's World (poem and essays), Library of Congress, 1995.
Seven for Luck (song cycle with lyrics by Dove and music by John
    Williams), Hal Leonard Corporation, 2000

MALIN PEREIRA: There was a lot of excitement about your play, *The Darker Face of the Earth*, being performed at the Kennedy Center. I understand you made several revisions to the play after the first edition, and Story Line Press issued a revised edition. What kinds of changes did you make? How substantial are they?

RITA DOVE: Well, the ending is different. The revision actually came about after seeing some of the scenes kind of "put on their feet," as they say in the theater, which means actually having actors read the lines and try to walk through them. The history of the play is very strange for a play. I wrote it without knowing what the theater world was like, and there were other things happening in my life, so I finally decided, *no one will do this play because it's too big*, etc. And so I put it away. It's only because my husband kept bugging me every five years or so to do something that I finally rewrote it and Story Line Press published it in 1994. At that point I really did assume that that play was going to be on the page and that was it, and maybe someday when I was dead someone would do it out of pity or whatever. When the Oregon Shakespeare Festival was interested in the play, I realized I had this opportunity now to see if what I *thought* would work onstage would indeed work onstage. A lot of the revisions came about from just not feeling comfortable with some of the scenes and the pacing. I did add a couple of scenes as I realized that certain characters were more stock than essential, and that we needed to feel that they had a full life, even if you didn't know what the life was. These are complicated human beings who are bringing everything from their pasts to the pressure of that moment. For instance, there is now a scene between Phebe and Augustus, because Phebe just kind of became embittered over being left, and I actually liked her as a character. I was exhausted by the time I finished that version. I thought, "Okay, that's enough." Also, I did change the ending. It's essentially the same tragedy, except that Augustus does live at the end of this one, it's just not a life worth living. With this version, what happens is that Amalia kills herself; also Phebe is now in there, too, because I thought, this is essential, to have her there. As the three of them piece together, in this moment of craziness, what exactly the story is, that indeed Amalia's his mother, each reacts in a different way, and his mother then kills herself to try to save him, which means that the revolutionaries think that he did what he was supposed to do and he's a hero. But what kind of hero is that who's just realized that he's lost everything that could make him happy? That change came about because of my daughter, who had participated in all of the sessions at Oregon Shakespeare Festival. She loved it and would sit through all these rehearsals and make suggestions. It was great. And one night I was still perturbed at the ending. I had put Phebe in it, but I still just didn't like the way the insurrectionists came in, bang, bang, everyone was dead. So I was fiddling with it, and she came down (she was supposed to be in bed), and I said to her, "I was just messing around with this ending." And she said, "You know, I think he should live. There are worse things than death." This is a twelve-year-old who really doesn't know what she's saying, but when she said that I suddenly realized, yeah, that's even worse. It was interesting because in some of the workshops, that was one of the questions that was always presented to me, because in the original *Oedipus*, of course, he does live. People asked, "Why didn't you follow the myth exactly?" I don't follow it exactly because I didn't want it to be a kind of checklist against a Greek myth. I couldn't find the right way I could make it believable that he could live. I hadn't found the plot that would make him live and why that would be worth it for him, not just to fulfill the myth. And that was the moment that did it. So those are the major changes. Hector's part also has been deepened. I didn't want him to be merely a crazy man in the swamp. I really wanted everything that he said to make eminent sense if you knew the whole story. Since no one knew the whole story, he seemed crazy. So he does have a couple of monologues and things like that, but the basic story is still the same. And that all came about working with these wonderful actors.

MP: So it was the putting the play into production that offered these realizations; it becomes apparent that certain things need to be changed. I guess that's very typical in the theater.

RD: Yes, it is very typical in the theater, from what I understand. I found it really exciting because as a poet, someone who's used to doing everything in one circle of lamplight, this was exhilarating. It was also exasperating sometimes: too many voices. I can really understand now how people can lose perspective in the theater, because there are a thousand things to think about. Most of the time I had to just simply forget everything everyone said and go back out to my cabin and make my decision. So it was a fascinating experience. As a poet (because I really think of myself as a poet), one of the things artistically that I learned in rewriting the play was how much power in theater a silence or gesture can make. It's very close to poetry, how what you don't say has to be contained in those white spaces, but also in the sound of the word. That's one of the essences of poetry that always thrills me and keeps me going back to it.

MP: Your earlier poetry often was dealing with the historical past, but in *Grace Notes* and *Mother Love* you seem to have moved more into the personal present, and you've commented in other interviews about your willingness to now come into the personal a little bit more. You called it at one point "coming home," writing your way "back home." How does *The Darker Face of the Earth*, which I read as a play about the historical foundations of American culture, relate to that?

RD: Well, that's a great question. There are two parts to my answer. First of all, because *Darker Face of the Earth* has such a long history, in a very interesting way it's an early work that I came back to. I began working on that play actually about the same time that I finished my first book, *The Yellow House on the Corner*. So in that sense, all of the themes of *Darker Face* were very close to the slave narratives of *Yellow House on the Corner*, filling in the past, trying to get into the past as a person and to humanize it, so that eventually I could get to my own past without being self-indulgent. However, trying to go back to the play and rewrite it for production felt like another kind of coming home, because now I had to inject a lot of my own emotions and takes on things in characters to make sure they were alive and not just mythic representations walking around saying their lines and getting off the stage. The first version of the play is clean, but it's very quick, and it's more pageant than personalized. So there's a little bit of me in every one of those characters that wasn't necessarily there in the first version, particularly Amalia, and it was very important to allow her to speak. In the end I didn't want any easy answers; I didn't want anyone in the audience coming away thinking, "These are the bad guys, these are the good guys, slavery is bad, slave owners are bad, look at the noble savage," and all that. I wanted every one to be fighting for his or her own individual realization against the system. The big bad guy is the system, obviously. But that's all the kind of stuff I learned by finally coming around, coming home in the previous volumes.

MP: Interesting. So do you think that in some way the personal present and national history end up being connected for you?

RD: They've always been.

MP: Why or how?

RD: I think they both have something to do, a lot to do, with being female and being black. From as early as I can remember, I always felt that there was a world going on with lots of "historical" events going on, and that my viewpoint was not a direct one, but I was looking at it from the side. I'm talking about when I was small. First it started out as a female issue, because I think for most kids, when you're growing up, there's a point, when you're in a minority, when you *realize* you're a minority. It's very strange. It's kind of, "Oh, really, I'm not like you?" It usually comes from the outside somehow. But as a *girl*, growing up in a really traditional family, with a mother who is a housekeeper and a father who is a chemist, I always felt that there was this view of how the world should run, and then I was supposed to fit into this somehow, and I didn't think all the rules were quite right. Both of my parents would say, "Education is the key," and "You can be anything you want to be," and then I'd look at the magazines and say, "I can't be everything I want to be unless something's going to change." So that meant that I didn't take the historical at face value. Ever. And, of course, W. E. B. DuBois talks about the double vision when you're a minority. You see what the mainstream is immersed in, which is reality, but you also see the other reality. He talks about what advantage this kind of binocular vision gives you; it gives you perspective, it gives you depth. As I grew up I felt enormously lucky that, because of my circumstances, I had this vision. I always felt underneath it — I never believed that the newspapers were true necessarily — that was just one version of the truth and it's interesting, it's pretty good, but I'll wait to see what judgment is going to come in. So that's why the personal present and the historical past have always been connected for me. I think it's truly a part of my environmental influences.

On the other hand, language was always fascinating to me, even from a young age. I think with most children it's fascinating at a really existential level; the sounds that you make are wonderful, regardless of whether they make sense. There were several kinds of ways in which language was stylized in my life. I'm talking about storytellers in the family, the good ones, the ones who could tell the story you've heard three thousand times and suddenly it's a good story. From those storytellers to the kind of oral games you play on the street as a black kid, from the dozens to what that implies and how the language becomes plastic, all of that and then also the literature. To read someone like Shakespeare and think this language is part of the emotion, and there are all these different levels to language and different tones and qualities. All of that, too, was experience which is perceived directly as one part of life, but if you're going to be a writer or are going to be an artisan, you choose a medium. The trick is to use this essentially artificial, made-up medium to try to imitate that immediacy, which it can never do because it's never immediate, but you give the illusion of immediacy. I was fascinated by that from a very young age. It was probably part of the reason why, and I've talked about this in other interviews but I've never really talked about it in this kind of way, when I was in second grade I wrote this silly novel called *Chaos* where I took my spelling words and wrote chapter by chapter according to the list of spelling words. And part of the fascination with that was to see how the words themselves, the language, these symbols would build the reality.

MP: So in some ways writing your personal present is rewriting national history, adding the version that wasn't represented or writing from the center that was marginalized.

RD: That's one part of it. That's absolutely one part of it, with the understanding that my personal history is only one personal history. That is part of it. Also, I think that because I was acutely aware, even at a young age, that my perception of an "official" historical event was very different than that "official" version, I thought that this must be the same for every person if you really stop to think about it. There's a war, and people can talk about casualties in the war, but if you've had someone die in the war it takes on a completely different cast, and if you're a refugee from that war it takes on a completely different cast. All these kinds of things I think are really fascinating, and in the end, unless you have a writer, or artist, or an oral history, the only version left is the one that is the official version, and I really resist that. I just feel that all of us cannot ever forget that the official version is merely a construct that we may need to order our timeline, but we can't forget that there are human beings, all sorts of individual human beings to punctuate this.

MP: Which of course is what you're doing in *Museum*, writing poems of "unofficial" history. It reminds me of James Baldwin and how he talks about how the sad thing about white America is they often believe their own myths, they believe the official version of history, and I find that somewhat true when I teach. So many of my students just hang on to those official versions of history.

RD: And they can be utterly devastated when they realize that it's not true. I think that's why Vietnam and the sixties were so explosive and powerful. It was the moment when we realized that the myth didn't hold. Then the seventies and the eighties became this retreat to a perspective of *It's just me and I'm going to do this.*

MP: How does it feel now *not* to have all of those responsibilities of being poet laureate?

RD: It feels wonderful, actually. That's a terrible thing to say. It does feel wonderful. It also is not completely over, either, and I think that one of the hardest periods of time for me was right after it was over, because I naively assumed that Bob Hass was going to take this over and I could go back to my life, and I couldn't go back to my life. There are residuals and the letters and the requests keep coming, but you don't have the outside justification to say, "Well, I'm going to go on a half-time teaching load." So it took me, and it's still taking me, a lot of time just to figure out how to conduct my life so that I have one. And since I was raised to be a dutiful daughter I am someone who answers letters, and I think Toni Morrison is the same way. We're midwestern. We know how our parents raised us. In a way you get raised to try to fit into the northern world. The southern roots are very close; my grandparents came from the South. They came to the North and went into these factories and then had to build a new neighborhood, a new home, and the rules of social behavior were fairly rigorous. They say to the children, "This is how you have to be," and you do this because you honor yourself as well as your community, which really puts a double-whammy on you. So there I was, trying to answer these letters, and finally — I really think it took until about last year — I realized I don't have to answer all of these letters. I can actually just not answer, and they'll write again.

MP: Oh what a relief! It's apparent that music, your training in classical music, has been important for your work. It comes up thematically in so many ways. One thing that I'm curious about is, how does that training influence your work structurally? Have you thought about that at all?

RD: Oh, I've thought about it. I haven't thought about it in any kind of critical way. First of all, at a very basic level, I believe that language sings, has its own music, and I'm very conscious of the way something sounds, and that goes from a lyric poem all the way to an essay or to the novel, that it has a structure of sound which I think of more in symphonic terms for the larger pieces. I really do think that sonnets to me are like art songs. That's one thing. I also think that resolution of notes, the way that a chord will resolve itself, is something that applies to my poems; the way that, hopefully if it works, the last line of the poem, or the last word, will resolve something that's been kind of hanging for a while. And I think musical structure affects even how the poems are ordered in a book. Each of the poems plays a role. Sometimes it's an instrument, sometimes several of them are a section, and it all comes together that way, too.

MP: What we were considering in my class on your work, and I think we were applying this to *Yellow House on the Corner*, was that you sometimes have five-sectioned works, and we were wondering if you were structuring things along the idea of five movements for longer symphonies. You have moved away from that, of course, in more recent volumes, but especially since it was your first work, structuring a longer piece like that, I was wondering if you just went to that structure.

RD: This is fascinating, because the book I'm working on now has five sections, and I remember feeling like, "Oh, I like these five sections."

MP: Yes, comfy.

RD: Yes, really comfy. I think that three-sectioned books put too much emphasis on that middle section being solid and holding onto the ends, and when you have five sections, it kind of takes the edge off of putting such great importance into the beginning. One of the things about when I'm ordering and structuring the books is to try to thwart people's notions that the first poem is going to give you the key and now here we go! It's just an opening.

MP: Actually, I teach it that way.

RD: There's also this sense that if you take the first poem as the key, then what doors does it open further down? It's more like: here's an opening motif, and then it's going to be embellished, and then it may change, and then it may go minor, and then it does all these kinds of things, so it isn't like this is the truth, but this is just one truth.

MP: Very true of *Museum*, too. You play with the opening motifs along the whole way. It's really diverse; it's not just like the answer is at the beginning. Well, you've published a lot besides poetry: short stories and essays and plays, and a novel, and I know from other interviews that crossing genres, you feel, is very necessary and a good thing as a writer. I've wondered whether you find that there is a specific relationship between your poetry and your nonpoetry that you'd be able to articulate. Do you think, for example, are certain subjects inappropriate for poetry that then you turn to other venues?

RD: Well, actually, when an idea occurs to me, sometimes it's an idea, sometimes it's a line, sometimes it's a word, sometimes it's a character, but at the moment when a piece begins, gets its genesis and I feel that something is going to happen and become a piece of writing, I know what form it's in already. I can't think of an instance where I've tried it out as a poem and said, "Oh no, this should be a short story," or something like that. The only case I can think of where there are almost duplicates is the scene in the novel on a beach playing the guitar, and then also in the poem "Summit Beach," but I deliberately decided to try it both ways. It was willed. The story came first, and then I thought I really would like to try this from a different angle, just that moment. So there hasn't been that kind of crossover where I've said, "Oh, this didn't work, or that didn't work." I think it must happen farther back in the brain, a series of thought processes so that by the time it comes to my consciousness, all those decisions have been made. I think that has something to do with the way that the language itself then gets used in various genres, the weight of each word, too. Because I remember when I was working on the novel, at first, and I knew it was going to be a novel, and I thought, "Oh I don't want to write a novel — too big, too many words, it's such a waste." This is just how you think as a poet. Then, until I could figure out how the weight of each word and the weight of each sentence wove the story, I was just writing a lot of verbiage. Once I figured out two things, the key signature and the time, then it became much easier. I figured out how each individual note — you've got me talking in musical terms! —how much weight each different note had, what kind of time signature I was going to have in this piece. All artists can fall into the traps of whatever we do well, and that for me is to write a poem. To write in other genres offers stretch and a counterbalance to that trap. The other genres help remind me that there's a value to length, there's a value to overload; there's something to lushness, too, and it can be just as powerful as something austere.

MP: Which is mostly your aesthetic in your poetry.

RD: It is.

MP: You don't tend to go on and on and on.

RD: No I don't, but someday . . . The thing is that if you go on and on, it has to have a purpose. I get really frustrated with poems that go on, but the words can be kind of sloughed away. I think there's a way to go on and on and still have it —the intent. But I do find, in relationships between the genres, that when I'm writing poetry I very often read prose and vice versa.

MP: You don't want to be influenced by the poets when you're writing poetry.

RD: It's not just that I don't want to be influenced, because when writing a poem I will go to the bookshelf and take a book up because I know there's something in there that I need to read again. But I don't want to sit down and read lots of poetry books while writing poetry. It muddies the water. It must have something to do with the musical training, because when I'm in another country I can pick up languages fairly quickly; I do it mostly I think through imitation and the intonation of the language, the way it falls. For example, I speak German fluently, but I have a great difficulty if we go somewhere and someone speaks German with an accent, like a Swiss-German, or someone who speaks English with an Afrikaans, South African dialect. After an hour I start to talk like that, and I have to go away! Wales and Ireland were a nightmare because I would start doing that, because I also loved the way it sounded, too, so that tendency in me would mean that if I were reading exclusively Adrienne Rich for days, then I would start to write like Adrienne Rich. That's not necessarily me. That's not my voice, that's her voice. So I have to not read much poetry while writing it, for self-protection.

MP: I've been interested in your recent focus on the work of Breyten Breytenbach. You just translated his Li Po poem, and I noticed you dedi-

cated a poem to him as well in *Mother Love*, called "Political." I was curi-
ous, first of all, how you picked up Afrikaans. Did you go to South Africa,
or how did this all come about? And I'm curious what interests you in his
poetry as well.

RD: Well, a lot of it is just circumstance. First of all, I don't know Afri-
kaans. I know German; I know a little bit of Dutch. If I listen to Afrikaans
long enough I can get into it. The way that the translations came about
was that I was at a poetry festival last summer in Rotterdam called the
Poetry International, and this has been going on for twenty years; I've been
there once before. And each year they've had writers come from all over
the world and have this week-long festival, just poetry day and night. But
also sometimes in the mornings they have a translation workshop for the
week, and they choose a poet who is either Dutch or Dutch-related in the
language, and all the other writers come in and translate the work, and
the idea is to try to bring some of these works to the translators' respec-
tive languages. So Breyten Breytenbach was the poet for this last summer,
and it was great because he was there, and they also had provided literal
translations in a host of languages, in English, in German, in French, in
Spanish. And he gave a reading. So I used the French and the German and
the Dutch and the Afrikaans and the English, of course, to try to put it
together. Again it gets to my fascination to try to find the approximation
in the language. Breyten Breytenbach I find interesting because of his lin-
guistic standpoint — he knows so many languages. I like a lot of his poems,
but there are also others that I'm not that crazy about.

MP: Yes, he's published a novel in French as I recall.

RD: Right, and he's lived in Paris all these years, and I've met him at
several conferences. When you go to these international conferences, you
meet the same people all the time. I think he lived in Spain sometime, too.
So I can't help but feel all those languages influenced his work. So that's
really where all that came from, and it's less a fascination with his work
than it is just the way the circumstance presented itself. With dedicating
"Political" to him, that occurred after, I think, the first time I met him, in
Mexico, and as I was working through those poems about mothers and
daughters. I remembered a description from his memoirs, his *Confessions
of an Albino Terrorist*, when he talks about the black political prisoners
singing as someone's being led to execution, and that really was powerful. I
was trying to get into the sense of Demeter going down into hell and what's

going to sustain you if your daughter is going down into hell. That image came back up to me.

MP: I remember reading in an interview, it must have been at least ten years ago, that you were interested in going to South Africa, but I guess you never got there yet.

RD: I have never gotten there. Actually, I'm going this May [1999]. There's going to be a writers' conference in Durban, so I'm going to go this May.

MP: Are you going to get to go around a bit?

RD: A little bit, but not enough. I can't stay long because of my stupid schedule — I'm only going to be there for ten days. But I'll probably go back sometime next year to the University of Cape Town. There were a couple of instances when I was supposed to go to South Africa through USIA [the U.S. Information Service or Agency], but they could not assure me that I and my husband could travel together and that I would be speaking in front of mixed audiences. So I didn't go.

MP: A writer you've mentioned throughout your work is Derek Walcott. What would you say has been important for you about Walcott and his work for you as a writer?

RD: It's interesting because I'm still trying to figure that out. I love his work, but I don't think that he is influencing me. I mean, I find that his work is *very* different from mine, but I love his work. The first time that I came in contact with his work was through his play *Dream of Monkey Mountain*. I read the play — I must have been a junior in college — and I just thought it was phenomenal; I just never knew that theater could be like this. I was surprised to discover that he was a poet as well. I thought, "Whoa! I get a double treat here." Part of it is the fact that he's always dealing with this, I don't want to call it a *dilemma*, but with this *position* of being in love with this island, in love with his people but feeling also separate from them because he's gone off to school and that he's writing these amazing poems that they won't read. And also wanting to honor where he comes from but at the same time not wanting to be another colonizer of the experience, and he's always very conscious of that. I think he is even conscious of it all the way to the level of language, because he has earlier poems, particularly, where he puts in a lot of patois, and even places in later poems where, in the middle of this absolutely gorgeously constructed English, this British turn-piece sentence, comes one of those "*he no be this*" phrases, which happen in the culture a lot. I just think that he is an exquisite writer.

MP: But technically you don't feel that there is a debt there or any kind of influence?

RD: Well, I think technically there is a debt in the sense that I wish that I could write that well. I think that the language is just gorgeous, and it's not my voice, it's not my style. But, in general, I admire his trying to mix in all levels of the language, because this is what he has grown up with, and his making it work on the page. That was something that I aspired to. Trying to get the more syncopated rhythms into the more classic iambic pentameter.

MP: So it's that mixed heritage and the mixing of the traditions that you like.

RD: I think it's a wealth rather than a problem, and it's so ass-backwards to say that there is a black way of writing and then there is a white; this is madness. Every black person that I know speaks at so many different levels all the time, and why not use all of that? All of it. Why not? I do believe that [racial essentialists] will come along; even if they haven't heard it that way they can think of it. We've done it so long with other ethnic groups. If you think about all those attitudes and expressions that we've gotten from Jewish Americans, for example.

MP: It should be a both/and equation, not an either/or.

RD: Exactly.

MP: Which brings me to one of my favorite poems.

RD: Which one is that?

MP: "Upon Meeting Don L. Lee in a Dream" from your first volume, *The Yellow House on the Corner.*

RD: Oh.

MP: Critics have noticed this poem.

RD: I know.

MP: You can't help but notice this poem. Arnold Rampersad points out that this piece might show a bit of hostility to the Black Arts Movement. It's an early poem of yours, and I wonder if you've moderated your stance toward some of the Black Arts Movement aesthetic views or prescriptions over time.

RD: Yeah, *moderated* is a difficult word. It implies . . .

MP: Extremism to begin with.

RD: Right.

MP: Well, you do fry him alive in the poem. [Laughter.]

RD: He and I are friends, too, you know.

MP: Have you come to a broader prospective now?

RD: I think of it more as a generational poem, as opposed to one that deals with aesthetics; that as a young girl, insecure as a writer, in a sense I was doing that killing-the-father thing. I remember having someone ask me, "Well, why do you say, 'in a Dream'? Why don't you just say it directly?" I answered, "No, I want it to be dreaming because it is a psychological poem. It is a poem that works on that kind of psychic landscape." It wasn't an excuse for the surrealism in the poem but a way to say not to take it at face value. I *do* think that when I was beginning to write or beginning to contemplate putting the writing out into the world (which is a different thing altogether) when I was in college, just beginning to think seriously about writing for publication and stuff like that, I *was* terrified that I would be kind of suffocated before I began. That I would be pulled into the whole net of whether this was black enough or whether I was denigrating my own people and all this kind of stuff. This is a pressure, not just from the Black Arts Movement, but this is a pressure of one's whole life, to be a credit to the race. When I was in my twenties, I think I knew instinctively I was not strong enough to be able to take that, that I would probably just stop writing, and I didn't want to stop writing. Which meant that I didn't publish for a while and that I really kept back and didn't want to get out into the fray, so to speak. I didn't want to get into the political stuff because I felt like I had to figure out what I was doing artistically, and if I didn't write my particular take on the world, if I could not find that conduit before I got out into the fray, then I was lost. So that poem, which is a very early poem — in fact I wrote it in college — was kind of clearing the way. It was this feeling of "I'm gonna be strong enough to stand up to you, at least in a dream. I don't know if I'm gonna be able to do it later." I think I was really lucky that I wasn't born a few years earlier, too, because when I began to develop I *had* to publish, I had to see if it mattered to anyone else, and luckily for me by that time there was more leeway being allowed. I have nothing against anyone in the Black Arts Movement.

MP: Not personally.

RD: No, no, not at all. Not even artistically. I see how it was absolutely necessary, and I think a lot of it is really wonderful, too.

MP: Perhaps it was the hegemony of some of their proscriptions that was upsetting to you.

RD: Yes, that's what it was. It was a feeling of "don't fence me in." And yet part of me could also see that given the stereotypical ways in which mainstream America looked at blacks, it was necessary to build the base first before you started admitting more complexity into that, and perhaps even some negative things and negative characters. I feel that it is anathema to an artist to tamp down the truth for any kind of poetic goal. I don't see how you can be an artist at that point; I think you compromise yourself very severely. I think of Seamus Heaney's essay that he wrote about the eastern European writers, the poets, and the way he felt that the pressure of the political situation forced them to find a way to say the truth. And there is something to be said for that. There are ways, if you are dealing with any kind of constricting or restrictive artistic system, to pull through, but it takes an enormous character. It takes a very strong character, and I believe there are writers who have been lost because they simply could not take that. I don't think that it is anything to be ashamed of, either. Some people are stronger than others in that sense. So, that poem was really when I first put my foot outside of the door. You know, put it in *The Yellow House on the Corner* and said, "Okay." I was tempted to take it out of *Selected Poems*, and I thought, "No, that's not fair."

MP: It's a good poem, too.

RD: It is a part of how I developed, and so I thought I had to be honest.

MP: There is another place in your work where it seems like you're answering back to something that could be read as a Black Arts Movement proscription. The opening sequence of the novel *Through the Ivory Gate* — the Penelope doll scene — is answering Toni Morrison's *The Bluest Eye* and the whole obsession with the doll that goes on there. But in your novel, Penelope, the white doll, is kept, and the other doll, the black doll that the parents are so eager to give Virginia, is thrown out the window.

RD: Just thrown out the window.

MP: So what issues were you thinking about in that scene? Did you have some of those things in mind?

RD: Well, it's true that I had read *The Bluest Eye*, and that book really struck me very deeply for several reasons. I stumbled across it in a stack in the library when I was in graduate school. I didn't know who the author was. I take the jacket covers off, so I didn't even know that the author was black. I just saw the title. And I picked up this book, and I started to read it, and I thought, "Oh my God, she's telling my life." It was the first time that I had ever read anything that dealt with blacks in the Midwest. At that point I had felt very alone because I had experienced so many instances where people assumed that I either came from Harlem, you know, or from the South. You wonder, "Do I have to go to the burden of explanation, or can I just start where I am and write this story?" Here was someone who was doing that. So I felt suddenly not alone.

MP: It was a bridge.

RD: Yeah, it really was a bridge. The story of the doll was a bridge, too, because that's an autobiographical moment in the novel, although many are not. It was a moment in my life I had always felt ashamed of, that I had thrown the doll out the window. Why did I do it? It's not a justification to answer *Why did you throw the one doll out?*, but what does this show you about how society's expectations and judgments impinge upon a small child? In a way it was, for me, it was confession. And it *was* an answer to Toni Morrison, but it was more like an "Amen." It's like saying, "Yeah, I know where people are coming from. This has happened to a lot of us."

MP: An "I've been there, too."

RD: Right, exactly.

MP: What's implied in Toni Morrison's novel is that the doll represents the white aesthetic of beauty, which can be so destructive for young black girls growing up. You are agreeing with Morrison, then, in your sequence, you feel?

RD: Yes, I am agreeing with her. I'm agreeing with her at that level. There is another part of it, too, and that is that with those two dolls, in my novel, the white doll had real hair that you could comb. And the black doll had painted-on curls, and it was one of the first efforts at mass production of black dolls, but it really wasn't a very good likeness. It wasn't beautiful, not because it was black but because whoever had made it had decided that that's what a black doll looks like. It didn't look like a *person*. When I went back and started to remember the scene and write it, I realized that was what disturbed me about that moment. For years I had felt ashamed because I thought that I had rejected the black doll. But it wasn't that at all. It just wasn't a *good* doll. They made an ugly little doll, and it wasn't useful. I couldn't comb its hair. That's essential! Obviously, there was not a big market for black dolls, so they felt they didn't have to put in a lot of effort. But at the end of that section of the novel, the protagonist, Virginia, has grown up and runs across that doll, the white doll again, who has gotten waterlogged and who stinks now. She throws her away, and for me that was a moment when she kind of got rid of the guilt and was feeling that she could move on as an individual, which was why it was important to have that at the beginning of the novel.

MP: Yeah, I thought that it was really a powerful scene for her. In relation to this, you might be familiar with Trey Ellis's essay in the winter 1989 issue of *Callaloo*, where he talked about the new black aesthetic, an aesthetic born of the black middle class, which he sees as combining all kinds of aesthetic influences — white and black, counterculture and high art, and so on. He argued that the central feature of this was the artist, the black artist, as a cultural mulatto. What do you think of his idea that now we are in the midst of this new black aesthetic? Do you think that's true of your work or of a lot of what's happening now?

RD: Well, my first impulse was it was all sort of *manifesto*. If you have to write a manifesto, fine, go ahead. It gives people something to bounce off against. I tended not to pay much attention. I read it and I thought it was interesting, but it didn't help me. I just don't feel the need artistically to have to take a stand all the time. I think that taking such stances *can* be important in the whole critical history because it gives people points around which to swirl and to fight, and . . .

MP: Publish.

RD: . . . and publish and to burst out against. But I do think that my artistic temperament is really to be a moving *X*-marks-the-spot, to keep going. I try not to think about the cultural history of literature right now. That doesn't help me as an artist. I would much rather be in the middle of it, totally confused.

MP: I found interesting his reinvention of the term *mulatto*. It has had such a history with it, from the turn of the century and then the Harlem Renaissance "tragic mulatto," who was often depicted as a pathetic soul who self-destructed, to the pejorative use of *mulatto* by Black Arts Movement writers such as Amiri Baraka in 1965. Ellis reclaims *mulatto* as a positive term for contemporary black writers from middle-class backgrounds. It seems an attempt to give voice to something that I think was a closet issue for some black writers: "Yes, I can freely draw on iambic pentameter," as you were saying earlier. I think it does link back to Derek Walcott.

RD: Yes, it does. I think that is what he is saying, and you are absolutely right. It does pull it out into the open, and it needs to be talked about. I had difficulty with the *mulatto* aspect only because — and this is a poet being obsessed with detail — *mulatto* implies that this only happens to one aspect of humanity. When we say *mulatto*, we only think of a black who has white blood in him, or that kind of mixture, but never the other way around. I mean, never that there are whites who have all sorts of ethnic things mixed in. It's the way that it marginalizes again that makes me uneasy with that *term*, that's all. Not with what he's saying.

MP: Not pluralistic or truly multiple . . . well, he's claiming this group as *black*, and I see it as actually a kind of pulling toward blackness. I saw Ellis as trying to keep blackness a center in the artistic lives of these artists. But you are right, it leaves out a whole other range of possibility, doesn't it?

RD: It does, but it is the nature of manifestos to claim a certain ground and then say, "Okay, come what may," and that's fine, too. I mean, even the surrealist has to say, "This is what is claimed as the center." I recognize that, given our society, it is hopelessly naive still to imagine that one's own heritage will not disappear entirely or be ignored if we are not constantly reminding people that it's important, and I'm very grateful that there are people who are doing that work, and I'm glad I don't have to do it.

MP: This also reminds me of that short story of yours, "The Spray Paint King," in the collection *Fifth Sunday*. That is sort of your portrait of the artist as a cultural "mulatto." I know you've said elsewhere that he was based on a Swiss guy who was going about doing this graffiti when you were in Germany, but is it possible that you had Jean-Michel Basquiat in mind, or was he not impinging on your world then?

RD: He wasn't impinging on my consciousness then. When I was working on that story there were these graffiti going up all over Germany and Switzerland, and no one knew who was doing them then. I made up a mixed-race artist to do them. In that sense I think certainly that this artist is my symbol of the artist as a cultural "mulatto." I used the word *mulatto* there because *mulatto* also implies an oppression. It implies a psychological oppression. That's one of the reasons why I'm having problems with Trey's use of *mulatto*, you see. But in "The Spray Paint King" he has that oppression that he keeps trying to fight against or feel his defiance.

MP: One thing I would like to talk about is one of the very first things we exchanged correspondence over: the incest motif in your work. It appears in your work in all genres.

RD: Yes, it does, doesn't it.

MP: It's *everywhere*. So would you like to talk about this incest motif?

RD: I was baffled about it. I must say that I wasn't even aware it was there, and it was very obvious, once you brought it up. I thought, "Oh, my God!" There is no incidence of incest in my family, there is no autobiographical or even close-friend incidence of it. So it is something that I can't explain. I have decided that eventually I'll figure it out.

MP: And it remains exclusive to your work before *Grace Notes* and *Mother Love*. I was very much looking for it there, and I can't find it. It's in the short story "Aunt Carrie" in *Fifth Sunday*; it's in the novel, *Through the Ivory Gate*. It's in the play, *The Darker Face of the Earth*, and when you tell me that that is an earlier piece, now I see that motif fitting there. It's in Beulah's life in *Thomas and Beulah*. Now there we really have to look for it, because it could just be physical child abuse, but for the mother's righteous anger, "I will cut you down." With Beulah, I wonder how much you *consciously* thought of her as being a victim of incest with the father and then negotiating this marriage with Thomas, or did it just end up in there somehow?

RD: I didn't think about it at all. In fact, I can't say that the poem "Taking in Wash" in *Thomas and Beulah* was ever on a conscious level for me about incest. I knew that it was about that moment when the mother comes in between the father and daughter; whether the mother has always come in between or not was not, for me, the issue. I felt the mother always managed to come in between them.

MP: Except there is evidence to the contrary. I mean, I can't argue with the person who wrote the poems, but Beulah has nightmares where she goes and sees herself in the mirror as this monster figure — nighttime terrors. There's also "Promises" and "Anniversary," which are two poems that have a lot to do with her marriage, but they also suggest she's overly involved with her father.

RD: The father is always there.

MP: What's the father doing in her marriage?

RD: I think there is probably an element of, not incest necessarily, but there's that unhealthy attachment of fathers to daughters, or even mothers to sons, that starts really surfacing at the time of marriage. It is almost built into the whole tradition of bridal showers and weddings in the fact that the father can give her away. Give him something to do so that he doesn't freak out or whatever. Part of me also feels, and I think that this is why the Aunt

Carrie stories are in *Fifth Sunday* and *Through the Ivory Gate*, that our fear, as a society, of incest and of sex in general fuels excessive guilt when we feel our love toward our children. I'm not talking about sexual love toward children but just that feeling of clinging and then not wanting to show too much because that could be cloying, and that could be interpreted some way. We are really messed up, actually. I know I've seen it in me in my feelings with our daughter. As kids grow up they don't want you to touch them just because they are growing up, and we are almost ashamed that we wanted to touch them. That's very natural to want to stroke her hair again. But we've gotten to the point now where we can't do that, and maybe we really should be doing it. I remember I wanted to be on my own, but I wanted to be held, too. It just was unseemly to be held. You are supposed to grow up. That's part of why the incest thing comes up all the time, though it is obviously a very extreme example. I just can't give you any more because I don't know if it's over yet.

MP: It's unconscious.

RD: Yes, unconscious, and I don't know if it's over. I don't think it is going to come up in a poem any time soon.

MP: I don't want to have you thinking about it, because then it might never come up! Now another writer who comes up on several occasions in your writing is H. D. And it's interesting to me that every time you've cited her, you haven't cited her poetry. You've cited her prose. When did you become familiar with her work, and what about her work interests you?

RD: I became familiar with her work in graduate school at, actually, Iowa.

MP: Via Louise Glück?

RD: I'm trying to think if it was Louise or not. I don't know who mentioned it, but I did study with Louise and that would make a lot of sense. But I just don't remember if she was the one who mentioned the book. Well, I'll tell you the first thing that fascinated me about H. D., though I can't remember who said it or who mentioned the book. Someone mentioned *Hermetic Definition*, and I thought "H. D. . . . hermetic definition — in just that tension between her initials and that . . ." I just thought, "Oh, I gotta read this person, she must be very strange and wonderful." It's interesting, I do only quote her prose, but I love her poetic work. It's so much itself, if that makes any sense, and it's so very musical in its own insistent phrasing and stuff that I take her in very small doses, otherwise I'll start sounding like her.

MP: Do you read her poetry now?

RD: I do read her poetry. I haven't read it for a long time now. And part of that was that I wanted to (it sounds so practical but I guess I am in some ways), but when I was working on the *Mother Love* poems I did not really want to reread her because I did not want to approach myth in any way like the way that she approached it, so I wanted to forget and I haven't gotten back to her yet. I will.

MP: She is very intense.

RD: Yes. What I admire about her is the way she could take the outrageous circumstances of her life sometimes and write a poem or sequence that was absolutely beautiful; I thought she could do that and it was not self-indulgent, it was not really confessional in any sense, and I'm glad I don't have that situation in my life.

MP: You've produced a pretty large body of work now, especially in poetry. Do you see any kind of development or phases? Do you feel that things got to a certain point and now you've turned somewhere?

RD: I try not to look to see if there is any kind of development, because that'll stop me doing the next thing, *but* the other kind of language you were using about turning corners makes sense, and I do see those kinds of directions — like feeling that it is time to turn a corner to stop going down this road. Then there are certain things that I'll do sometimes very deliberately, technically, to try to pull me down a different road. When I finished *The Yellow House on the Corner*, the next, *Museum*, was on the one hand inspired by my living in Europe at that time, living in Germany mostly, and what that did to my perspective of a history of the world. But the technical thing that happened was that almost every poem had its title first, and in *The Yellow House* it was always the other way around. I had great difficulty with titles, and I despaired of ever being easy about titles. For some reason, in *Museum*, the thing that began to happen was that the titles were almost there first. It was very strange. When *Museum* was finished and I was already working on *Thomas and Beulah*, but I didn't know it was *Thomas and Beulah*, the technical task that I gave myself was, I said, "Okay, you don't want to write an *I*," because everyone was writing an *I* at that time, you know, "and you don't want to write in *You*," because you know everyone was doing that, too, and it seemed so weird. What's left is only *he* and *she*, and so I thought I should try to write poems in which there were characters, in which there was the *he* or the *she*. It wasn't that I would throw something away if it had an *I* or a *you* in it, but I just did that and it happened to come together with these poems. After *Thomas and Beulah*, this expanded narrative, this poetic sequence, I had a great desire to write songs, something that was a lyric, which is what *Grace Notes* came out of. I enjoyed it. The mother-daughter poems in *Mother Love* were both a product of my life, obviously, with a daughter growing up, but also the fact that I had been reading Rilke's *Sonnets of Orpheus* — I suddenly started writing sonnets. There have been other things I've tried. I've said I want to try to write a long-range poem. It just didn't work, I felt. I said, "That's not gonna work right now, I think I'll just wait awhile." This way of assigning myself little technical things is just a means to push me somewhere else, such as the emotional or the artistic, but it's the emotional artist push that I don't want to define. So I'd rather just define the technical and let it fall where it may.

MP: So what are you working on now? You said it was a five-part . . .

RD: It's a book of poems. I'm still at the point where I can't really give you an idea of it, though it's almost finished. In fact, it only has one or two poems that need to go in it. But I don't know what it is exactly, because the poems have occurred over a great period of time, as opposed to the other books, where they were much more concentrated. There's a point in *Mother Love* where I was only writing those poems, and I had the sense of the hook. This book is different. There is a very early poem, a long poem, in it that I've always tried to put in books and it never fit and now it's found its way. Then there are some very recent poems. And because I haven't been publishing a lot of these poems, I just didn't publish them. I didn't feel like I wanted to hear where they were going yet. I didn't want someone to start commenting on them before I could figure out where I was going with all of this stuff. A lot of them are short, *Grace Notes*-short kinds of things. A lot of them are really lyrics, but they have a different sense to them. They aren't private lyrics, it's more like Wittgenstein's "to take yourself as the case" — to take it so the personal is more like the existential eye in the universe.

MP: Getting to the universal through the particular.

RD: Getting to the universal through the particular, but also assuming that the universe *is* a particular as well. Sounds kind of big and grand. Some of them I feel are kind of lonely poems. No, not lonely. *Alone* poems.

MP: There is a difference.

RD: Yeah, quite a difference. At the risk of over-interpreting myself, I think that some of my experiences about the schizophrenia of being a private person and a public person have informed these poems. Not in any autobiographical way, but just in that sense that I think every one of us is alive in our skin, and at the same time you feel completely insubstantial. I want to get at that.

MP: It's always a shock how people perceive one; you must have gotten a heavy dose of how people perceive you in the last few years. I'd like to pick your brain for a minute about two poems we had very interesting debates about in my class last semester. One of them is "Shakespeare's Say" in *Museum*. What I read this poem as being about is that he, Champion Jack, is creating art out of his sometimes brutal experience, in the blues tradition of lyric expression coming out of this brutal experience, and that he does create art out of this. A couple of my graduate students launched a very interesting counterargument, though, where they claimed his art actually was false and failed, and they hung their argument on, particularly, the stanza that reads "going down slow crooning," and then the part where he sings that Shakespeare says, "Man must be careful, what he kiss when he drunk," and then the repetition of going down and how nobody's listening to him. I wonder how you see Champion Jack in this poem, and his art?

RD: I never thought about it consciously this way. At the beginning of the poem, we see the facade of Champion Jack and his myth, in a sense — in debt and in his walking suit and all of that stuff, them leading him around. This is the public Champion Jack. Yet they don't understand him at all; the essential Jack Dupree is not there and is never there for his audience because they don't have any reference points. At the moment when he's going down and he's not in good shape physically (the man is a drunk, you know, and he's not at the height of his powers), you could say he's at his worst. But the mistakes sound like jazz. I think at that very moment he comes back to what makes him an artist in the beginning, the blues. He comes back to, "My mother told me there would be days like this." At this moment he feels, again, the blues. Before that he's got his act, he's got his little rap, everything is fine, and he can say all this stuff about Shakespeare. I don't think it's great, but at that moment, when he's drunk, he can't hold his piss — "My mother told me there would be days like this" — that's where the art and the life come together. The blues lyric fits, and he feels it. So he does the whole trajectory, but in the end, at the moment when to the outside world he's washed up, that is really a moment when he's found his art again.

MP: Which is the blues tradition. It can't be an external thing, it can't be a facade, it can't be a show.

RD: Right. On the very, very physical level he's going down into the cellar, to do this stuff, and it's scary, but to *go down* means to get deeper, get deeper into something. With Persephone and Demeter in *Mother Love*, I always thought that *going down* meant, if this hurts a lot and it doesn't feel good, then most people don't want to be there, but you gotta get there in order to be able to know what you are walking on when you're above ground, not to just assume that that's all of reality. In contrast, *going up* for me is often a place of great loneliness. You know, the only dark spot in the sky.

MP: The other poem is "Roast Possum," from *Thomas and Beulah*. When I taught the poem last semester, I talked about how Thomas is in an honored role as the storyteller who's giving the tale to the grandchildren and using the animal tale as that mechanism to talk about race and survival and racism. Two students in the class really wanted the whole issue about Strolling Jim to be brought in a lot more into the reading of the poem than I had been doing. At the end, Malcolm interrupts — that's an important word, *interrupts* — asking, "Who owns Strolling Jim and who paid for the tombstone?" Then Thomas corrects him, firmly recenters him on the main topic, which is the possum: "We ate that possum real slow." I had always read that moment as indicating that Malcolm had gotten distracted by the story that was supposed to be for embellishment. Two students pointed out that Strolling Jim brings issues of enslavement and ownership into the poem, and that maybe Malcolm is not so wrong to be paying attention to Strolling Jim. So I'm wondering how you read this showdown, man to man, between Malcolm and Thomas. What's going on?

RD: It's a complex showdown because it is a generational showdown, too. Neither one of them is necessarily right, but they are right for their time, which is why I chose the name *Malcolm*, too. What Thomas is doing is telling a story the way I'd heard it as a child: you are given all these elements, and you have to decide what is important in the story. All of the tangents are important, too. But it's really up to you, as the listener, to decide which one of the tangents you are going to be frustrated by, or if you are going to listen to them, and they kind of change it as the years go by. One becomes more important, or not. So he brings in Strolling Jim, and he tells his story against that possum. It is about a horse who did unique stuff, and remember horseback riding is an elite sport for the rich and for the white. Then the horse gets buried under the ground like a man, and, of course, *man* is a charged word for African Americans. So when Malcolm interrupts Thomas, it is very important to ask who owned Strolling Jim. It is about ownership, and it's also about who qualifies as a *man*. Is a horse a man? Is a black man a man? It's a little bit of all that, too. Are you a boy chasing a possum? Thomas doesn't contradict Malcolm, necessarily, but he tells him, "Don't forget the possum, that's all. It's not like you shouldn't remember the horse. I'm not going to answer this question because if I answer this question, to tell you who owned him and paid for the tombstone, you're going to get wrapped up in the details of that, or you are going to get so angry about the fact that this horse got a grave as a man, that you are gonna forget how to catch the possum, and you've got to know that, too." Now Malcolm is ready to go and demand stuff, and the grandfather is saying, "Sometime, if you just look really closely, you can see that someone is playing the possum, and that's how you catch him." So both of them are right. It's a moment that, hopefully, Malcolm will remember later on in his life. It's probably too early right now for him to like that answer.

MP: Because he wants to be a hothead.

RD: Yeah, he wants to put the count on a man, you know, like Strolling Jim did. And he wants to be outraged, and he should be outraged, because what Thomas has in *his* head, too, is the fact that in the encyclopedia this is what they are saying about black people, and even though he's an old man, at that point, he's seen the changes that are happening in the country with the whole civil rights movement starting up. So things have obviously changed from the encyclopedia saying that black children are intelligent until puberty, then they are lazy. But he's got to let Malcolm figure it out on his own. Malcolm has a different history. Thomas's history goes back; Malcolm's is going forward.

MP: Yeah, looking at it from different directions.

RD: Yeah, and then meeting at this moment. It's so interesting because so many of the stories that should have had morals in my childhood, didn't. They never told us the moral. They just told us a story. You wanted to try to get to the moral, so you'd ask, "What happened to them?" They would say, "I don't know." I can't tell you how many times I asked this. There are a lot of things that could have happened to them, but you go through the story to figure out what paths they would have taken.

MP: You've been living in the South now for over a decade. I don't know if you realize that. Is that right?

RD: Oh my God, it's true.

MP: And, like me, you were raised in the Midwest. How has being in the South affected you or your writing?

RD: Well, Virginia, particularly Charlottesville, is very strange South. This is the land of contradictions and nexuses, I think, and that's one of the things that I love about this place. You have Thomas Jefferson with all of his contradictions. You've got the cradle of democracy and the constitution; you've got the cradle of the Confederacy.

MP: Your assistant told me about Lee/Jackson/King Day, how in Virginia Martin Luther King Jr. Day is used to also honor white Confederate heroes Robert E. Lee and Stonewall Jackson.

RD: It's astonishing, but that's really who we are as Americans. We contain all these contradictions in our whole concept of what this country is, and our great myths about America are just riddled with these kinds of contradictions. So I like being at this kind of place. I can't tell you what it's doing to my writing yet. It generally takes me a good many years before I start writing about wherever I'm at. I think it will do something to my writing, I just don't know if it's there yet.

MP: The South is a point of origin for so much. Understanding the South helps me understand how everything else got to be the way it is.

RD: That's right because, you know, the really bizarre thing is that we are more racially divided now in this country than we've been in I don't know how long, all because we've never dealt with the Civil War. I really think it's because we haven't done our work. When I was a kid, the South was this land of terror. I had relatives in the South, and we went down to visit them when I was ten and again when I was fourteen. I was absolutely convinced that I was going to be lynched and terrible things were going to happen. What I didn't understand, but what really impressed me, was that blacks and whites interacted, though there was great caution on both sides. They knew each other better than blacks and whites in the North.

MP: They lived in proximity.

RD: I realized that we didn't live in proximity in the North, where I had assumed that we would be this great integrated dream. That was amazing. I'd say Charlottesville is an academic community, mostly. It's a very strange place here. It's really almost Washington, and so it's an odd place to be, in that sense. I taught at Tuskegee for a semester, 1982, and that was much more like being in the South. That was Real South.

MP: I wonder if being in the Real South would do anything for your writing at all.

RD: I think that, maybe I hope that, one of the ways being here will influence my writing is the interest in exploring our myth of ourselves as Americans, because I do feel that all the time here. I feel we're constantly rubbing up against what we've always, in our hearts, thought America was, and how we contribute to this or fight against it, and what things aren't resolved. Here Jefferson's everywhere, and the vehemence of the arguments about Jefferson here is just absurd. When I first came here and went to a dinner at the president's house, someone stood up to toast Mr. Jefferson, and I was about to make a joke, and my dinner partner said, "Oh yeah, he's gonna toast Jefferson." But I realized they were *serious* and that every official academic function begins with a toast to Mr. Jefferson. That's bizarre. And yet you've got a whole influx of young professors and students who are coming in from all over the place who are kind of amused by all of this. Jefferson is a wonderful man, don't get me wrong; he had talents, but he was also a man. He was also a complicated and fallible human being. What startles me constantly is how it becomes a matter of life and death for people to have the Jefferson they want. Again we're getting back to the public person or the idea of a myth, whether you believe it or not. That's why I kind of like being close to all this.

MP: Keep an eye on it.

RD: Keep an eye on it. I don't know where it will go. I've often joked with my husband that someday I'm gonna write this play called *Jefferson* that will get me banned from Charlottesville, and then I'll have to go someplace else.

MP: Kicked out of paradise. Not quite?

RD: Not quite.

MP: It's the end of the millennium, as you know, and people are making a big deal out of this, and we're using it to structure our systems of meaning about all kinds of things. But it's the close of the twentieth century in American poetry. How do you see your work, coming at the end of the century in American poetry? Are there lineages you feel it fits into, and then how do you see it as starting a lineage for the twenty-first century?

RD: Well, first of all let me just say that I'm fascinated by the millennium because it's a boundary that's totally constructed. When I lived in Arizona, my husband and I would often at New Year's have a *ball* because we would just celebrate it every hour. When you have to find these points, to say we've crossed over somewhere . . . So that's something that is fascinating to me, and though there is no such thing as a new millennium, the fact that we *believe* that there is a new millennium means that there *is* a new millennium, it means that people are working toward it and all that kind of stuff. I haven't really thought of it in terms of a new millennium artistically, because I don't believe in these kinds of boundaries, but somewhere it's going to, of course, pull it together. I think in my own life of where I'm at because I'm forty-five, and you start thinking about this. At forty-five, you still feel like you have a foot in youth, but it's getting there. At *fifty* you can't do it anymore, or maybe — I just don't know, I'm working toward that. So it is true that there is something that I feel that is starting, not to close down. What I really find exciting is to be a bridge. I have had the fleeting idea, thinking, "Gosh, I'm glad that I'm not *seventy-five* at the end of the millennium." I mean, I'm really glad that I'm this age so that I can actually say that, "Oh, yeah, I've got a role." I like the bridge aspect of it. I just like to be going through it, and I'm really kind of excited to see how people are going to react.

MP: Well, you can actually be the one they react against.

RD: That's right.

MP: Or follow.

RD: Whatever, whatever.

MP: You can go back to DuBois opening the twentieth century with, "The problem of the twentieth century is the problem of the color line." If you use that as an arc to construct it on, I think some of your work is a very interesting segue then into the twenty-first century, because you're not interested in the line. Maybe you make it more of a dot-dot-dot or a blur.

RD: A demilitarized zone.

MP: You make it permeable?

RD: I make it permeable. And yet the problem is still the problem, the gray zone.

MP: Well, I don't think that people generally know what to do with gray areas.

RD: No, they don't, Unfortunately, DuBois's wonderful statement (and because it's so beautifully put) still pertains. It is not a line any more, but it's something else. I think that he was also dealing with the concept that people had to make a boundary between them. The fact is that we still think in terms of boundaries between peoples and groups and sexes and all that stuff and it's so depressing sometimes.

MP: The twentieth-century boundaries, have they broken down?

RD: I don't think that the boundaries can be broken down until people go deeper into themselves and admit that there are no unique compartments in themselves. I really think we, as human beings, have had such incredible denial in terms of how much we're certain of. Why can't we admit uncertainty into our lives? I really feel that we don't admit it into our lives, and when someone does, it's something very daring, when it should just be the way life is. I think that that admitting uncertainty into one's life also allows you to not to be afraid of anything that feels mysterious, something that is unknown, which then translates into the Other. What is this Other? We have others inside of us.

[1998]

HARRYETTE MULLEN

Among all the poets in this collection, Mullen would be the one most likely to be labeled *experimental*, a label she would welcome. Mullen's oeuvre presents interesting questions about audience, language, identity, race, and the place of theory for African American poetry — and all poetry. Her poetry and literary criticism revitalize common topics such as the oral tradition, folklore, and the blues, offering new perspectives. Her publication history is a study in the dilemma of the black poet as expressed in the work of poets from Paul Laurence Dunbar to Rita Dove, as she has navigated among audience expectations and the conventions of racial identification, challenging what it means to be black, what it means to be a poet, and most especially what it means to be a black poet.

Mullen was born in 1953 in Florence, Alabama, where her father was a social worker and her mother a teacher. Her parents divorced when she was young, and her childhood was filled with family, school, and church (two extended family members were Baptist ministers). Moving at age three to Fort Worth, Texas, Mullen experienced segregation as well as a fruitful exposure to Latino/a culture and language. Mullen earned a BA in English from the University of Texas at Austin in 1975; she went on to earn in English both an MA in 1987 and a PhD in 1990 at the University of California, Santa Cruz. She held a range of jobs through her undergraduate, graduate, and postgraduate years that exposed her to an array of people and cultures. She taught at Cornell University from 1990 to 1995 and then moved to UCLA, where she currently is a professor of English.

Mullen's poetry appears to be very different from volume to volume, changing in voice, technique, and themes. Throughout, Mullen has been interested in language and also in the audience's relationship to the work. Her first chapbook of poetry, *Tree Tall Woman* (1981), shows affinities with the Black Arts Movement in its selection of racially marked themes, an emphasis on family and community, and an accessible voice (in what she terms the aesthetic tradition of the "authentic" voice). Following that first collection, Mullen's poetry became decidedly experimental and theo-retically informed, as she was influenced by Oulipo (a French experimen-tal collaboration between poets and mathematicians), language poetry (a contemporary avant-garde movement), and literary theory. *Trimmings* and *S*PeRM**K*T*, published in 1991 and 1992, respectively, draw extensively upon the techniques of Gertrude Stein, relying on puns and wordplay. While one can identify racial motifs in these two volumes, Mullen lost the predominantly black audience she enjoyed for *Tree Tall Woman*. Setting out to regain those readers and retain her new audience as well, Mullen in her next book deliberately joined the two traditions through the fig-ures of Sappho (lyric poetry) and Sapphire (a blues woman reclaimed from negative stereotypes of black women). In *Muse & Drudge*, Mullen fuses experimental techniques with the art of the blues, taking on the ways in which American society has constructed the idea of *woman* as either ideal or debased. Her fourth full-length collection, *Sleeping with the Dictionary* (2002), continues her play with language and social critique, highlighting her use of experimental writing techniques such as the Oulipo strategy N+7, which invites randomness into composition and a range of responses into interpretation. *Blues Baby*, published the same year, looks back to her earli-est work, reprinting *Tree Tall Woman* and publishing uncollected poems.

Mullen's work after her first collection can be placed in the lineage de-scending from Stein that flowered in avant-garde poetry. Her experimental poetic practice allows her to juxtapose multiple discourses and traditions and especially emphasizes the role of the reader in creating meaning. In her interview with Daniel Kane, Mullen explicitly identifies the following as among her influences: Langston Hughes, Gwendolyn Brooks, Melvin Tol-son, Bob Kaufman, Margaret Walker, poets of the Black Arts Movement, language-oriented poets, Nathaniel Mackey, the poetry of the New York School, Umbra, and Lorenzo Thomas. Mullen's wordplay and apparent acceptance of randomness join with a strong element of political protest based in gender, class, and race, a stance that is shared by many poets across several threads of the tradition. Mullen studied under Mackey, a major experimental African American poet of this generation whose work can be situated in relation to open form and jazz poetics.

As one could imagine, Mullen's work has been well received by scholars of experimental poetry, several of whom have published essays on her work and interviews with her. Criticism has focused on her wordplay, theoretical underpinnings of her work, African American cultural elements, and issues of audience. She was also the subject of a special section in the journal *Callaloo*. Only one year younger than Rita Dove, she has yet to see a book-length critical study of her work published. Her comparatively later poetry publishing career, which didn't fully commence until the 1990s due to her pursuit of a PhD, may mean significant attention in literary criticism will come a decade later than it did for Dove. As we see in the interview with Komunyakaa, there still exists some considerable skepticism about experimental poetry's capability to express political, cultural, or personal truths. The question of the extent of Mullen's contribution to this generation may be answered by how well Mullen's poetry overcomes its doubters within the African American poetic tradition.

Mullen's work is beginning to win the notice of prize committees: *Sleeping with the Dictionary* was a finalist for the National Book Critics' Circle Award, the National Book Award, and the Los Angeles Times Book Prize. *Recyclopedia*, a collection of her last three books, won the PEN Beyond the Margins Award. She also was awarded a Guggenheim fellowship in 2005.

I interviewed Mullen via an e-mailed list of questions during the summer and fall of 2008. She sent her responses, to which I replied with some follow-up questions, and she, with follow-up answers.

Selected Works by Harryette Mullen

POETRY

Tree Tall Woman (chapbook), Energy Earth Communications, 1981.
Trimmings, Tender Buttons Press, 1991.
S*PeRM**K*T, Singing Horse Press, 1992.
Muse & Drudge, Singing Horse Press, 1995.
Blues Baby: Early Poems, Bucknell University Press, 2002.
Sleeping with the Dictionary, University of California Press, 2002.
Recyclopedia, Graywolf Press, 2006.

MALIN PEREIRA: I hope you don't mind if we start with a seemingly frivolous or "light" question. While teaching your poetry (most intensively, *Trimmings* and *S*PeRM**K*T*) in a graduate seminar this semester, several of my students kept coming back to the question, "Where does Harryette Mullen shop?" When I think back to my own experience of graduate school, I understand this as a period of reconstituting oneself as an intellectual in relation to the dominant culture, especially our American consumer culture. In doing that, we look to models, whether the professors standing in front of us or the professor whose work we are reading. So I think what my students (most of whom were female) were asking is, given your critique of consumerism in relation to two areas closely tied to definitions of femininity, clothes and food, how do you as a woman, and a black woman, negotiate consumerism in your own life? And what might they be able to take from that for their own negotiations of consumer culture?

HARRYETTE MULLEN: In some ways I'm a typical American consumer, although I was raised to be frugal. To stretch a modest family income, my mother was an organic gardener, and we were recyclers before I'd ever heard the word *recycle*. I've long been accustomed to shopping at discount outlets, thrift stores, and flea markets; but I also like to find unique or handmade items at artists' co-ops. Our growing concern about sustainable production, waste, pollution, and global warming compels us to consider our behavior as consumers and its impact on the world. With the rising cost of food and fuel, we're cutting back on consumption and reconsidering what it means to live "the good life." It's unclear whether this is a temporary adjustment or a fundamental shift in collective consciousness. Rather than despair that nothing can be done to save us from destruction, I've tried over the years to make gradual changes in a positive direction. It's not all about sacrifice either. I'm eating better since I've begun to buy more of my produce at local farmers' markets. Here in Los Angeles nearly every neighborhood has its own weekly market. California, with its proximity to the Mexican border and the Pacific Rim, has also been a focal point of struggle over wages, rights, and working conditions of migrant and immigrant laborers, another issue to consider as consumers, even when purchasing products made in the USA.

MP: One longtime interest of yours is subjectivity, especially in relation to the body and the text. Your dissertation at UC Santa Cruz explores issues of gender and identity in slave narratives, and you've spoken in interviews about how your poetry resists conventional notions of subjectivity. It's interesting to note that, in your poetry, poetic voice — as an illusory yet traditionally recognized vehicle of poetic identity — refuses to take on a consistent perspective across your work or even in one volume. You break from so many of the assumptions associated with lyric poetry that there's an *I*/eye behind the utterance, that the words are the vehicle for identity, etc. Could you talk a bit about how you see poetic voice and how you are manipulating it or moving beyond it in your poetry, and why?

HM: Lyric subjectivity is partly an attempt to overcome the separation of the word from the body and intention of the poet. That separation occurs not only in the publication of the poem, and the eventual death of the poet, but [in the process of composition, because separation] is a condition of poetic language, with its deliberate balance of precision and imprecision, so that the meaning of the text expands beyond the poet's immediate intention. The separation of the writer from the word begins as soon as the text is written. Even when I read my own words back to myself, the reader and the writer are no longer the same. There is a separation between the one who reads and the one who wrote. Over the years I have tried not to forget that separation but to rely on it. The lyric subject might be an apparently unitary construct, a persona that might or might not represent the "voice" of the poet. My work often includes language borrowed from others, or language obviously altered from its original purpose, and readers may interpret my work in a way that doesn't depend on the convention of a singular lyric subject whose authentic emotion or sincere intention the poem expresses. Critics Elisabeth Frost and Juliana Spahr have suggested that my work invites alternative ways of reading, particularly for communities of readers sharing their respective interpretations.

MP: Right. Quite different from E. M. Forster's dictum, "Only connect." Why do you value this separation between writer and word, lyric subject and emotion in the poem, poet and reader? Is it simply about opening up alternative ways of reading, or do you have a project to uncover the falseness of these conventions? Is one goal empowering readers and generating multiple meanings?

HM: It's not so much an ideological objection that I have toward the lyric subject, which is to some extent an artifact of history, culture, and tradition. Subjectivity in poetry is part of the grand illusion of artistic creation. I may want to believe in the illusion, but I rely on a critical awareness of how such illusions can be constructed or deconstructed. I've always been intrigued by the legend of the sybil, a female oracle whose poetic utterances were interpreted as prophecy. This idea of poetry seems to be both ancient and postmodern. I am aware of the distance that separates the poet and her intention from the reader's comprehension of the poem. This allows a sense of clarity, confidence, and freedom in my relationship to readers. While I hope to connect with readers, I am aware that not all readers are ready or willing to give their attention to a poem. Readers, including the most attentive, could interpret a poem in ways the poet could not anticipate. I hope those who encounter my poetry feel that it is worth the time and effort to read and to consider what the poem might mean. There's always something on my mind when I'm writing; but it's often difficult to pin down exactly what the poem communicates or how readers comprehend it. As a writer, teacher, and critic, I'm aware that interpretation relies on cultural and historical context. The poem takes advantage of the gap between intention and comprehension, expanding the range of possible meaning. Whatever I've intended to say, I hope the poem says something more.

I'm not hostile to the idea of convention. I'm interested in the relationship of tradition and innovation. Language itself is a system of rules and conventions. It belongs to all of us but can't be entirely possessed by any of us. We are born into language and it keeps on going after we die. Yet it is one of the tools we can use to fashion a personal identity. A poem purposefully obeys and disobeys the rules of ordinary speech and language as well as the conventions peculiar to literature and poetry. Whether we're talking about poetry or ordinary speech, we selectively follow certain rules while bending or breaking others. That's a part of how we fashion what we think of as a distinctive voice or style. What's interesting to me is how language can include and exclude, connect and disconnect at the same time. A poem that is immediately comprehensible to some readers will leave others scratching their heads in puzzlement.

MP: Somewhat linked to the above question is another question from a traditional way of thinking, this one about your poetic "development." So often in literary criticism, and I myself am guilty of this in my book on Rita Dove, we construct a story about how a poet and his or her work develop over the years. There are several ways in which it's difficult to write a narrative of development for you or your work: your effort to "return" in your fourth book to themes of interest to readers of your first book; the republication of *Tree Tall Woman* (originally published in 1981) as part of *Blues Baby* (2002), which also includes previously uncollected poetry, so that these poems in a sense now "follow" the three volumes that many readers first encountered (*Trimmings*, *S*PeRM**K*T*, and *Muse & Drudge*); and of course your revoicing of Gertrude Stein in *Trimmings* and

S*PeRM**K*T — all these complicate a development narrative. Even the title of the 2006 collection reprinting those three volumes, *Recyclopedia*, suggestions a continually shifting and recreating cycle rather than a linear narrative. The closest you have come to articulating a narrative of development is in your discussion of how *Muse & Drudge* was prompted by your desire to bring together your two audiences, the primarily black female audience of *Tree Tall Woman*, and the predominantly white avant-garde poetry crowd of *Trimmings* and *S*PeRM**K*T*. Now, in *Sleeping with the Dictionary*, might it finally be possible to construct a narrative of development for you and your work? One perhaps based upon an ever-deepening interest in linguistic core structures and the play of possibilities they enable? Or, do you hope to always escape such a narrative?

HM: Yes, it is difficult to narrate my development as a poet. I really haven't given it much thought. I just tend to do whatever comes next. Maybe there's an implicit narrative in my responses to your other questions.

MP: There are several really good interviews published with you that I'd direct the reader to for more information about some of the theoretical issues informing your work and some of the poetic schools or influences of certain poets on your work. But one issue that hasn't been talked about in those interviews is the particular period of black poetry in which you are writing. Since this interview is expected to be part of a book collecting interviews with some of the most significant poets in African American poetry following the Black Arts Movement (born between 1945 and 1963), I'd be interested in hearing your thoughts about this period of black poetry in which you have been writing, mostly in the 1980s and 1990s, and continuing into the twenty-first century. In rather stark contrast to the Black Arts Movement, this period cannot be characterized as a unified movement; in fact, the diversity of themes and aesthetics is quite broad. How would you characterize this period and the poets writing in it? What contributions to the changing same of the black poetry tradition are being made?

HM: African American poets are still reacting to the intensity of the 1960s–70s. The desire of black artists to represent and affirm black identity propelled the Black Arts Movement. That era's emphasis on unity has given way to diversity and complexity. African American poetry today might be characterized by more speculative and inclusive discussions of "blackness," more nuanced attention to socioeconomic, sexual, cultural and aesthetic differences, more expansive global consciousness. The Black

Arts Movement allied itself with urgent political goals of black solidarity and empowerment. Today there appears to be no aesthetic or political consensus of African American poets, yet I would not go so far as to say that we are "post-black" or that we lack political consciousness. We are still perceived as different from other Americans, although we are somewhat integrated into "mainstream" culture. African American poetry has shifted from declaring to interrogating "blackness," expanding "black experience" and "black expression" to include a greater range of "human" experience and expression, and representing "human experience" from a globally conscious "black" perspective. African Americans, traditional and innovative, are freely exploring divergent ideas and poetics.

Even during the 1960s–70s, there were political and aesthetic disagreements among African American poets. At a certain point, not only the aesthetic manifestos but also the poetry itself became a forum for bickering and mudslinging. The rhetorical urban vernacular emerged as a representative voice or dominant style of black poetry, but it was by no means the only poetry, drama, or literature produced by African Americans in those decades. The movement made black artists and writers visible as a collective, even as it tended to eclipse individuals with different aesthetic or cultural values, whose work is gaining attention from writers and scholars today.

Without the cultural work of the Black Arts Movement and the earlier 1920s Harlem Renaissance, which accompanied the political activism of their respective civil rights and black empowerment organizations, I doubt that we'd be where we are today. It seems that we needed to proclaim a collective cultural identity, to delineate what we might share in common, before we could turn to diversity. Having accomplished significant political gains and defined a collective cultural identity, African Americans have the self-confidence to look beyond ourselves in our work as artists, writers, critics, and scholars. I think this is due in part to the continuing influence of black-identified movements (such as politically oriented hip-hop culture and a broad spectrum of social activism organizations), along with the emergence of black cultural studies, literary canons, and networks of scholars and writers at academic institutions, the presence of widely influential black figures in mainstream media culture, and the recognition of black writers (African, Caribbean, and African American) with Nobel Prizes in literature.

Black Arts writers learned from shortcomings of the 1920s Harlem

Renaissance, when writers often depended on wealthy patrons. Since the 1960s–70s, African Americans have continued to organize vital networks and institutions that support the work of black writers, including *Callaloo* Creative Writing Workshops, Cave Canem, Dark Room Collective, Furious Flower, the Hurston-Wright Foundation, Soul Mountain Retreat, and Voices Workshops for Writers of Color. Literary journals such as *Callaloo*, *A Gathering of the Tribes*, *Hambone*, *Nocturnes*, and *Obsidian* publish an exhilarating array of poetry.

A flourishing African American literary culture took root in the 1970s. Between then and now, several authors have published "how to" handbooks for aspiring African American writers, including self-publishers. Commercial publishers finally are persuaded that a market exists for black books, including popular literature and nonliterary titles. Major cities offer black bookstores, such as Eso Won Books here in Los Angeles, a product of the cultural renaissance of the 1960s–70s. Like other independent bookstores, it is endangered by competition from chain stores and internet sales. In chain bookstores, interestingly, fiction by black writers is likely to be shelved separately, apart from other fiction books, while black poets' books tend to be integrated with others in the scant space allowed to poetry.

Compared to past decades, black writers today may be somewhat more integrated into the "mainstream" literary culture of creative writing programs and workshops, writers' retreats, reading circuits, literary journals and reviews, book publishing, and awards committees. Major publishers such as Norton, Oxford, and Gale have brought out companions to African American literature, literary biographies of African American writers, and anthologies of African American poetry. Books by black authors receive attention in *African American Review*, *Black Issues Book Review*, *Black Renaissance*, *Callaloo*, *Drum Voices Revue*, *Quarterly Black Review*, and *Transition*, as well as other periodicals aimed at "mainstream" audiences. The black literary culture exists to encourage, coach, and call attention to African American writers who might escape notice of the "mainstream" literary establishment.

MP: As a follow up or linked question to the previous one, what do you think of poetry literacy or definitions of poetry that are dominant in parts of the black community today, such as the emphasis upon spoken word or performance poetry? I know in one of your poems the speaker talks about wanting to be a performance poet. Also, how do you see your own work, which has reemphasized the graphic/written dimensions of the tradition (in response to an emphasis on the oral), in relation to black popular culture's dominant definitions of poetry today?

HM: That poem, "Playing the Invisible Saxophone en el Combo de las Estrellas," is dedicated to Evangelina Vigil-Piñón, a writer I've known since we both worked as artists in the schools in Texas. I wrote it after seeing her in a performance when she read a poem about jazz and improvised a musical solo on "air saxophone." I've seen Amiri Baraka do similar kinds of vocalizing while drumming on a lectern, when he isn't performing his poetry with instrumental accompaniment of actual jazz musicians. Vangie might have been inspired by Baraka and other African American poets, possibly when she was a student at Prairie View University. Her experience as a Mexican American included listening to jazz at this historically black college, just as my experience as an African American included reading Spanish, Mexican, and Latin American literature at the University of Texas.

The first "experimental" novel that I recall reading with excitement was Julio Cortázar's *Hopscotch*. Before then I'd read and enjoyed poems by e. e. cummings. At the time I didn't think of them as "experimental" or as poems that privileged text over speech or voice. I understood that such things as his grasshopper poem were possible when composing on a typewriter, not realizing at the time that Apollinaire had done something similar with his handwritten calligrammes. I was just as interested when *Dial-a-Poem* and *Black Box* came along as formats for voice and sound. I have no particular bias for or against the graphic or performative aspects of poetry. I want to move freely across those boundaries. Baraka, a leader of the Black Arts Movement, allowed himself that freedom.

MP: While you speak of Zora Neale Hurston in several interviews as a key figure, I haven't seen anywhere that you explained in any detail your perspective on Phillis Wheatley as in some ways the foremother of the African American poetic tradition. Her emphasis on written literacy and Christianity might make for some interest to you? If her work isn't something you think about much, why is Hurston's, especially since Hurston is not a poet?

HM: I look to Hurston as a creative writer who heard poetry in the everyday language of black folk, and also as an adventurous scholar. Hurston's folklore collections and Clarence Major's dictionary of African American slang were important sources for my book *Muse & Drudge*. Wheatley is monumental, a founding mother of American, African American, and African diaspora poetry. I realize now that my response to her was influenced by June Jordan's essay "The Difficult Miracle of Black Poetry in America" and Alice Walker's story "The Diary of an African Nun." Before Gates ever read *Deep Down in the Jungle*, Wheatley was signifying on the classics. Before DuBois ever gave it a name, Wheatley was exploring the complex terrain of double consciousness. Her brilliance illuminated the inconvenient truth of a freedom-loving nation founded on slave labor and provoked founding father Thomas Jefferson to reveal his own double thinking about race in *Notes on the State of Virginia*.

MP: I will be interviewing Yusef Komunyakaa next, and in preparing for that interview I was somewhat surprised and very interested to see that he speaks quite negatively against experimental poetry in two interviews. In a 2002 interview with Tod Marshall, he says: "Many of the experimental poets — it seems as if those poems come out of everything but experience. The poems come out of certain kinds of cultivated practices that have to do with reading the right books. Consequently, we can probably program computers to write those poems based on the intake of certain details from theory books and encyclopedias and what have you. That kind of experimentation is riddled with false notes. I agree with Pound. Emotion says that there is a person there" (155–56). Now, I'm not trying to start a fight here, but when I got to the word "encyclopedia" I had to wonder if he is directly speaking about your work. As a black poet whose work is identified strongly with experimentalism, including use of theory and reference texts such as dictionaries and encyclopedias, how would you respond to Komunyakaa's concerns?

HM: Komunyakaa is a poet whose work I often teach and have long admired. His description of experimental writing is literally true of certain texts, including poems generated by chance procedures or composed with the aid of computers. His opinion of such practices is widely shared by many readers. Komunyakaa's acknowledged influences include surrealists, jazz musicians, and others who once were considered avant-garde, experimental, anti-aesthetic, bizarre, inscrutable, and so forth — the usual reaction to art that challenges or alters how we perceive and make sense of ourselves and the world. His complaint is directed at poets whose formal or technical experimentation takes precedence over expressive content. He's not opposed to poetic invention, computers, or encyclopedias. He's only declaring an aesthetic preference.

As to his comment about reading "the right books," if poetry is a cultivated practice of people who read books, it's my understanding that "the right books" may be different for each reader. Besides alluding to s+7 or n+7, language games associated with writers of the experimental Oulipo group, references to dictionary, thesaurus, and encyclopedia in my own work also foreground the habitual recourse of readers and writers to such authoritative reference works and literary "companions," particularly as we face the difficulty of diverse and conflicting cultural literacies. The Encyclopedia Project, cofounded by Tisa Bryant, invites creative writers to contribute to a repository of alternative knowledge. I might add that, on first reading Komunyakaa's *Taboo*, my UCLA students found its eclectic allusions and jazzy improvisation quite challenging, yet intriguing and rewarding with subsequent reading and discussion. The "authoritative reference work" they used most often to comprehend the poet's allusions was Wikipedia.

MP: Let's break from all these heavy poetic tradition questions. I noted that in a couple of interviews you express great interest in and love for travel. I wonder if you could share with us what travel gives you and how it might enrich your work. We are becoming a far more global society, and I wonder if a transnational sensibility might be coming into your work, which up to now seems infused with American culture.

HM: Travel entices me to overcome my fear of the unknown. I have many places yet to visit, and still more fear to conquer. I've especially enjoyed traveling with other writers and scholars, as I've done in trips to Canada, Costa Rica, Cuba, France, Germany, Jamaica, and Mexico.

MP: Another life question: There's about a decade span between your first book and your second. While of course you must have been in graduate school during part of that time, since your dissertation is dated 1991, what else did you do? How did you make a living while writing poetry before you became a professor? How did any of those experiences contribute to your work?

HM: I was trying to figure out how to live — exist and survive — as a writer. That interval was filled with poetry readings and literary festivals, artist residencies, fellowships, conferences of writers and critics, arts council meetings, graduate studies and dissertation writing, academic and nonacademic jobs. While earning a meager living I was getting to know diverse communities of writers, artists, musicians, dancers, and scholars, and (in those days before the internet) searching for hard-to-find books in libraries and used bookstores. I was also writing, revising, and sending out poems, short stories, book reviews, articles, and essays for publication in assorted journals and anthologies. My jobs included cocktail server, fast food worker, typist at a law firm, tutor, community college instructor, university teaching assistant, artist in the schools, office worker and aspiring journalist at a weekly newspaper, and temporary receptionist at Goodwill Industries, where I trained a recovering heroin addict as my replacement. Between jobs, I slept on my sister's sofa and applied for artist fellowships. In my best year as a struggling artist I was accepted for six months at the Dobie Paisano Ranch near Austin, Texas, and for six months at the Wurlitzer Foundation in Taos, New Mexico. At a certain point, I wanted the stability and intellectual stimulus of an academic life, and I arrived at graduate school in a ten-year old car packed with all my possessions, with less than one hundred dollars to live on until my first paycheck. I'd been trying to find a publisher for my *Blues Baby* manuscript, but I put that on hold when I applied to graduate school.

MP: Do you use elements from this wide array of work experiences in your poetry or literary criticism? If so, in what ways? Has your work in the food and beverage or communications industries (both of which are about the public sphere) contributed in any way to your sense of who your readers might be?

HM: I can see a connection between my work as a junior journalist and the kinds of writing I'm doing now. I was on the staff of my high school paper and several student publications at University of Texas, as well as a newspaper for the African American community. I even worked briefly for *Sepia*, a magazine modeled on *Ebony* that was published in Fort Worth. I could compare myself in some respects to Paul Laurence Dunbar, Gwendolyn Brooks, and Langston Hughes, poets who also wrote for newspapers. They were interested in bringing vernacular language, as well as a journalistic or critical-documentary perspective, into literary poetry. Certain poems in *Sleeping with the Dictionary* allude to widely reported news stories, including the mass suicide of the Heaven's Gate cult, the bombing of the Chinese Embassy in a NATO air strike on Belgrade, and the police shooting of Amadou Diallo in New York.

My other jobs may have heightened my attention to diversity expressed through language, along with a sensitivity to the division of "town vs. gown" in the range of my experience serving college students, from my time as a fast food worker and cocktail server in Austin, Texas, to more recent faculty positions at Cornell University and UCLA. I do recall how difficult it was to work in a food service job, where it was common for male patrons to request "a waitress with no dressing." I also recognized University of Texas students I'd served before, when I worked at a summer resort for rich Texans. My fellow employees were working-class kids with no plans for college. I used to practice my Spanish with one of my coworkers, who told me it is nicer to say *blanquillos* (little white things) instead of *huevos* (which literally means eggs but is also slang for testicles). I left the drive-through burger franchise on "the Drag" across from the University of Texas campus to work in a pub where I thought I could earn more with tips. But I had to quit after too many drunken college boys skipped out without paying their tab, and the manager deducted it from my earnings. When I worked at the bar, I had to refer to a chart on the wall to decorate the drinks with the proper garnishes. Since I don't drink alcohol, I had no idea which drinks were supposed to be served with a cherry, an olive, an onion, a lemon or lime, or a tiny paper umbrella. One of the poems in *Sleeping with the Dictionary* includes parts of a recipe for making margaritas, but the poem itself was inspired by a series of murders of young women in a Mexican border town. I refer to another cocktail recipe in a poem about visiting Havana as a tourist, "Drinking Mojitos in Cuba Libre" (published in *Callaloo*). Mixed drinks, like the margarita in Mexico and the Cuba libre, daiquiri, and mojito in Cuba, have historical significance, as each was created to popularize national exports such as rum and tequila. In particular, rum has a historical resonance for me, because some of my ancestors worked as slaves on sugar cane plantations.

MP: I was pleased to see that you have published an essay on Julie Patton in *American Poet*. I met Julie when she was on a North Carolina Humanities Council grant doing poetry outreach here in Charlotte a few years ago. She came and spoke to one of my classes and she and Lee Ann Brown gave a reading. I remember being quite struck by the fascicles (poetry packets) she was creating, which are reminiscent of course of Emily Dickinson's work. My graduate research assistant has been unable to procure the essay for me — "Truly Unruly Julie" — which would mean it would likely be difficult for others to get. I wonder if you would mind telling us what you had to say about Patton's work in that essay. What's important about her work?

HM: My essay in *American Poet*, "Truly Unruly Julie," is a version of a guest poet's column I wrote for *Boston Review*. I think that was a direct result of a week I spent with Julie Patton, Lee Ann Brown, and Jonathan Monroe, an esteemed colleague from my time at Cornell University. Thanks to Jonathan, we were all together at the Virginia Center for Creative Arts, in the company of visual artists, musicians, and song writers. That was the first time I heard Lee Ann sing her "Ballad of Susan Smith." It was the first time I heard Julie sing "Your Language Is Too Flowery," and heard her speak at length about her work with musicians such as Don Byron, Uri Caine, and Ravi Coltrane. (Sadly, it was the last time I saw Reetika Vazirani, who was writer in residence at Sweet Briar College, just down the road from the VCCA compound. [Reetika Vazirani was Yusef Komunyakaa's partner; she killed herself and their three-year-old son in 2003.]) As you may know, Julie Patton's North Carolina residency was initiated by Carolina Circuit Writers, an organization founded by my sister, Kirsten Mullen. Lee Ann Brown's Tender Buttons Press published my book *Trimmings*. Julie and Lee Ann are multimedia or intermedia artists whose work encompasses visual arts and electronic media, music, poetry, and performance. Tracie Morris is also notable for innovative performance and sound poetry. We met through our association with Cave Canem.

MP: Julie's visit to my class was a highlight for my students, who marveled at meeting someone with such creativity and originality. Her reading later in the day included Lee Ann as a surprise bonus. She performed "The Ballad of Susan Smith," which moved our North Carolina audience considerably. Both she and Cornelius Eady have done fine work with that horrible story.

I had no idea Kirsten Mullen was your sister (although obviously I could have seen that from the name). I sat across the table from her at the Afro-American Cultural Center here in Charlotte a few years back, planning with Julie and the director of the AACC the Charlotte portion of Julie's residency. My brother and I sometimes talk about how we both went into closely related fields, me in English (with psychology as a second area of interest) and him in social services (with screenwriting as a second area of interest). Have you and your sister ever considered why you both work in writing? What about your childhoods fostered these talents?

HM: My sister and I agree that we became habitual readers and writers as children in part because our parents divorced when we were very young. Our mother, a lifelong learner and educator, taught us to read and write before we entered the first grade. We were at the public library every week, checking out the maximum limit of books. We took books along with us everywhere, to entertain ourselves when our mother was taking care of business. At the time, our only communication with our father and our paternal grandparents was through letters. I believe I still have every letter they sent me, stored in boxes in my garage. I've become the family archivist, inheriting the correspondence saved by my maternal grandparents, including letters from my great-grandmother Hattie, whose parents had been slaves. Hattie was born after the Civil War; her husband Walker was born a slave in Virginia and became a church pastor in Pennsylvania. They were the first generation of my mother's family to attend school and become literate. I have one page of Walker's handwriting, a brief autobiographical statement.

I think Kirsten and I are writers because of the separation from our father, and also because of a foundation of literacy in a family of teachers, ministers, office workers, printers, and others whose employment required reading and writing. Our mother has retired from her career as a teacher and administrator in the public school system, and as founding director of a community school. She is currently learning Spanish, Tai Chi, and computer skills.

MP: I'm also interested in your essay on Sylvia Plath, in *Chain*, mostly because I've been delighted to learn in the course of this project that most of the female poets in this book have a significant regard for Plath and her poetry. Both Elizabeth Alexander and Wanda Coleman have poems about Plath, and Thylias Moss tells a story in her interview about her MA thesis on Plath and Ai. Now I would like to add you to that list of Plath appreciators. Could you talk about Plath's poetry and what's important to you in her work?

HM: Juliana Spahr and Jena Osman, editors of *Chain*, published a version of "Nine Syllables Label Sylvia," my essay on Plath's poem "Metaphors." I've used this riddle-like poem from time to time to show my creative writing students how economically the form, content, and figurative language sum up the speaker's perplexing position. My students frequently name Plath as a favorite poet, but many of them were unfamiliar with this

particular poem. I suppose it's one of her minors, but I like it. It's interest-
ing to see how she adapts such conventional forms as riddles, clichés, and
euphemisms, and how she moves from simile to metaphor to synecdoche.

MP: Do you admire Plath's poetic skill generally in her poetry? Her path
from the conventional to the experimental (insofar as confessional poetry
was experimental)? Or is it just that poem as an illustration of devices that
attracts you?

HM: Plath was a gifted and passionate poet. My difficulty is separating
the creative and destructive impulses of her art and life. It's interesting to
compare Sylvia Plath and Anne Sexton with poets such as Adrienne Rich
or Sharon Olds, who have the benefit of feminist consciousness and more
effective psychotherapy.

MP: While in several published interviews you talk about your 1990s
published poetry, there's not much about specific poems or themes in *Blues
Baby* or *Sleeping with the Dictionary*, both published in 2002. So, I'd like
to talk about poems from those collections for the rest of this interview.
One poem in *Blues Baby*, "Painting Myself a New Mirror," comes at the
end of the section "Tree Tall Woman," a reprinting of your first volume of
poetry. To me, this poem reads as an early ars poetica, establishing some of
your interest in experimentalism, subjectivity, representations of women,
and the nature of art. Could you talk about this poem for a bit, and what
ideas about your own poetic you were articulating in it?

HM: "Painting Myself a New Mirror" was my way of revising a tradi-
tional representation of vanity in allegorical paintings: a woman grooming
herself while gazing at her reflection in a mirror. Typically the male painter
used a nude female model to portray the sin of vanity. Sylvia Plath's "Mir-
ror," a poem with a riddle structure similar to "Metaphors," might be her
reflection on this image of vanity that conventionally links woman, mir-
ror, and death. The speaker in my poem is a young woman who dreams of
becoming an artist rather than the artist's model, brushing paint on canvas
instead of painting her face with cosmetics. She envisions herself as a child
seeing her image in the mirror for the first time, and as a girl turning the
mirror away from herself to signal others.

MP: I myself have been fascinated with the question of how women writ-
ers shift from objects of beauty to creators of beauty in their art. How do
they create an aesthetic that does not objectify as they themselves have
been objectified in traditions such as literature and the visual arts? It was

the subject of my dissertation and first book, *Embodying Beauty*. "Painting Myself a New Mirror" from this perspective, then, would serve as a pivotal poem in your development as a female poet, articulating your movement into female artistic agency and voice. What do you think? When you say, for example, that the girl turns the mirror away from herself to signal others, is that a turn away from lyric subjectivity as a poet in order to keep the objectifying gaze at bay? Do you think female poets have to keep lots of aesthetic distance in their work between themselves and the art to avoid being read as the final subject or ground of the poem, rather than the poem being read as an art object?

HM: I'm not certain that we can entirely escape objectification in art and literature, but I'm certainly interested in the ways that women and people of color, individually and collectively, have adapted, challenged, and transformed male-dominated and Eurocentric traditions and practices of art, criticism, and scholarship. I'm not hostile to the lyric subject or the embodiment of beauty and desire. It's just that, for me, the mirror is more entrancing when it's turned away to catch the light. I do think of "Painting Myself a New Mirror" as a poem about self-awareness and artistic vision, about the development from girl to woman, and the movement from the model or muse who serves the artist's imagination to the artist empowered to create and communicate. I've always had an interest in these muse, model, and artist figures, from "Painting Myself a New Mirror" and the "Siren" series in *Tree Tall Woman*, to Manet's *Olympia*, Josephine Baker, and a "strayed mermaid" (wearing fishnet stockings) in *Trimmings*, to the lyric poet Sappho and a chorus of women in *Muse & Drudge*, to Eurydice and Jayne Cortez in *Sleeping with the Dictionary*. "Fancy Cortex" may be the first blazon that praises a woman's brain. It's dedicated to the poet Jayne Cortez, whose husband Mel Edwards is an American sculptor. Her previous husband, jazz innovator Ornette Coleman, got his start in the I. M. Terrell High School band, along with musicians Dewey Redman, Charles Moffett, and Prince Lasha. One of their fellow band members was my mother, Avis, who played clarinet and marched as drum major. My mother, by the way, later went to Talladega College, where her classmates included the writer Calvin Hernton, and her teachers included the painter David Driskell. She still has an oil painting she made in Driskell's class.

MP: Continuing this discussion of specific poems, in *Blues Baby* I was interested to see a number of poems with male personae. A good example would be the siren sequence, where there are two different male perspectives on the sirens, followed by a poem from the siren's perspective. Can you talk about writing from a male point of view?

HM: A male persona can represent a partner in a duet or dialogue. *Blues Baby* was envisioned as a sort of blues symposium of male and female speakers discussing the pleasures and hazards of love, sexual attraction, and erotic relationships. The siren sequence alludes to a well-known episode in Homer's *Odyssey*. In my version, the siren is an artist figure. The two sailors have conflicting responses to the siren and her song: the first is fatally attracted; the second, repulsed by what appears to be a monstrous combination of warm-blooded woman and cold fish. She could be any female artist, but I imagine my siren as a blues singer, like Billie Holiday in her autobiography *Lady Sings the Blues* or Ursa in Gayl Jones's novel *Corregidora*.

When I read *Corregidora*, which is really a blues novel, I felt that Ursa was based on Holiday, who accepted the title of *Lady* although she had worked in a brothel. Growing up in the Bible Belt, I observed that a great divide separated "blues women" like Billie Holiday or Bessie Smith from "church ladies" like my grandmother. Like Gayl Jones, whose grandmother was locally famous for writing church plays, I was steeped in religion as a granddaughter and great-granddaughter of Baptist ministers. Like Jones, I turned to the blues tradition as an archive of information about sexual relationships. Her work explores how gender, sexual, and socioeconomic relations in the Americas are shaped by four centuries of slavery plus another hundred years of Jim Crow USA. The same could be said of the blues.

Breaking sexual taboos did expose women writers to personal criticism. For Gayl Jones, it might have been particularly difficult, coming from a fundamentalist religious community that suspected Hollywood films and mainstream novels as products of a "wicked" secular world. To be an artist, novelist, actor, or filmmaker might have seemed almost as scandalous as singing the blues in bars and nightclubs. So in *Blues Baby*, this female blues singer becomes a dangerously alluring siren or Mami Wata. I imagine her as Billie Holiday wearing a sequined fishtail gown.

MP: A number of poems in *Blues Baby* address sexual and physical pleasure. Compared to previous generations of female poets, this seems a new directness. Did you think about that at all as breaking new ground? Is it that both sexual frankness and the male personae mentioned above are partly the result of the blues impulse informing the volume?

HM: When I was writing my early poems, quite a few taboos were broken already. The "sexual revolution" began in the 1960s as the widely available birth control pill allowed women more sexual and reproductive freedom. Already by the 1970s, African American novelists such as Cecil Brown, Steve Cannon, and Clarence Major had explored frankly erotic or explicitly pornographic themes in their work. Melvin Van Peebles had made a splash with *Sweet Sweetback's Baadasssss Song*, a pornographic film with a "revolutionary" political message.

Now that you mention it, perhaps the forwardness of *Blues Baby* was relatively new in women's poetry. Sharon Olds published her first book in 1980, but I didn't know her work until later. My models of earthy sexuality were in the tradition of blues and R&B music, and in women's prose writing of the 1970s, including fiction by Rita Mae Brown, Gayl Jones, Erica Jong, Toni Morrison, and Alice Walker. The stark and shocking poems in Ai's *Cruelty* were akin to Gayl Jones's prose in *Corregidora*; and poets Jayne Cortez, June Jordan, Audre Lorde, Sonia Sanchez, and Ntozake Shange boldly proclaimed their womanhood in language that, like Tina Turner's music, could be "nice and easy" or "nice and rough." In college I was also reading books like *The Joy of Sex* and *Our Bodies, Ourselves*. By the time I was publishing poetry I felt that acknowledging women's sexuality was a worthwhile feminist project. However, I didn't find a publisher for the *Blues Baby* manuscript until Cynthia Hogue requested permission for Bucknell University Press to reprint my first book, *Tree Tall Woman*. I suggested that the new edition should include the *Blues Baby* poems, which I was writing when *Tree Tall Woman* was published originally.

MP: One poem that seems to compare your generation to the previous, civil rights generation is "You Who Walked through the Fire," in *Blues Baby*. It reminds me of poems by Cyrus Cassells and Elizabeth Alexander that pay homage to the bravery of that generation and express appreciation for the possibilities they enabled for those who followed. Your poem, though, seems to questions the results of this generation's greater freedoms. The poem seems doubtful that this generation is living up to the sacrifices made by those who came before. Of course, it somewhat takes on the perspective of the civil rights generation in the first two stanzas, but when you shift in the last stanza to two questions and an *I* first-person speaker, the poem seems self-critical. Also, while lacking the traditional end rhymes or stanza structure of a sonnet, it is an adapted fourteen-line sonnet — which seems unusual for you. Could you tell us what you see going on that poem?

HM: It would be tough to live up to the bravery and sacrifice of previous generations whose courage and determination made our lives easier. Compared to our ancestors we are more comfortable, but less heroic. Likely literary influences for "You Who Walked through the Fire" were Gwendolyn Brooks and Lorenzo Thomas. Brooks often used the sonnet's formality to underscore the dignity of everyday people. Something similar occurs in "MMDCCXIII 1/2. " by Lorenzo Thomas, a fourteener that begins, "The cruelty of ages past affects us now." I've continued to be interested in variations on sonnets and quatorzains by poets such as Ted Berrigan, Wanda Coleman, Beverly Dahlen, Rita Dove, Robert Hayden, Terrance Hayes, A. Van Jordan, Bernadette Mayer, Marilyn Nelson, Evie Shockley, and Natasha Trethewey. A recent anthology of collaborative poems includes "Sprung Flung," a free verse fourteener I cowrote with Douglas Kearney. Some of my prose poems are rewritten sonnets. An anthology of contemporary sonnets published recently in the UK includes two poems from *Sleeping with the Dictionary*, "Dim Lady" and "Variation on a Theme Park." Both are rewritings of Shakespeare's "Sonnet 130," which begins, "My mistress' eyes are nothing like the sun." My poem "Broken Glish" (published in *VOLT*) is an "inverse translation" of Pablo Neruda's "Soneto VI" that begins, "*En los bosques, perdido, corté una rama oscura.*"

MP: Yusef Komunyakaa's most recent collection, *Warhorses*, opens with a section of adapted sonnets. The sonnet seems to be getting a lot of attention these days from African American poets. Thanks for the heads up about your prose poems being rewritten sonnets and the reminder about your two rewritings of Shakespeare's "Sonnet 130"— I will have to read them at our annual Sonnet Slam on campus next year, which should interest our early modern faculty and students. What about the sonnet attracts you?

HM: It might seem counterintuitive, given the prominence and prestige of sonnets in lyric tradition, but the sonnet appeals to me in part because of my interest in prose poetry. It was very easy to move back and forth between the sonnet and the prose paragraph. I want my prose poems to be less prosaic and more poetic, so I like the energy of a sonnet. The structure of a sonnet is like a paragraph in verse, laying out a concise argument, but the sonnet also sings and swings.

MP: Last, I'd like to get your comments on two of my favorite poems in

Sleeping with the Dictionary: "Exploring the Dark Content" and "We Are Not Responsible." I think I like these poems so much because they each use experimental poetic techniques to political ends. Both these poems challenge the stereotype some people have that experimental poetry is just a lot of word play and doesn't have any "meaning" and isn't about anything "real." I read "Exploring the Dark Content" as a poem playing around with ideas about blackness, in the lineage of poems about heritage, black identity, diaspora, and black folk culture. There's a tension in the poem between acknowledging these aspects and viewing them with a skeptical or even critical eye. Some of that is enabled by playful punning. But there are also some pretty direct assertions in there. Can you talk about some of the politics of blackness you are addressing in that poem? And, in "We Are Not Responsible," you create a chillingly familiar *1984*-ish picture of our present-day society, reusing popular discourse to reveal endemic social injustice. In particular, you finger language and cultural choices or behaviors that read as "oppositional" to the dominant social order as the markers authority uses to identify threats they must quash to maintain power. Could you talk about this poem and what your concerns are about our society today?

HM: Every poem in *Sleeping with the Dictionary* started with something "real" that is meaningful to me, although in some cases the origin of the poetic idea has receded into the background by the time the piece is finished. In several of the poems, playing with language allows a critical subversion of authoritative discourse. As you have indicated, "Exploring the Dark Content" and "We Are Not Responsible" echo recurrent discussions of identity politics, multiculturalism, immigration, assimilation, and racial profiling, along with poems such as "Bilingual Instructions," "Bleeding Hearts," "Coo/Slur," "Denigration," "Elliptical," "Natural Anguish," "Resistance Is Fertile," "Souvenir from Anywhere," "Suzuki Method," and "Xenophobic Nightmare in a Foreign Language."

Generally speaking, my outlook is optimistic. Since you ask about my greatest concerns for our society, I'll list them here. As a writer, I'm concerned for the future of literature. As a citizen of the U.S., I'm concerned that fear is driving us to destroy everything that makes our way of life worth defending and preserving. As an earthling, I'm concerned for the survival of earth and its inhabitants.

[2008]

THYLIAS MOSS

Thylias Moss's poetry has changed dramatically across her oeuvre. Her intellectually and aesthetically complex multimedia experiments stand out in this generation of poets. Her twelve books, while focusing mainly on poetry, span memoir, verse narrative, children's literature, and drama. She is the only one of these poets to win a MacArthur Fellowship (popularly known as "the genius grant"), in 1996.

Moss was born on February 27, 1954, in Cleveland, Ohio. Moss's childhood was both nurturing and traumatic, as she had a stable, affectionate family life with warm and loving neighbors, yet during her elementary school years she was sexually abused by her babysitter (detailed in her 1998 memoir, *Tale of a Sky-Blue Dress*) and witnessed the violent deaths of children. Her experiences with racism in a mostly white school district worked against her advancement as a highly gifted child, and high school became a hostile place to her. She experienced a lot of personal problems in her high school years, which she traces to the experiences of trauma and abuse. Moss attended Syracuse University from 1971 to 1973, and married John Moss in 1973. Moss returned to college in 1979 at his urging and earned her BA in English from Oberlin in 1981, then an MA in English from the University of New Hampshire in 1983. She has two sons, Dennis and Ansted. From 1984 to 1992, Moss was on the faculty of Phillips Academy in Andover, Massachusetts. She is currently a professor at the University of Michigan, which hired her in 1993. She now holds a joint appointment in the English and Art and Design departments.

Moss's earliest work showed the influence of the Black Arts Movement in its emphasis on social commentary and employment of a mostly narrative style. The early poems are accessible, reflective, and grounded in attention to everyday humanity. Her poetry today transcends the page: writing within an aesthetic frame she terms "Limited Fork Poetics," Moss's "poams," as she calls them ("products of acts of making"), draw upon olfactory, visual, sonic, and tactile dimensions. Her current work is available on her blog at http://tinetimes.blogspot.com. Moss's poetry as a whole has drawn upon a range of mythologies and religious symbols, African American life, scientific discourses, the current realities of racism, and the history of slavery.

Moss may be the Elizabeth Bishop of her generation, standing uniquely alone in the tradition. The highly allusive and juxtapositional quality of works such as *Last Chance for the Tarzan Holler* and *Tokyo Butter* is reminiscent of Ezra Pound and T. S. Eliot's major experimental modernist works. The intellectual abstraction and individualized character, however, pull these works back from being epic "tales of the tribe" as much as confessional exposés of how the poet's mind works. Moss's early interest in the poetry of Sylvia Plath and Ai suggests she might be a confessionalist of the mind and systems of meaning, rather than of emotion and the physical body.

Literary criticism has mostly overlooked Moss's poetry. While her work has been well reviewed and has won numerous awards, including a Pushcart Prize in 1990, the Witter Bynner and the Whiting awards in 1991, a Guggenheim in 1996, and a MacArthur "genius" grant, only one literary critic has published an analysis of her poetry. Jay Winston shows how Moss plays the metaphysical trickster in her poetry, freeing up from colonized signifiers a potential for truth. Productive areas for further exploration include her depiction of slavery in *Slave Moth*, the experimental structure of *Tokyo Butter*, and a developmental study of her work. The density and complexity of her work will challenge many and may prove a deterrent to a full flowering of critical attention.

I interviewed Moss via e-mail for more than a year, from July 25, 2007, to October 17, 2008. We had multiple starts and stops due to her health and family responsibilities and my administrative work, but we persevered. I sent her each question separately until the last three, which I sent at once so we could wrap up the interview process.

Selected Works by Thylias Moss

POETRY

Hosiery Seams on a Bowlegged Woman, Cleveland State University Poetry Center, 1983.
Pyramid of Bone, University Press of Virginia, 1989.

At Redbones, Cleveland State University Poetry Center, 1990.
Rainbow Remnants in Rock Bottom Ghetto Sky, Persea Books (National
     Poetry Series), 1991.
Small Congregations: New and Selected Poems, The Ecco Press, 1993.
Last Chance for the Tarzan Holler, Persea Books, 1998.
Slave Moth: A Narrative in Verse, Persea Books, 2004.
Tokyo Butter: Poems, Persea Books, 2006.

OTHER

Talking to Myself (play), 1984.
The Dolls in the Basement (play), 1984.
I Want to Be (children's book), Puffin, 1995.
Tale of a Sky-Blue Dress (memoir), Harper Perennial, 1998.

LINKS

http://tinetimes.blogspot.com
http://forkergirl.typepad.com/
http://itunes.apple.com/ns/podcast/limited-fork-music/id192523404
http://www.4orked.com

LINKS TO THE "BUBBLING" COLLECTION

http://www.youtube.com/forkergirl
http://www-personal.umich.edu/~thyliasm/ProjectGenealogy(w.sung
     narration).m4v
http://orelitrev.startlogic.com/v2n2/MossBubble.pdf
http://orelitrev.startlogic.com/v2n2/OLR-moss.htm

MALIN PEREIRA: I'd like to start off focusing on your earlier work. I'm
fascinated by the revision process behind *Small Congregations*, a collection
of new and selected poems from your first four books, in which you sub-
stantially revise several poems, retitle some, and rearrange all of them into
a new order. When I think of selected or collected poems volumes by other
contemporary poets, I cannot think of another poet who has been so will-
ing, even eager, to rework and reorder his or her art. The result is a magnifi-
cent re-creation of more than a decade of early work. Can you talk about
why you did such extensive revision and how the process unfolded? At that
time, how did you see your art and creative process and its products?

THYLIAS MOSS: I think that I took "selected" much too seriously when Ecco approached me with the idea; I thought about what it would mean to choose poems at the time that I was choosing, having become someone a bit different in circumstances a bit different from those circumstances prevailing at the time that the poems were initially written and published; I saw this as an opportunity to showcase the current limitations instead of the previous limitations, making true something I stated frequently in 1993 (and much less regularly now): "I want to write to my limits; I try to locate my work at the boundary of what I know, the edge of comfort, the end of expertise so that I am on the brink of discovery or collapse, embracing the raggedness of embrace. Everything I write will give evidence of the limits of my abilities at the time and circumstances of the writing." In this way, I could be more sure that I was thinking and writing to capacity; in this way I could be more sure that I could not have produced anything better at that time.

I was also eager to seize an opportunity to repair, revisit, and rethink. I was "selecting" or deciding how to configure poems that evolved to be products of the moment in which they would be repackaged and reconsidered, not replacing their previous incarnations, but existing beside them, like school pictures tracking changes, some of which would be growth.

Each poem is an iteration of a moment, and *Small Congregations* is true to its moment, which is not the same moment as the moments that produced the poems that *Small Congregations* contains. There's also the need to integrate the past into the present, an integration that is an intertwining, the one shaping/reshaping the other. The revived past is revived and revised in the present, so is subject to what prevails in the *now* of its revival. It was great to explore some of what would happen if I worked on the poems in a new *now*; how much would be retained in a form that seemed necessary in two different *nows*? Such questions still interest me. And there's the boredom factor; how boring to just reshuffle the poems without a little tinkering! The thrill factor: yes, risk tinkering and possible destruction, possible ruination of the poem, rendering it no longer *Best American Poetry* worthy, or a fate even worse! I am a maker still trying to figure something out, and my willingness, my need, my eagerness to rework and reorder is evidence that I haven't figured it out yet. To be honest, I don't want to arrive at the "all figured out" stage; that sounds like a terminal boundary, and I resist those. I don't know of a boundary that can't be transgressed.

The Thylias I had become was preparing the new and selected volume. *Small* because the "Congregations" poem previously published was greatly reduced, and because of the apparent reduction in size of something considered as distance from that thing increases. Entering the poems again enlarged them again, so there was also the joy of expansion of thought, the swelling of idea.

It was also important to act on how, in a system of existence, nothing's ever really finished. If something was really finished, would reworking be possible? What does publication render impossible? Publication of a poem is not the end of an idea's generative possibilities. Publication indicates the location of where I was and where I took an idea at the time that the writing stopped. Over time, I acquired more information, and the transformed versions reveal the implementation of that information, and of transformed beliefs. I changed/change my mind. I made/make mistakes. The poems are evolving organisms, and ecosystems/subsystems. The transformations are records of the travels of my thinking. They expose what I thought was possible at the time.

Just how long the "new" of "new" poems endures is interesting and amusing to me. Also, it seems that "new and selected" is, in addition to what many of us know it is, an invitation for that which is *new* to also be *selected*, and for that which is *selected* to also be *new*, so I was just honoring what that phrase mandates: new poems, poems selected from previous publications, and poems that are new forms of previously published poems. There's no comma between *new* and *selected*, so there's no reason for me to assume a boundary; instead, I'm encouraged to overcome a boundary. I like to think that the phrase requires me to be bad, a little naughty in my approach — I need that for my image of myself.

Maybe if *Small Congregations* had been only a selected volume, I wouldn't have been as persuaded to tinker, but the old and new were expected to coexist, so there had to be interaction, and without the possibility of the interaction changing what's meeting in some way, one of the best possible outcomes of elements meeting is thwarted. The influence of a changing neighborhood. The ability of poems to adapt to new surroundings and circumstances, including the thinking of the poet. They had to mingle. A meet and greet requiring even some minimal attention to compatibility and compromise, minimal attention even if domination on some level prevails. The collection could be called, I guess, an experiment in adaptation.

Not only is writing a process, writing is a system; the poems are part of a complex whole that changes over time. The changes can be of a more subtle variety of course, how the poem is read and interpreted, changes that also occur when the re-created poems are experienced in some way.

One of the consequences of this re-creation was my being served with a subpoena because Persea sued Ecco over a contract violation. *Small Congregations* was published by Ecco in 1993, only two years after Persea published *Rainbow Remnants in Rock Bottom Ghetto Sky*, so it wasn't easy to convince Persea to allow some of the *Rainbow Remnants* to appear in a competitor's book, making it unnecessary for someone interested in the *Remnants* to purchase *Remnants*, since so many of its pieces would be in *Small Congregations*. An agreement was carefully worked out as to which *Remnants* could be included in *Small Congregations*, an agreement based on the manuscript that I submitted to Ecco, a manuscript I treated as a new book altogether, writing and revising just as I would have for a book whose content was all new, for the content was all new to the moment of the book's construction and reconstruction. I didn't know and didn't suspect how formal this agreement was. I didn't realize that it was an actual legal contract — my literary poetry simply didn't demand such thinking. I was used to payment for poetry in contributor copies, not advances. So the nature of the agreement didn't seem significant to me. It didn't occur to me that it could be a problem that some of the poems were so thoroughly reconfigured, reconsidered, so fully re-visioned that the resulting retooled poems were, well, *new* poems bearing no resemblances to their parents. No one at Ecco or at Persea realized that three poems in the manuscript were descendants of poems from *Rainbow Remnants in Rock Bottom Ghetto Sky*. There were no obvious links that screamed "evolution" or "derivation." These three poems said "new."

Then the galleys came to me, and I corrected the acknowledgments, indicating that there were three additional poems that had been previously published in different form in Persea's volume. I believed then, as I do now, that I, as the author, could alter the poems, could work on them at any time. Poems are free to evolve, even if only when they are experienced by someone, including the writer. Someone at Ecco made the changes in the acknowledgments, but no one at Ecco informed Persea that there were three additional "remnants" that had been there all along, just not properly identified as from *Rainbow Remnants in Rock Bottom Ghetto Sky*. Both

Ecco and Persea had seen these three poems in the manuscript at the time that the agreement was being made, but neither of them had recognized these three as "remnants."

When the book was published, Persea saw that the acknowledgments contained three poems not in the agreement, so sued Ecco for violation of the contract. Ecco responded by blaming me, the one who revised. I was served a subpoena to appear in court with all versions of the poems in dispute so that it could be legally determined at which point a revision became a new poem and not a revision or version of an existing poem at all. *How exciting!* I thought. *How scientific the proof!* I had no idea how this was going to be proven or who might be called upon as expert witnesses for both sides — imagine! Interim versions did not exist; by then, I worked exclusively on a computer, and previous versions were overwritten by new ones. I thought that my computer might be confiscated, the hard drive dissected, and the remnants and fragments of interim versions presented in court as evidence. I decided to manufacture versions, some interim steps, leading to the disputed forms appearing as simplifications of solutions of algebraic equations. The *New York Daily News* picked up the story — it was so ludicrous, a publisher of literary poetry suing a publisher of literary poetry — just how many dollars had Ecco robbed Persea of when it "stole" three more poems than the agreement allowed? The *Daily News* delivery person asked for a copy of *Remnants*, I was told, when he delivered the papers to Persea. The litigation turned out to be great (and temporary) publicity; sales (briefly) increased for both Ecco and Persea. The cost of litigation was immediately greater than any profits the publishers could reasonably expect from sales of the literary poetry. The *Wall Street Journal* picked up the story. As a result of this attention, I thought I was headed for the Oprah Winfrey show. Not bad for literary poetry, I thought; Oprah and court. I was expecting coverage on the nightly news. I was looking forward to an audience for (my) poetry unlike any audience I'll ever have (at least not while I live).

MP: I really enjoy the turn your answer takes — I didn't know about the lawsuit over the revisions. I love it! And as a scholar with a sidecar interest in Oprah's Book Club, I especially would have liked to have seen the whole thing play out on Oprah. I have long wished she would include poetry in her book club. That lawsuit confirms my sense of the uniqueness of your multiform and multilayered revisions. I think you see the poem *not* as an artifact, much differently than several of your contemporaries. That sensibility is in your process and aesthetic right from the beginning.

TM: Unfortunately, Persea didn't want me to endure that nasty court appearance, since I was being accused on some (minor) malfeasance — revision as wrongdoing. Wouldn't that have been ideal? A legal precedent for defining the boundaries of revision. Perhaps taken to the Supreme Court one day? Ah, the implications that ruling would have had on genetic engineering! (which could be considered as a form of revision), but Persea didn't want to subject me to emotional damage, and assured me that the motivation for the lawsuit did not include my being accused of anything improper, so they settled out of court. That settlement made me incredibly uninteresting, and promptly reinstated literary poetry's unpopular and irrelevant status, leaving me without an opportunity to endear myself to America as the most beloved literary poet ever, perhaps interviewed from jail after being found guilty of revising.

MP: In *Small Congregations* you often evoke religious moments in the everyday, and find the sacred in common, or even highly negative events. I know from your memoir *Tale of a Sky-Blue Dress* as well as your poetry that your mother was a churchgoing and devoutly religious person, and I wonder if the religious sensibilities of that collection might have been shaped by her influence, and by extension by your own storefront church experiences. In particular, I am thinking of Craig Werner's "gospel impulse," an idea that he traces in the black church and gospel music (manifesting in literature as well), a process of (1) acknowledging the burden, (2) bearing witness, and (3) finding redemption. As he puts it, "The gospel impulse half-remembers the values brought to the new world by the men and women uprooted from West African cultures: the connection between the spiritual and material worlds; the interdependence of self and community; the honoring of the elders and the ancestors; the recognition of the ever-changing flow of experience that renders all absolute ideologies meaningless" (28). How might *Small Congregations*, and perhaps your memoir, be inspired by a gospel sensibility?

TM: Of course I have been influenced by anything to which I've been exposed. What I cannot articulate for you with accuracy is the degree of influence. And as for measuring it, the tool used will conspire a bit with what is being measured, so will extend what is there to be measured, which is to say that most overlays placed upon my work and life will fit; the overlay and the life plus work will adapt so that there will be some intersections able to be interpreted as meaningful. I love this quality of human intellectual ability, this marvelous cognitive mapping skill — we are defined by our ability to define and by the malleability of definitions. There is so much entanglement, so much influence as outcomes of so many incidences of contact on all scales that collaboration prevails; to write is to write about something, is to come into contact with something, so I collaborate with content. The entirety of my thinking, of the content of my work, does not spring only from me but is response.

This is part of the reason, by the way, that I place so much of my current "forked work" in online places, why I have extended accessibility to include a wider range of visual forms and sonic forms — even tactile forms (the cover of *Slave Moth*, for instance, is a hand-made dress that an eighteen-inch American Girl doll I own wears — the embroidered letters have texture, are structures that can be read by touch though they are not in Braille patterns). My forked work is not mine alone but also belongs to its contributors, to sources of the content, to that which the poems are about of reference in any way, and by extension also to that which the contributors are also connected.

I don't intentionally associate aspects of the black church (or with black cultural experience in general) with *the burden*. Even considerations of slavery bypass burden status for me in that any Black American descended from slaves is also descended from survivors. That is incredible to me. I am from lines of multiple forms of survivors. Part of the purpose of *Small Congregations* is to revel in pockets of survival taking shape in small circumstances. It is to recall sources like Val Hermosa Springs, where small communities thrive in their way of configuring survival (as in "Maudell's Moon," for example). It is to look at the small universe of the storefront church, at these transformations that lack the magical aspects of transformations in fairy tales and in biological processes of complete metamorphosis, yet are thorough, effective, the best evidence of them manifesting in the shout that occurs when there is overfilling of the space allocated for spiritual transport systems. There is a bursting, a flooding, a gushing, a flowering — sudden and obvious expansion that can fold back into itself, responding as some flowers do when out of contact with light.

My favorite transformation of a neighborhood late-night and after-hours establishment into church is the one in my mother's rapidly declin-

Doll representing the character Varl from *Slave Moth*, wearing dress handmade by Thylias Moss. Photo courtesy of the poet.

ing neighborhood that retained the barstools as perches for the deacons. *Retained* not in the sense of needing to be saved, but in the sense of exchange; for this contribution, something else is received. Redemption also as a form of elevation and extension. The prosperity of the spirit (often in locations that lack economic fertility). I should note here that what I mean by these apparently directional terms is not directional. Because these processes occur in space without a dedicated center, movement in any direction has opportunity to be perceived as upward motion. To bore down through the earth entirely and find the sky still above. Circularity is so promising. When I've read "Poem for My Mothers and Other Makers of Asafetida" to an audience of any size, I've read it as a sermon. I won the Dewar's Performance Artist Award in Poetry in 1991 for reading that poem to an in-house audience and to the Bravo TV audience. The energy of the sermon is infectious (the energy of the gospel music too). Viral, I should say, because particles of the virus can affect/infect, as the particles expand, members of the congregation in whom the particles burst, the expansion manifesting as the shout, the dancing of the virus out of the body. I find these to be remarkable processes.

It seems fair to say that *Small Congregations* was written for my mother. It is a praise book, as are most of my other books, with *praise* defined and redefined in many structures that determine, with help from the content, how the content can occupy the structures. It seems fair to say that my years of exposure to small and large black churches spills in this book for me to study.

Influence of gospel music? My voice was amplified on a Sunday while I wore a stiffened Sunday dress that flared out from the waist to its widest point at the hem, crinoline-powered solid foundation under the white choir robe. That Sunday, I became a power singer. My voice lifted the roof so that its rudimentary modeling of the most generalized wingspan of a bird of prey could also model a simplification of flight. My voice was bigger than the pastor's when the sermon peaked. I was a soprano; I could produce Mariah Carey's signature stratospheric notes, the last time at Phillips Academy for a Martin Luther King Jr. Day event under the direction of cellist and conductor William Thomas.

MP: In *Small Congregations*, you draw upon and directly reference autobiographical elements such as your husband's affair, your parents, and your abortion. (At other times, you use personae, but that's a different question.) The poem, "A Catcher for an Atomic Bouquet," originally in *At Redbones* and then revised and positioned near the end of *Small Congregations*, seemingly addresses this issue of the confessional element in your poetry, stating, after a list of autobiographical events, "This / personal maze is not the prize" (15). (In the revised version, the word *personal* is left out, I should note). My question has two parts: (1) how do you see the confessional element in your poetry, and how has it changed over time?; and (2) what influence did Sylvia Plath have on your views about confessionality in poetry?

This second part to the question derives from the story you tell in your memoir about how Charles Simic had you write your final graduate school paper on Plath (and you added Ai, for reasons you discuss fully in the memoir). There, you detailed the limitations of their "celebration of darkness," realizing you were really talking about your own work. I wonder if you came to similar conclusions about the limitations of a confessional mode for your work, and if when you speak of beginning to "sever those ties" to Plath's and Ai's "darkness," you also began to make different choices about auto-biographical materials in your poetry. Or, have you retained an acceptance of the confessional mode throughout your work, with the addition of joyful moments to the dark ones?

TM: I've long considered poetry, certainly my own, as part of nonfiction, always quite revelatory and celebratory regarding disclosure of the structure of thought, and through that, the architecture of my identity, fluid within boundaries. I had wanted the author photo in *Tokyo Butter* to be a scan of my brain; no other image of me would offer as much authenticity of self, but the publisher rejected this idea, and rejected also my idea to feature a photo of my shadow. Because the poetry concerns genuine preoccupations, discloses limitations active at the time of the making of poems, exposes what I dismiss easily and hesitatingly, because the poetry deals openly with the juggling of truths, it is always confessional even when not directly implementing facts from the life of the writer.

I'm not especially interested in recounting the details of my life and would not have thought to write a memoir on my own: were it not for the lawsuit, the *Wall Street Journal* article would not have been written, and Avon Books would not have been inspired by the article to solicit a memoir. I would certainly write the memoir differently now, or maybe I wouldn't write it at all, since it's too much of a detour from my interest in connecting, not myself with myself, but with what is available for contact. It just interests me more.

That said, in my mind, it's not often that I am confessional when *confessional* means disclosure of the facts of what is usually defined as *personal* or *private* life. And because of interactions, of extraordinary processes, outcomes, and configurations of entanglement, details of my personal life are not easily separated, not easily distinguished from details of other lives, so elements of the personal data of other lives are simultaneously disclosed, and not necessarily in the manner in which those persons would configure the disclosure if those persons made decisions to disclose. I avoid, memoir aside, certain disclosures. The patterns and structures that my imagination arranges and builds are perhaps even more revelatory of my identity than the disclosure of facts. The mind itself is a location that hosts events, that co-makes, co-houses my poems.

The confessional element in my writing extends to all of it; I confess what concerns me, what I notice, what I do not, what I find embraceable negatively and positively. It becomes clear what I am willing to be intimate with, the cohabitations in my mind. What I eat with the fork and what I don't eat, won't eat is clear. Full disclosure of my intellectual diet — that is far riskier than to admit to an affair, to an abortion. My intellectual diet reveals identity; to have an abortion reveals only something that happened, an event, not a trait, not a quality of being. I am not an abortion; I am a dancer with bits of flux, with partialities in transit.

In Plath I found not only this, I found the force behind words, similar to what I found the Sunday of my "Battle Hymn" solo in church when I led the choir, the deliciousness of authority; in Plath I did find endorsement for blabbing, for spill, for messiness, for telling with so much force, consequences (apparently) (temporarily) subdued — *wow*. I saw more force there than in Ai, who seemed not able to seize power and control from darkness. Sometimes it seemed shared, but never fully taken; the full weight of such terrible reins was not hers. The full weight *was* Plath's, too much weight perhaps, but in her hands for a time. But such reins do fill the hands. The hands cannot hold anything else, and that is unfortunate since there is so much else.

Know me through what I notice, how I notice and what I do not.

You can call *Tokyo Butter* autobiographical because it is; it had and discloses some autobiographical roots. I honor the cousin who died. My Toyota 4-Runner was totaled when I left home to buy a copy of the Koran during a winter storm advisory — that happened. The long, centrally placed poam "DEIRDRE: a Search Engine" documents a Google search — but these moments, and others, including my pleasure in completing the "theft of Kinnell's sow," a theft I openly contemplated in the essay "Contemplating the Theft of the Sow," and that I referenced in varying degrees in "The Extraordinary Hoof"; these facts, these autobiographical details (more of which appear in "Ghee Glee," and many other locations) occur in the context of my efforts to answer a larger question, my efforts to reconfigure the universe around answers to the question, "What persists?" In which forms is it still possible to access aspects of Deirdre? Of any flux? What lingers and how? What is the form, the residue available for influence and shaping? I was investigating persistence, and in that investigation examined details of personal life.

Slave Moth began as response to concerns voiced by parents [about slave history being discussed in class]; one mother (of a ninth-grade boy) in particular shaped and funneled what was possible to endorse, at an African

American focus group at my son's private school. The video poam "Project Genealogy" (available in the Limited Fork podcast, and the poem featured in On the Same Poem for the annual Community Reads project in Forsyth County, North Carolina, in 2006) is subtitled "Why I Wrote *Slave Moth*." The book occupies some of those negative loops of omission formed when parents, in their willing submission to the shaping of opinion dominated by one mother, linked themselves and their ninth-grade children to slavery in only one way; they needed more models, exposure to more of the range of possibilities that existed even in the limitations of slavery. Their imagination resided only in the terrain of the model of slavery that had been both configured for them and by them. Got to have a range, Malin.

MP: Let's talk about your poetic development in terms of style, techniques, and aesthetics, focusing on your work prior to your current invention of Limited Fork Poetics, which we'll come to later. When I look at *Small Congregations* in relation to *Last Chance for the Tarzan Holler*, I notice several things: a movement from bigger stanzas and poems of similar length (in *Small Congregations* and the early books) to a wide array of stanza shapes, line lengths, and overall poem lengths, as well as increasing use of other typography shapers such as indenting and italics (in *Last Chance for the Tarzan Holler*); a movement from poems grouped into general sections with approximately the same number of poems (in *Small Congregations*) to a highly complex structure including epigraphs, a prelude poem, image-based patterns in the groupings of poems into sections, thematically titled sections, and an epilogue poem (in *Last Chance for the Tarzan Holler*); and a movement from a mostly associative aesthetic to one that has become more densely and specifically allusive and more image laden. (Several allusions even have endnotes.) Do these generalizations sound about right to you? How do you see your aesthetic and style changing in the five years between those two books — 1993 to 1998? What continuities remained?

TM: Your observations about stylistic and aesthetic development are keen, Malin. Yes, those were exciting years to me, because I was aware of an unfurling that permitted gestures formally not apparent in my work; I mean not even any clues that something might be gestating. A little big bang. I consider *Last Chance for the Tarzan Holler* a breakthrough; in some ways, my first book, the one in which the ways in which I process experience and information became the organizing principles in my literary work: *my* book at last.

In *Last Chance for the Tarzan Holler*, I had agenda; the book is the outcome of an investigation of the boundaries of humanity. I set out to determine whether or not evidence of humanity could be found in the pathological. Each poem is an outcome of a facet of that inquiry. The need to investigate preceded any plans to compile the investigation into a book. As the investigation progressed, one day I realized that about eighty pages of investigation had accumulated on my computer — a book.

For the first time, the complexity of my identity was indulged; I was playing, not taking so seriously the intellectual necessity of any human product. I was enjoying the arbitrary nature of meaning, the ability to assign it anywhere, the marvelous flexibility of rationale, the ability to create theory, systems of thinking, systems of meaning that can not be proven. During these years, I'm reading more and more about complex systems, fractals, chaos theory, and so forth; I'm aware that I love nonlinearity, that the swirl of the funnel is what attracts me to it, that every idea is a tornado in my mind, that an idea is not stored in one location in the brain, but is filed simultaneously in all the locations that house any part of any of the components of the idea. As information is added, the network adjusts, more connections and layers become active, and the structure of the idea is reconfigured.

During this time, I was developing more sensitivity to how space is occupied — of note are parallels to my University of Michigan office assignments, initially (1993) an office shared with someone who did not get tenure, the office where I was served the subpoena for *Small Congregations*, with a view of the physical plant roof, a trapezoid of sky visible, a small trapezoid; it seemed that any section of a cloud completely filled it. Then comes 1994 and tenure — I was only the second Black woman to get tenure in the history of the University of Michigan Department of English (Gayl Jones was the first) — and a semiprime office, one on the remodeled third floor, a view of the bricks of another wing of the building. To see the sky and ground, I had to flatten myself against the extreme right end of the window, practically fuse my face with the glass, almost duplicating an Alice *Through the Looking Glass* experience, something best undertaken intentionally. Then the MacArthur, immediate promotion (within days) to full professor, making me the first (and the only for several years) Black woman at the full professor rank in the history of the University of Michigan Department of English, and a prime office: full view (one whole windowed wall) of State Street, visual access to trees, multiple forms of traffic, multiple simultaneous ecosystems, meteorological systems, seasons, steeples that emerged after the leaves fell, stars at night.

My thinking had room to expand, was unleashed, configured and reconfigured itself in space that included what was beyond Angell Hall. I had visual access to much more; the visual abundance strengthened mental connections forming between the many streams contributing significantly to my emerging understanding of existence. The *wow* factors were restored. I was the Thylias I had been in second grade, I had been when at nine I ran a summer school to enrich the minds of children in my neighborhood. I abandoned the protocols of poetry that I had, blindly, I concluded, accepted; why wasn't I questioning more of rules? I was as capable of making rules as anyone else, so I made my own that were more consistent with my emerging beliefs about experience and existence. *Last Chance for the Tarzan Holler* is *my* first book.

Last Chance for the Tarzan Holler contains the foundations of my recently emerging theory, Limited Fork. It is full of links, takes advantage of connections across scale, acts upon more of the implications of metaphor, offers a rudimentary understanding of how twists and folds can increase surface area and create flexibility — in a previously flat (even with content, especially in the form of flat poems) piece of paper. So *Last Chance for the Tarzan Holler* is the first tine. From that book, Limited Fork becomes inevitable.

I also was overcoming acquiescence to publisher preferences — some of which were related to definitions of *Blackness* that deprived me of the complex structure of identity. If I am capable of an endeavor, then that endeavor evidently falls within what is possible within a definition of *Blackness*, or I couldn't execute that endeavor. So I define *Blackness*, redefine it, reconfigure it, as it must be able to embrace anything I do, anything I think, anything I imagine. I got deep into the possibilities of rejection during those years. I stripped myself naked and then out on whatever I wanted. *Last Chance for the Tarzan Holler* is also a literary fashion show. I modeled my own designs. I reconnected with some of the arrogance I had enjoyed at various times in my childhood. I savored my own power without exerting my power over others. I put some of my adoration of the ideals of subversion back on the table.

As to the development of the long lines of *Last Chance for the Tarzan Holler*, for the depiction, within the linear limits of Persea's publication protocols, of roller coaster tracking; as to the emergence of poetic lines that synchronize themselves with patterns of coastlines, that offer aerial views, and then, on that same eagle course, move in, the possibility of details increasing, the eagle eye turned microscopic, the navigation of electrons becoming meaningful, apparent as feathers encounter scanning electron microscopes — Malin, I was trying only to offer an honest assessment of the curvature and interactions (forms of motion) that ultimately can bring us back to ourselves, the humanity everywhere, the millions of mirrors, the microbes that "sour milk" hosts showing us our basic structure, re-minding us of some of the benefits of clumping, clustering, unifying here and there now and then, and because of that, having something worth remembering.

MP: Your answer has confirmed for me my first reactions to Limited Fork and *Tokyo Butter*: that conceptually they were drawing upon fractals. A friend of mine shared with me years ago some theory about fractals, and it's great to reengage with that way of looking and thinking. It helps me to know I'm on the right track.

TM: Fractals indeed. From time to time, my classes study fractals as their formation, especially in the form of idealized, generalized computer-produced models of the more irregular naturally occurring fractal forms and fractal motion, which serves well to teach notions of symmetries and attractions across scale, space-time scales as well as space and time scales. Metaphor actually becomes a tool for navigating the basically fractal structure of moving from proximity to distance — from any location to any other location. I like to demonstrate these possibilities with strands of beads, beads as cells, beads as planets, as galaxies, as universes, gears, etc.

More broadly, my current focus on Limited Fork Poetics is poetry as a complex adaptive system, and fractals are examples of complex systems. There are many other kinds of dynamic systems of course, fractals among those associated (primarily) with visual beauty, even for some mathematicians. The Mandelbrot set is among the most recognizable and most du-plicated series of fractal images. It is the navigability of systems and the motion of systems that fuel and sustain interactions. Thought's navigation of the brain is largely fractal, linking beads of neurons, firing them in mul-tiple locations simultaneously, components coming together on Saturday afternoon, the dots linked, and the emerging structure is a fork.

MP: *Last Chance for the Tarzan Holler*, despite many specifically Christian religious allusions, seems a deeply archetypal text, with symbolic dimensions transcending any one religious belief system.

TM: Yes. I see particular belief systems as splinters of the spiritually bifurcating fork. I am interested in the ways in which humanity seeks to extend itself, to be more. I am fascinated that such expansion becomes necessary. A lifting, a boost. A religious belief system counteracts inertia.

MP: I am thinking, for example, of the movement from images of fire, bone, water, rock, and light in the first section, about the dark side of childhood and infanticide, to imagery of breasts, milk, and food in the second section, about art, resurrection and faith, culminating in the third section's images of flood, loss, suffering, and cleansing, suggesting rebirth. Could you talk about the questing, monomythical themes of that book?

TM: Movement is crucial. The poems consistently make decisions that hope to refute stasis. There is activity. Without motion, there can be no possibility of transformation, which is movement from one state to another. There is a preference for movement — even if away from an ideal form — because what is eligible for ideal consideration changes as knowledge changes, as the observable and detectable and noticed and detected change.

MP: How might *Last Chance for the Tarzan Holler* be connected to your memoir, published just the year before? Does it in part represent a symbolic rebirth after working through your experiences with childhood abuse — and its repercussions into your adulthood — in the memoir? Or, perhaps birth into a new poetic, as your answer to the previous question suggests?

TM: If connected to the memoir, the connection would be subterranean, present, active without my active awareness; if connected, then the memoir functioned as blasting material whose detonation cleared a space in which I could work without biographical impediment. Not that details have stifled work.

It's interesting to note that my recently acquired identity as "forkergirl" does not descend from the memoir; I am now an evolutionary branch of my former self. This is for me a paradigm shift. *Tale of a Sky-Blue Dress* does not tell the tale of forkergirl, does not have to lead to forkergirl; the memoir does not present the inevitability of forkergirl. There's no indication in the memoir of her possibility. I rather like that.

To be able to speak somewhat objectively about the past indicates that my relationship with those years had become a relationship with history.

Part of ancestry, but not my self-enforced identity. One achieves distance from the incidents, relocation of the self. It is a placement of self where I wanted self to be. A relocation of the self that allowed self to expand. When *growth* did in fact happen, I don't remember swaying, I don't recall any seasickness. Very much symbolic. Not just rebirth, but more like reincarnation; I was born as forkergirl (some years later). An indirect symbolism. I was reincarnated and not named until the new identity gelled and the trajectory changed. This path is not accessible from the previous path.

MP: Returning to the aesthetic thread of our discussion now, *Slave Moth* presents itself as an anomaly in your work; as a verse novel, how does it fit into your poetic development after *Last Chance for the Tarzan Holler*? What stands out to me is your extended use of the persona/character Varl, and of course the other personae/characters in the book, a distinctly different mode than the confessional or even the lyric poetic *I* you often employ elsewhere. Can you expand on your comments to me earlier about the creative process behind the idea of that book (the parents' group that embraced a narrow definition of *slavery*)?

TM: If *Slave Moth* is an anomaly in my work, it is an inevitable anomaly that logically follows *Last Chance for the Tarzan Holler's* pursuit of evidence of humanity within the pathological, as the system of slavery may be constructed as (even if it were not one) a pathological system. As a descendant of slaves, I have personal motive for being able to locate evidence of humanity in that system that contributed to my existence. My thoughts, as outcomes of such inquiry, are that humanity has remarkable ability to survive. African Americans who are descendants of African slaves are also descendants of survivors. That is a *wow* for me; we are descendants of survivors, descendants of those whose strategies to exist within or despite of or because of their circumstances succeeded.

Any of us who exist are products of bloodlines that reach back to the start of humanity. We are from lines that survived epidemics, catastrophes, disasters — all who exist have a legacy of survival, and this legacy functions as fortification for me. Someone in Africa was captured or sold into slavery, survived the capture, survived the voyage, survived to become my ancestor. How incredible; this ancestor did not succumb to the situation. Surviving a situation is a form of defeating that situation; surviving is a most potent weapon, can be such an act of defiance, and ultimately so powerful. There are times when I feel this power, when I'm aware of it, and my awareness of it allows me to use it. I have been unable to ever feel inferior because of this powerful legacy. No one's heritage is any older than mine, which also has been here from the beginning of humanity. No one's heritage is more powerful than mine, which also persists. I need no other license to give me access to whatever humanity can access.

I suspect that this attitude, if it is anomalous, comes to me in part as part of my inheritance, my father's mixed-race family in a small town in Tennessee. In documentation from the 1880 census, I learned that my paternal great-grandmother, identified as a white-Indian mulatto, married a black man who adopted her mixed sons, including my paternal grandfather, who died as did his father from a rare neurological disorder for which there is still no cure. I have a longstanding association with anomaly, a history of anomaly. I quite enjoy departures from standards, especially when those standards serve double duty as expectation, triple duty as limit or boundary and therefore function — improperly — as definitive models. My paternal grandmother was the daughter of a literate black woman raised by Quakers in West Virginia. My son is named for a West Virginia location linked to the life of a woman who practiced her literacy with written and oral diatribes against slavery and discrimination. She refused to forgive or excuse any owner of slaves.

This is the mindset and attitude that accompanied me to a meeting of the African-American Parent-Teacher Focus Group at my son's grade six through twelve private school. My attending that meeting was anomalous, as usually I was teaching class on Monday nights, but I was there listening to very vocal black mothers, one in particular, complain about a ninth-grade genealogy assignment that her son found too embarrassing to complete, since it would require him to publicly admit to having slaves in his past. Indeed, his ancestors possibly could have been owned by ancestors of his affluent Caucasian classmates. Her son was not going to suffer that kind of embarrassment, so damaging to his self-esteem and his status with his peers in a school with about, at that time, a 98 percent white student population. He alone in that class would have a genealogical tree with dead ends instead of fruit-producing branches. So for the love of drupes his mother would ban the assignment. Once her son arrived at slavery, this ninth-grade black boy would be able to go no further. His downfall would be a tree of denied and forbidden knowledge. The payoff for his research would be servitude and the companion, confirmation of his inferior status. That was too much to risk. She was a responsible mother who had raised her son to be proud, and an acknowledged ancestry of slavery would contradict that pride, would expose the fraudulence of that pride. She suggested that this assignment, part of the ninth-grade curriculum for years, be abandoned, and was joined in a demand for abolition of the assignment as soon as she made it. The black parents present vocally supported this mother in her quest to spare her son from the overwhelming and damaging embarrassment of public acknowledgment of slave ancestry. The Head of School (I never have referred to him as Head*master*) was on the verge of being convinced by the argument, as he conveyed his sensitivity to the issue. It wasn't necessary for me to do anything; resolution was imminent, a pathological resolution I thought, but humanity was manifesting itself within that pathology. I could have allowed abolition of the genealogy assignment, but I was embarrassed by something else: the embarrassment of these parents.

The embarrassment was the system of enclosure that gave shape to a vision of humanity that was way too narrow, way too constricting for the mind to inflate, unfold, blossom, expand. I too was limited, but my limitations permitted more wiggle and unfolding room, and in that greater expanse, I couldn't locate any supporting logic for the embarrassment. I was impressed by the ability of slaves to survive and employ a range of survival strategies. So I spoke, and informed the parents, teachers, and administrators present that my son, new to the school as a sixth grader, had been given an ancestry assignment that he had no trouble completing. He was not embarrassed by history, I told them. If my son is put in a box, I said, he would enjoy discovering ways to get out of the box or to transform the box; he would invent windows, doors; he would raise the ceiling, explode the roof. My slave ancestors survived long enough to produce the generation that ultimately produced my generation, my son's generation. I then added, before I left the room, that my son had no problem with slavery being in his past; he traced his ancestry *all* the way back, I said, *to the big bang!* He wrote a poem about it, which is part of my video poam "PROJECT GENEALOGY: why I wrote Slave Moth" which you may see at http://www-personal .umich.edu/~thyliasm/ProjectGenealogy(w.sungnarration).m4v and/or in my Limited Fork podcast.

There was a failure of an ability to imagine history beyond certain popular constructs, constructs that might indeed be valid. I believe that there is accuracy to prevailing notions of slavery in the general black community. Certainly among the meeting's attendees, an inability for the enslaved to maintain dignity was assumed. The inferiority of the enslaved was assumed. The weakness of the enslaved was assumed. The cowardice of the enslaved was assumed. The powerlessness of the enslaved was assumed. The ignorance of the enslaved was assumed. There was nothing associated with slavery that the attendees could seize to use as indicators of the fortitude of the enslaved. The ability to endure the circumstances was not assigned any value that could compete with the status of the ruling class evidently admired and coveted by the attendees. The enslaved were necessary emotionally and intellectually subservient as well as physically subservient. The attendees in 2002 felt as demeaned as they were certain their enslaved ancestors felt.

The model of inarticulate uneducated slaves brutalized and physically victimized by affluent white owners was so fixed as the only possible fact of the slave experience that no imagination could assist them in visualizing a range of human experience within the slave experience. They accepted the inhuman status of the slave.

Since this group was unable to recognize a range of human experience within the slave experience, I realized that more models of slavery exploring that range were necessary. The vileness of slavery wasn't the forfeiture of humanity by the enslaved; I contend that no humanity was lost. The vileness exists within the concept of ownership, the human treated as property, so even if an owner were benevolent, there would still be ethical bankruptcy in the act of owning a person. And for that which is enclosed in a system of ethical bankruptcy, the possibility of a benevolence not filtered or defined by ethical bankruptcy is not possible.

Therefore, in *Slave Moth*, to demonstrate the insidiousness of the system of slavery did not require a setting of physical brutality; that Varl was owned was sufficient. I removed as many popular constructs of slavery as I could, replacing them with an accurate (within the range of human possibility in the antebellum South) alternative model of an enslaved adolescent female whose loss of virginity occurs whenever it occurs by choice, not force. She is literate, manages to cultivate an identity that is hers even though being cultivated within enslavement as a system of enclosure. The identity cultivated may be assumed to be different from the identity she may have cultivated from within another system.

Varl's courage comes from the reinforcement of that identity that penetrates cloth, that is locked into cloth with her stitches. This is a slow and deliberate form of making text; there is much effort required beyond the mechanics of knowing how to write. Stitched words are thread sculptures. The words are raised on the cloth just as healed scars are raised on the skin. There is ceremony implied here, transition from childhood to adulthood, which is also the accepting of the responsibility of an identity. There is toil, the pushing of the needle through the thickness of cloth. There is the possibility of the pain of the needle prick, but the reward is identity. The reward is self. And once Varl acquires identity, the system of that acquisition becomes her immediate system of enclosure, literally through the cocoon of her words, her ideas, her proof of identity. With that proof, although she is still legally owned, she is not mentally or emotionally owned, and it becomes inevitable that at the moment that the system of metamorphosis is complete, she will emerge from the cocoon capable of flight to a location beyond the legal reach of the slave system.

It is because I accept the plausibility of Varl that I made (by hand) the dress that appears on the cover of *Slave Moth* and is worn by an eighteen-inch-tall Varl doll.

MP: How does writing a verse novel fit into your larger trajectory as a poet?

TM: It is the reality of the identity and life of Varl that mandated my use of such a "distinctly different mode" for the delivery of idea via characters. So intense is my commitment to these lives that the intensity reconfigured itself into characters that exist beyond me. It is as if I found Varl's shed cocoon and restored it layer by layer.

It might interest you to know that I have other anomalous writings; the work you know about is what publishers committed to; I have work that my primary publisher considers unmarketable, and my delving into more experimental forms is leaving me, for the moment at least, without a publisher. I have a prose-poam experimental novel print thing that my (former) publisher won't touch — an economic decision since there's no clear market. Some of the prose-poam "chapters" have been published in various journals, but the LFMK (Looking for My Killer) book won't be published unless and until I find a more generous publisher who will support my artistic growth in multiple directions and on multiple scales.

I hope to complete *Enchanted Essay* this summer, and this book too will be one that my publisher is not likely to want. I also plan to fork *The City of Margaret* and *The Holy Circus of Decent Girls*, two other novel-length works of mine you do not know, so *Slave Moth* isn't anomalous in the context of the range of what I make; it's an anomaly only in the context of what has been published.

The writing of a verse novel helps convey the idea of an idea as a dynamic system. I consider *Tokyo Butter* a verse novella poam. The verse novel is as a Platonic or Archimedean solid; the presence of volume is unmistakable, obvious. There are intertwined lives, roots and branches. The aesthetic expression retains the modulations of poetry, so language, syntax, and punctuation are choreographed, but the ambition is to cover more territory than a poem usually covers. I find the sculpting of language appealing, otherwise my work would utilize the default margin parameters of typeset prose. Perhaps my form would be better described as sculpted essays. *Slave Moth* would be a narrative sculpted essay presenting a case study of an alternative authentic model of slavery.

I plan to do further work on poetry as sculpture (not concrete poetry; I mean something quite different, more related to movement, the sculpting done by erosion and cancer); my *Bubbling* collection (in progress) explores this. Some of the *Bubbling* poams will also exist as a huge quilt that I hope to make this summer. Verse novels are important contributions to my range of making, and a range of making helps me attempt to understand existence better, the complexity of its scales and levels and structures, all of which are not apparent at all times in all locations in all circumstances.

MP: How do you see *Slave Moth* contributing to the ongoing body of work of contemporary neo-slave-narrative novels such as *Beloved* and *Dessa Rose*?

TM: *Slave Moth* brings to light more of the complex facets of slave experience that neo–slave narratives such as *Beloved* and *Dessa Rose* also reveal. There is a richness in the slave experience that is finally being imagined. I believe that Varl offers a perspective that otherwise would probably be neglected, as she remains outside of what is likely to be imagined in the construction of a model of a slave, although instincts such as Varl's must have prevailed, as the protection of a self is crucial to most strategies of survival. In each of these novels, there are slave heroines who determine what they will not sacrifice; they determine the point at which they will not yield and defend that boundary, acts that also endow them with the privilege of individuality instead of category, a privilege that in turn helps expose more of the complexity of the humanity of the enslaved. To be unable to entertain the possibility of a Varl is to also reduce the humanity of the enslaved and the humanity that descends from the enslaved; there had to be a Varl. I hope I have done her justice.

MP: One of my favorite stories in your memoir *Tale of a Sky-Blue Dress* is when you found out that your professor expected you to express black rage, in the mode of the Black Arts Movement, in an assignment for which you had explicated a Robert Frost poem you admired. You made up a new Black-Power-type poem marching all white people into hell, and wore an Afro wig to perform your reading and explication. This tells us a lot about the expectations governing black students and black poetry at the time. How did you navigate in your early poetry expectations that you should align yourself with Black Arts Movement proscriptions (whether promulgated by white professors or black poets)?

TM: This is necessarily a tough response. You refer to a period in which I'd have to say my writing was not mine (and this is something I also say now, but with an entirely different configuration of intended meanings and implications). To align myself with Black Arts Movement proscriptions would mean that I assigned a public status to my writing. Writing meant for private therapeutic or aesthetic expression would not require acknowledged alignment, but in an academic setting that taught aesthetics and literary analysis, transfer of taught ideologies, to some degree, can be assumed. Indeed, the entire purpose of my poem "Harlem Rap" was to secure for myself the grade already earned with work done on Frost. It was when I accepted a literary role of marginally located militancy that I could be assured of producing work that would receive consideration appropriate for a marginally located, culturally based literature. To have my work taken seriously when shared was a basis of sharing, which is to say that rejection or dismissal was not the target of the gesture to share. But I also was not seeking approval; that is, I gave myself permission to write, and had provided that permission since I was six or seven. So it was ten years of the practice of writing later that I found myself in the situation you ask about. This decade is significant; a decade of practice was also a decade of fortification. Granted, there were chinks in the armor because of certain maltreatment from sources inappropriate for intimacy with someone my age, but enough armor remained intact for the function of armor not be completely overcome. I felt, therefore, some confidence in fighting back.

Now in the fight with the professor, the fighting back looks suspiciously like something else, because it was. This event during my first or second year of college, the first and last year in which I auditioned for a role in a play, the role assigned according to assumptions about the appearance and cultural authenticity of the actors chosen for roles that were intended, according to prevailing interpretations, for actors of a specific physicality and cultural authenticity. My initial audition for a role in *A Midsummer Night's Dream* did not get me a speaking part at all, but I was selected to play a pixie who was on the stage reacting to everything, invisible to the other characters, for the entire play — this generosity of silent stage presence a tweaking of the actual script. I was led to believe that my performance integrated the primary productions of the primary theater department at this New York state university from which Vanessa Williams graduated some years later. I did want to speak on stage, and to do that, I had to audition for a role in a black production offered by the Black Studies Department. No problems there. The right complexion, the right hair, the right figure: I was promptly cast for the lead role in a play whose title I've forgotten by a black male playwright whose name I've forgotten, and let me tell you how pleased I am to have forgotten. This lead role was of a prostitute, Francine, maybe? I was either seventeen or eighteen years old, on stage using language I still choose not to use in my speech, and almost not at all in my writing, about sexual practices I would not feel a need to document.

As I recall, this was the world premiere of the (un)forgettable play. *Midnight* may have been part of the title, unless I use this now in a logical association of my first two years of college with the nadir of my academic endeavors. The playwright was in town for the world premiere, and pleased with my having been cast in the part, the first Francine. He took me to dinner. To respect the scholarship of the Drama Department and the Black Studies Department I was compromised. I participated in the Black Arts Movement both with and without choice: I auditioned, without coercion, for the play, and I accepted the part so that I could speak on stage and say nothing of enduring consequence and nothing that affirmed anyone's humanity. I said nothing I believed in or wanted to tacitly support, but I spoke convincingly of the pleasures of Coke bottles and received unwelcome attention from men, including another (this time declined) celebratory, post-debut dinner engagement with the playwright, just us two. Mythic creature on the legitimate stage or salacious cultural icon? Such choices. The artfulness of the Black Arts Movement as practiced in my local learning sphere did not offer much for someone who'd studied AP Biology (Genetics), AP English, AP French, Calculus, and so forth, in high school with the intention of pursuing further study. But for the sake of art, I chose to act like someone I did not want to be in any reality. Though not denied an audible voice in the black production, I was still denied identity.

It was quite an odd location in space and time, one exempt from having to relinquish control over depiction of black women to black women, and where I was when I was, black women did not verbally reconfigure what was possible for us in scripted circumstances. While I might have been discharged from completing the week's run of the play, I could have improvised in the performance one night. I could have spoken, made real within the make-believe (which seriously disrespected the power of imagination), what I and Francine, given the chance, would want to and need to say, which also would have been what the black male playwright, black male student director, black male student actor pimp needed to hear. My obedience to script was also acquiescence to elevation of the pimp.

My guilt extends to my shameful solicitation of a friend of mine who differed significantly in superficial physical assessments. Her complexion much darker, her hair much coarser, her weight much heavier, so she was as perfect for her role as useless wife to the pimp as I was to my role as the pimp's favorite prostitute, Francine. Both the pimp's wife and the pimp's prostitute were being physically abused by the pimp, but nuanced so that the abuse of Francine would reveal the pimp's love for her, whereas his abuse of his wife would indicate he had no positive feelings for her at all.

Was the department too seduced by the "world premiere" element? All ethics and scruples discarded just to claim that "world premiere" status? Francine was not the only one who sold herself, the self configured for her, and a self not able to function as a self off a stage caught in a time and logic and self-respect warp that was also a whip beating all of us into submission to undesirable situations we made for ourselves without objection from those outside the movement. While I would not censor the production of anything that is able to be classified as any form of art, at the age I was, and in a movement in which choice was emerging as a possibility, I did not get off the sinking ship into a boat headed for life. I opted for oppressive situations; I sought them, despite what I'd experienced with a female babysitter and a young married choir director and deacon. So art was questionable indeed, and the politics of the Black Arts Movement was offering me nothing better, just something louder and much more crude, than American canonical exclusions offered. Expectations and stereotypes du jour only.

Accordingly, I was in a position where it was in my best interest to not align myself with either of the available camps. After my first and last theater performance, I left that academic institution, left academia altogether for five years, got married to a man scandalously older than me when we became involved. How did I navigate? I got the hell out of Dodge. I would not compromise the belief that I deserved more than was available where I was. I left Sodom; I left Gomorrah — and I did not look back.

This decision does not mean that I applied the intellectual, social, and cultural deficiencies I observed at that university to the larger and presumably more reasonable and healthy Black Arts Movement, but it did mean that I valued individual identity more and used complex definitions in determining the boundaries of permissions for this complexity. Just as I did not applaud the denial of Francine's sacred womanhood, sacred sexuality, I refused more complicity in systems of denial of possible meanings and recourses for complex identities that were not confined to one defined area. The wholeness of identity was not a concern of the arts movements where I was, but I wanted that wholeness for myself. That wholeness was in my home with my parents and extended families, which I didn't mind tracing back to the beginnings of the universe.

MP: How do you see the relationship between your race and your poetry today?

TM: My race has not changed. It's a pretty steady state. Black remains something so powerful that whatever I do invites an opportunity to consider race; it is an issue whether or not I act upon genetic "facts" in ways that may be understood as active. I either embrace or reject the classifications. In some way, I respond. My need to respond is a function of already being classified as belonging to what I either embrace or reject. No further classification is necessary, as any actions interpreted as rejection would not remove me from the category. Just by existing, I am classified. What is not escapable is racial scrutiny of what is perceived as my aesthetic product. Fantastic. All is well (within me) with the racial worlds to which I belong. My poetry is everything that my poetry can be with limitations. I refuse to deny myself access to what's possible. And these (racial) worlds (of mine) can be just as infinite as any others. My Limited Fork Theory is a black concept. So Limited Fork Theory is a mixed (up) concept. So Limited Fork

Theory is a boundary-eating virus, reconfiguring boundaries with its waste products that are gobbled up by whatever feeds on that, so the Fork goes on making connections, building symmetries and super cluster geometries of realities without the (dis)pleasure of building something heading for permanence.

MP: In a biographical essay by Eve Silberman about you on the Modern American Poetry Web site, she relates that you are "chary of being classi-fied as a 'Black Female Poet,'" quoting you saying that your ancestors were brought here from Africa, but "it has not very much of anything to do with how I view the world" (par. 20). Given that this interview is planned to be part of a collection of interviews with major contemporary black poets writing after the Black Arts Movement, how might you characterize the position of race in the poetry of this generation of African American poets?

TM: Race can be an asset in terms of the access presumed peculiar to that perspective. Race exists. The poetry knows this, but race is not all that exists, and the existence of it does not disqualify any race from function-ing as a center from which allnesses in any direction may be accessed. Race exists; there's no necessity to deny it, but it is emphasized and conspicuous only on certain scales. Race is not confining unless configured that way. Unless there's no reason, no interest, no incentive, no means to go any-where. I happen to like to travel — and to make myself at home.

MP: I love the last line of your answer, about how you like to travel and also to make yourself at home. That understanding fueled so much of my book on Rita Dove's work. I think that flow of energy between travel and homes is a key trope for much of what's underlying the contemporary Af-rican American poetry I study.

In *Last Chance for the Tarzan Holler* and *Tokyo Butter*, your increas-ing fascination with medicine and science becomes apparent. For example, in *Last Chance for the Tarzan Holler*, in the poems "Ear," "Crystals," and "Sour Milk," and in *Tokyo Butter*, in the epigraph from Lucretius on atoms, and throughout multiple poems, all use vocabularies of the sciences, engage scientific discourse and concepts, and describe various scientific proper-ties and processes. Could you talk about how your interest in science and medicine has developed and what you feel it brings to your poetic diction, allusions, and metaphors?

TM: Origins of my interests in science surfaced in walks with my father after I returned home from attending church with my mother. These were long walks, perhaps because of what my father perceived might be necessary to permit me to bend toward formal religious structures concerned with the destiny of my soul and/or toward his spiritual philosophy, in which hell could not logically exist so did not; lean toward either/both without falling in all the way, drowning in either one.

During these walks, we stopped at a drug store so that he could purchase for me the Golden Book of my choice, head-to-head with the books of the Bible. I chose science books, technology books: energy and machines, the solar system, rocks, mineralogy, meteorology, prehistoric animals, mammals, polar regions, automobiles, amphibians, medicine.

So I am now the girl my father walked with. Not the same girl, but one of the possible outcomes for that girl once her possible paths were limited/shaped by choices/interactions then. In these travels, maybe in part not to lose my way, I make connections.

My poems, whatever form they take, document investigations, configurations of outcomes of tethering expeditions, which are necessarily incomplete, inconclusive since so much falls through, flies over, is not detectable by the tines; those tines apparently attached to the same fork handle may bifurcate across/within scales, dimensions, realities, forms. So I work with what I manage to get off a (section) of tine(s), perhaps changing it so that in interacting with me (collaborating) it may not be (any more) what the limited fork forked, but is what the limited forker forks around with.

MP: Reading *Tokyo Butter* made me realize how much you reference food throughout your poetry. You really like food!

TM: I do indeed like food, and happen to have a genetic base to support this love without excessive visible damage: a high metabolism inherited from my father, passed on to my son, in which there is a failure to accumulate fat deposits, so we look to be in better lipidic shape than we likely are. Naturally, I've been attracted to *Top Chef*, a program that has extended my interest in the artistry of a plate's edible content, the poetry of serving, the writing of the spatial arrangement of edible poams. Related to this also, in a sponsorship capacity, is the program *Monk* for the title character's open preference for the integrity of each food, the respect of the boundaries of each food, sometimes a respect taken to separate plating for each item. This elevated me to an appreciation for gourmet serving protocols, course by course, elegant isolation of good tastes offered plate by plate instead of an efficient melange or comprehensive edible mishmash on a single plate; I like this poetic space, this art of formation of the poetic food lines delineating tastes that coalesce and connect into a more singular source for nutrient extraction in the digestive system. Selective combining and isolation of tastes to be performed by the diner, not prescribed by a ladle of fused flavor difficult to sort. I often request and serve sauces on the side, am suspicious of gravies and other masks, prefer mixing bits here and here, in small quantities, these tests of taste combinations visible, and as aesthetic as I can make them, on my plate. I don't eat fast.

MP: I suspect you are a fine cook, or at least a highly refined eater. How many poets, for example, would write a poem called "Ghee Glee"? I recall, too, in your memoir, the delicious lunch you prepare for your husband. Could you talk more about your love of good food and how you see it in relation to your art?

TM: Certain tastes connect to ideas in my brain, become fully dimensioned so that there is a physicality associated with each bite of food, initially related to the presentation on the plate and reconfigured by connections in the brain, usually to shapes of pleasurable experiences. I believe that sound, the singing, the speaking of language is also tasted; my sonic poams (made track by track, each sonic "food" trackable and isolatable, even after the sonic flavors are combined into a single sonic meal) are the building of separate flavors into meals, the exploration of preparing complex flavor combinations so that new tastes may emerge from flavor components often used in only customary ways, and difficult to use differently if consistently mixed into an "allspice" so that that mixed state is considered a singular taste state, reducing opportunities for reconfiguring what no longer seems a composite. Sound and taste wrap up each other with the tongue, obviously intimate gestures, related to visuals, the architecture of which suggests what might occur when a particular visual experience is reconfigured or reframed as taste, olfactory waves also shaping the architecture of taste even before there is direct physical, intimate contact with the tongue, part of the pleasure of cooking as reactions of food with heat release scents into the air that enter the body before the physicality of the food. In this way, I am able to cook what I don't actually eat, building tastes and taste options/possibilities based on olfactory architectures. Some people thump melons, I sniff them (and any food under consideration for purchase) before making decisions.

Because I hear what I write, what I silently compose; because I hear this in my mind, I am also saying this content, tasting subtle flavor kernels, peppers that is to say, that oral iterations crack, the spice then surging literally, interacting physically with the tongue, but until such aural explosions, olfactory taste is more apparitional, patterns of easily configurable structures some of whose scent becomes visible in the mapping of steam, choreographed by temperature fluctuations, cooking method, amount and timing of spice introductions, etc.

Also, momentous occasions in my life have associations with food, have been the reason certain foods were eaten, have accounted for all of my encounters with wine. Indeed, the first activity with my son after his birth was breastfeeding, the milk of my body personalized for that child. Two days before this birth, on the anniversary of our marriage, my husband and I were in a restaurant I favored, and I ate Arctic char, grilled to perfection, a medium location in which the center still bears evidence to what the flesh of char was like before transformed by heat, spices atop the char there like freckles, a magnification, I like to think, of cosmic interactions not often visible, yet we are bombarded all the time by stuff in the cosmic soup we are part of, spin and rotation the stirring that helps maintain the machinery of existence, which is very much like a kitchen. Interactions are a form of cooking, a form of collaborative cooking.

MP: *Tokyo Butter* has a highly experimental structure, evidenced by, among other elements, the poem (titled "Lake Deirdre" by my best guess from the acknowledgments page) running along the bottom of the pages of the poems on pages 3–22, but not listed in the linear table of contents, and the hypertextual experience of reading it, in which one must stop reading and reference other texts in order to piece together the meaning. I was reminded of T. S. Eliot's *The Waste Land* (a highly experimental text in its day), as if this were an internet-age parallel, with search engine technology rather than endnotes. I used the internet a lot to read it. This seems a rather major shift in your poetic, one which you tie to your new ideology — Limited Fork Poetics — at the end of the book, although now that I've seen your podcasts and blogs since *Tokyo Butter* it seems a precursor to full expression of Limited Fork Poetics. How did you imagine this experimental structure in *Tokyo Butter*, which is still on the page, yet manages to move off it as well?

TM: A precursor, indeed. Limited Fork Poetics, which I now refer to as Limited Fork Theory, which I consider a more generalized theory of making.

My thinking about Limited Fork Theory eluded me until a Saturday in October 2004 when my husband took me to the Quality 16 cinema to see a film whose title I do not remember. At the end of the film during the credits, I had the revelation that compacted what I was understanding into a more practical form of a generalized theory of making with implications in most if not all events of making, a theory of approach not confined to a particular medium or field of inquiry, one that would permit the practitioner to approach experience as a single linked system of supercluster geometries that interactions form and reform. Why that moment, why those credits of that film collaborated to host the event that was the birth of Limited Fork Theory, I cannot say, but I was receptive to interacting; I wanted to understand how to put something together, how to assemble a viable something out of the components I had. "Of course!" I shouted to my husband, grabbing his arm. "The credits are moving," I said, as I received an understanding that exposed universes by reconfiguring the frame I used for the nature of existence into a more flexible system from which acts of making, including the making of meanings, could draw from anything, because there was a path (or logic) linking anything, direct paths and indirect paths. Making connections, and identifying patterns made by linked paths, was another way of ordering experience, bringing things together, making communities, and moving, traveling, navigating existence, which included: error, falsity, mistake, imagination, failure, for these were also temporary hosts to temporary events as seemingly real as any others. A misreading is a form of navigable engagement. How information, experience, and poams are framed is flexible, the perceptual framing system determining boundaries of possibility and impossibility. What is impossible does not happen; only the possible. A flexible framing system makes sense in an existence in flux, in motion (as humans are able to perceive existence).

MP: One key word in *Tokyo Butter* is *culture*, which appears in the titles of fourteen out of twenty-six poems (or out of twenty-seven poems if we count "Lake Deirdre"). While the salient definition of *culture* is a particular form or stage of civilization, it's also about the cultivation of microorganisms or tissue for scientific study, denoting as well the products resulting from such cultivation. How do you see culture as a key metaphor, concept, or theme for the text? Were there any connections to poststructuralist theory or cultural materialism that influenced your thinking?

TM: *Culture* of course refers to a medium that supports the growth of colonies, communities of microorganisms that a shifting of scale can render enormous, can reveal in complexity of detail, even revealing the apparent aesthetic aspirations of a virus. Culture is an environment that supports and sustains, that feeds its inhabitants, that welcomes interactions. *Tokyo Butter* cultures are populations whose numbers and interactions have given rise to protocols that seek to maintain the circumstances that supported the initial bursts of proliferation. Those protocols are peculiar to mainte-nance of those cultures even when the numbers, when other interactions, even when other variables begin to reframe the boundaries (which are more flexible than many might like). A single idea is not singular; *culture* is a consequence of growth, domination of numbers, interactions; behaviors emerge, ways to explain those behaviors become possible. Language maps, from this angle or that angle, what is perceived about the populations on some scale at some moment.

Now, Malin, I have seen maggots form, in expected places, but also in the magical maggot culture of a kitchen sink when food in a garbage dis-posal had time to sit idle in the dark on the rubber daisy atop the drain-pipe. In that nutrient-laden darkness, eggs hatched; there was small writh-ing all over the black rubber daisy, too small for me to see, too insignificant a mass though it was indeed a mass, and a microscope would have revealed perhaps inspiring intricacies and possibilities, the formations and patterns of the writhing of drain-concealed maggots perhaps would have enjoyed a displaced symmetry with other patterns of activity and volatility, including massive cosmic events larger than the earth but far away; a look into the night sky doesn't connect with anything perturbative. The culture of mag-gots, through flexibility in the framework of writhing, may have writhed through forms and patterns that are also assumed by other things, the mo-ment of the connection intensifying some sort of impulse perhaps, maybe transmitting some kind of field, some kind of energy that is also a marker of the connection, of the distant interaction.

After a while, sometimes the scale of activity shifts so that evidence of the activity of a previously concealed culture becomes perceptible, enters the range of human perception as it did when there was an additional fau-cet in the sink, an updraft of small flies, babies the size of four-millimeter black pearls gushing out of the drain and into the kitchen, as if the black rubber hybrid daisy were releasing spores that finally grew in my imagination right now, an image of that scene mapped there, a shadow-type symmetry tethered to the event in the past by the information, by the delayed reception of what the event transmitted initially, the distance and logic and necessity traveled, the symmetry of the connection becoming kaleidoscopic with a connection to purpose, which happens here when the connection is made; the reconstructing of a version of the event of sink-born flies as if that was the purpose of the food being left in the drain, so that the past in which the drain birthed flies is also reconstructed as a collaborator of the metaphor that grows here as a response to your question.

All of this does give a nod toward poststructuralist theory; stability is a temporary state through which something passes. Stability and instability are navigated: states, as opposed to traits. Solidity itself may be perceived, and a rapid succession of mostly solid perceptions allows for the experience of something as solid to be reasonable, to seem a "fact" though that solid form itself is temporary, will be reconfigured on some scale, in some location, for some duration of time. A set of intersecting, overlapping, momentarily converging events can produce a form of consensus, a group perception of solidity that can be called "reality," but that too is configurable; the framing systems of existence are flexible, not fixed, and even outright error, to the erroneous extent that that can be determined, can configure a frame that can function as consensus on some scale in some location for some duration of time.

Shift the frames and there's latitude and longitude, shift the scale of the grids and framing systems themselves become the substance, the lattices apparently filling all the space, all the infinities so that there is a facsimile or approximation of thingamajig. No frames, no existence. Gravity, for instance, is a frame that is a product of things; forces exerted by things, on things, consequences of interactions, and so forth.

And this is what holds stuff together; the pattern of the sum of patterns of interactions on all scales in all locations for all durations/intervals of time is "universe." The *Tokyo Butter* universe. Many maggots there. And many astonishing flying four-millimeter black pearls.

MP: I'd like to bring up two institutions associated with your career and ask how they impacted it: Phillips Academy, where you taught for eight years, and the MacArthur Foundation, which awarded you a major fellowship in 1996. What experiences or opportunities were afforded you by these connections? Any limitations? How did they impact the direction of your art or the questions you pursue in your work?

TM: Phillips Academy was another necklace of black pearls. I was quite impressed with this institution's practiced commitment to educating "youth from every quarter." I was part of the most diverse community I've ever been part of while I was there; there was such a diversity of diversities: social, economic, geographic, national, religious, ethnic, gender. Adolescents who otherwise might not have met, might not have challenged each other, might not have had opportunities to interact did have them. In one of my classes, I had students on full scholarship from blighted urban areas, from a farm in Nebraska, a brother of Sade, and a member of the royal family of Kuwait, who was sent to Phillips during Iraq's invasion of Kuwait. It was an extraordinary classroom, so many framing systems to move about, and experience from both inside and outside the frame as we navigated our discussions. I learned that I loved teaching while I was there. Patrick Kennedy and one of Dick Gregory's sons were also among my students. I still hear from a number of them; in fact, just last week, I learned that my former student from Kuwait had given Phillips a substantial gift in my honor.

Because Phillips Academy's contract system did not rely on publications, I was able to produce work (despite the demanding teaching schedule: six days a week, and the need to supervise minors twenty-four hours a day) without feeling pressured to produce it in order to maintain my employment or to secure a promotion. My publications didn't seem to be a factor in contract and salary negotiations. The housing was provided; my last Phillips Academy house had three floors, ten rooms. My family was encouraged to take our meals in the dining hall so as to interact with students inside and outside the classroom. We had only student loans and telephone bills to pay.

Four of my books were written and published while I taught at Phillips Academy, one of them quite by accident. While my older son was at school, and I was pregnant with my younger son, I wrote a story that I planned to share with him when he got off the school bus, and that I'd already read to the growing baby, but I was so enchanted by the story that I rushed to share it with the school's Greek receptionist; she too was enchanted, and asked for a copy that I was glad to give her, thinking only that I had spread some joy until she told me that her sister-in-law, someone I knew nothing about, was the art director of the press that published *I Want to Be.*

Prizes I won for those books I wrote while at Phillips Academy allowed me to become quite attractive to a number of colleges and universities, resulting in six unsolicited offers the year I decided to accept the offer from the University of Michigan. One department chair told me that his department wanted to get me while I was affordable because he suspected that I would do something great, perhaps the "somethings" that helped me become attractive to the MacArthur Foundation.

The MacArthur Fellowship transformed my relationship with the university. While I didn't need the fellowship to feel intellectually empowered, the university needed my winning of a "genius" award in order for that intellectual empowerment to be openly acknowledged. Within this openness, I have more room to flex that intellectual muscle, to configure it into a bifurcating theory. Because Limited Fork Theory emerged along a path on which the MacArthur Fellowship occurred, it is as if the fellowship enabled that emergence. I had the intellectual space that such a dynamic system of thinking requires. Walls were knocked down — figuratively and literally: a prime office with a splendid view. And being in that office afforded me awareness of the simultaneity of systems interacting on different scales in different locations for varying durations of time. Certain conditions that could support the evolution of the theory had to precede that evolution. So without that office, without my husband taking me to the movie in October 2004, without my prior interest in complex systems, without the fellowship that secured me a key to that office, no Limited Fork Theory, no forkergirl — presently my most authentic identity.

Choosing the Limited Fork Theory path is unlikely in circumstances where the chooser worries about validation of the theory. There is a certain audacity needed to implement and practice the untested. I have some complicity in the transformation; my wanting to be forkergirl helps fortify that identity. Forkergirl sticks to me and I stick to forkergirl. I make no effort to break the bond. The MacArthur Fellowship was in part a grant of audacity. I am not afraid to make those connections that might be impossible for those not granted a healthy dose of audacity; I am not afraid to make those connections where the outcomes might be mutations or total transformations of structures in place before those wild (and sometimes discouraged) fusions (such as, as was once thought, mixed-race people). That the solidity of institutions might have to be forfeited in order to implement Limited Fork Theory is something I welcome, because even if I fall through one of the tines, I will fall somewhere, and that somewhere can be studied, and milked for possibilities: The Culture of Possibility, The Culture of (Re) Configuration, The Culture of Audacity, and yes, some intersection with a tine that is Barack Obama's Audacity of Hope.

MP: Let's talk about where you are now, in your investigations of the range and possibilities of Limited Fork Poetics. Your podcasts and blogs utilize new technologies and are taking poetry places it's never gone before. Will you ever publish in print again? Where do you think your poetry is headed?

TM: I think that the *now* of my expansion/reconfiguration into forker-girl has been part of every answer in this interview. I almost can't remember anything without forking it, (re)framing it. My years before fork have been reframed as guide tines that permit a view of Limited Fork Theory as an inevitable outcome. This theory is so close to how the mind works, how thoughts and ideas navigate the unlimited mind housed in a finite brain, how the brain processes information, locating and attaching or linking parts, echoes, reflections, shadows of components of an idea system to multiple locations of the mind; a network of neurons fire in these transactions. Interactions happen at nanolevels and at the level of Universe. This theory feeds and is fed by the movements, the behaviors, the patterns, the convergences, the divergences, the links, the activities in systems (in everything).

Limited Fork Theory is taking thinking (which includes poetry) where it could always go but wasn't. Limited Fork Theory can still produce known and familiar forms, including known and familiar forms of poetry, but in the study of interactions, Limited Fork Theory seeks to identify the patterns that temporarily emerge when any things are partnered. There are no boundaries that can't become flexible, even if only as a thought experiment in the laboratory of the mind. So new forms, hybrids, mergers, mutations are encouraged by the theory. And the poams (products of acts of making) that are the outcomes of applied Limited Fork Theory are systems, so may have many components in multiple forms. Print components, static visual components, interactive digital components, 3D components, sonic components, olfactory components, and these parts of an idea system that is a poam system may be miles apart, years apart, tethered by the strands, the tines of the idea itself, strands that can be pulled into graspable shapes, that can be expanded or collapsed, that can become metaphors for understanding other systems, that can be beautiful and inspiring maps of possibilities of existence: the other worlds, other meanings too often hidden.

I don't know where my work is headed — and that is useful; I'm pleased to not know, for to know would mean that not only do I intend to disregard any possibilities that unanticipated variables enable, I will also successfully disregard them, and I won't grow from the sharing that can be part of encounters or interactions. It is the nature of the mind to be flexible and to link to multiple locations in a single interaction event. That said, I don't feel anywhere near a "solid" understanding of all the predictions, intricacies, and principles of Limited Fork Theory. There is much to define, to investigate, and to articulate in any form that becomes possible and in multiple forms, multiple modes so as to construct a more robust linked-form map, which may be entered and explored and navigated in any way that entry can happen, any way that exploration can happen, and any way that is possible for navigation to occur.

Limited Fork Theory is already an evolution of Limited Fork Poetics; from a poetics to a more generalized system of thinking and toolset for making. Lately, I've been emphasizing flexible framing systems, and I am very interested in exploring forms of flexibility, and what happens at the boundaries of these forms. I find myself now split between the Department of English and the School of Art and Design at the University of Michigan. Perhaps, as a Proforker, I should belong to every department, a tine in each, for no matter what is studied, Limited Fork Theory has implications, and the work of a student practitioner will be a form of poam. The mind benefits greatly from the exercise of making and shifting/(re)configuring multiple framing systems, so maybe Limited Fork Theory will (also) be used as a form of mind sport, and will train thinkers. I wonder what the Limited Fork Theory marathon and triathlon will be like, or the Limited Fork Theory Olympics. Project Limited Fork Theory to replace the departing *Project Runway* on Bravo network? *Top Forker* might work well with *Top Chef* and/or *Top Design*.

Here's an example of my current work:

Recently, at Wayne State University, forkergirl had the opportunity to reprise an interaction with Nick Speed, a hip-hop/rap producer and sound illustrator with whom forkergirl had performed in the summer, an impromptu meeting of *Tokyo Butter* and hip-hop beats on an oppressively hot summer afternoon: Detroit Lit Fest, Thylias Moss invited to read, but reading seemed somehow inadequate when her turn came near the end of the event, given a sweat-drenched audience for whom words weren't as powerful as humidity intensifying in the hottest moments of the afternoon, sun coming through the tents like thigh-high slits in skirts, bifurcations in the fabric, a radiant tine, a limited fork from one of heaven's thermonuclear furnaces, the tent sort of there to catch some neutrinos popping out of the light, solar popcorn neutrinos, solar "popcorn" to acknowledge the birth of limited fork in a movie theatre.

Anyway, Nick Speed and crew and gear were on the stage, deejaying between spoken acts, sweaty heads nodding to his beats. My turn, the last poet, the humidity affecting my ability to make sound literary decisions, so I asked the MC if he'd mind my hooking up my words to Nick's beats, if he thought Nick would mind some interaction, and Nick was fine with it, even more pleased with forkergirl's naive willingness to accept as the musical punctuation and foundation of the *Tokyo Butter* content any beat Nick played, shifting the musical beat whenever Speed wanted to whatever Speed wanted, allowing Speed to shape the sound, to provide the sonic structure the words could inhabit, could claim and somehow customize — as if the words were made for those sounds that the words demanded. Forkergirl matched every loop, every twist, every divergence in pitch, tempo, instrument. Butter's like that, heat-softened without degradation into utter melt, sticky yellow fluid so much like urine — avoided becoming waste product; butter adjusted, configured itself, molded, sculpted itself over and over, became monument after monument in the musical phrases that praised the monuments.

Well, Malin, Nick and I plan to do more of this. Perhaps all of my readings will be buttery like this. Maybe.

MP: It sounds improvisational, and, while risky, quite freeing.

TM: Forkergirl is almost some kind of superhero for me. She flies; she transports me to forms of thinking and creative understandings that are outside ways of processing perceptual information that is too locked in trust of the sensor proximity. Such reasonable approaches to materiality don't necessarily do as much for the mind, which though it processes sensory interactions is capable of detaching from dependence on them when constructing possibilities. The mind does not require literal reenactments. It is always attached to the ground for existing within the grounded and finite brain, allowing for a most intriguing dichotomy, the finite and the infinite, the mortal and the immortal, intriguing because of the intimate relationship between these divisions, the finite roots of the infinite mind, the soaring kites of ideas and their strings that are moored in the brain. My physical body is not forkergirl. Forkergirl is mind. Forkergirl is idea. The spirit and energy field form of the theory.

Forkergirl is becoming convinced that not as much is done in U.S. educational institutions to encourage and utilize negotiations between the realities of mass and the realities of thought, which is not made of the same matter as the body. It is not that imagination or creativity are problematic; of course imagination and thought are not quantifiable in the same way as physical parts of the human body system: they're made of different stuff, and they do in fact exist. Harnessing the power of idea has incredible potential, and while I am not offering an equation of an idea to unlock it as other equations have unlocked aspects of the atom, I do believe that once thought is being understood as a force or energy/information field, then transforming technologies will emerge to support a physical existence that has little resemblance, if any, to what currently prevails.

Because forkergirl is some kind of superhero in her routine accessing of other dimensions, even if women can't access them, even if black women can't access them, she does deliver to them the objects of access, which include strategies of converting information from polydimensional experiences into forms that can exist in 4D space; so forkergirl does not forget her roots, and is, in fact, attached to them. Now, because forkergirl is some kind of superhero, I have been thinking of designing a costume, a forkergirl suit to adorn the body, acknowledging that body as the world headquarters of Limited Fork Theory. I suppose I need only a forkergirl hat, a forkergirl skullcap for sake of better accuracy, but I crave a physical dressing up, so I know the forkergirl suit will happen — and I will teach in it; maybe I will design uniforms for Limited Fork Theory schools and retreats.

[2007–8]

CORNELIUS EADY

Cornelius Eady's unique contribution to this generation of black poets lies as much in his founding of the black poets' workshop Cave Canem with Toi Derricotte in 1996 as in his poetry. He has written seven volumes of poetry, including *Hardheaded Weather: New and Selected Poems* (2008). He won the 1985 Lamont Poetry Prize from the Academy of American Poets for *Victims of the Latest Dance Craze*, and his musical theater piece, *Running Man*, cowritten with musician Deidre Murray, was a 1999 finalist for the Pulitzer Prize in Drama. Eady is currently an associate professor of English and director of the Creative Writing Program at the University of Notre Dame.

Eady was born in Rochester, New York, in 1954. He received a BA in English from Empire State College and published his first book of poetry, *Kartunes*, in 1980. He attended Warren Wilson's MFA program during the 1985–86 academic year but left without the degree for reasons we discuss in the interview. He has been married to Sarah Micklem, a novelist, for thirty years. Eady experienced a health challenge in 2004–05 when he was diagnosed with prostate cancer; he received treatment and has since recovered.

Eady's poetry draws upon the traditions of jazz and blues; *The Autobiography of a Jukebox* (1997) contains *Dreaming in Hi-Fi*, a CD of songs written and performed by Eady. His poems fuse music and the realities of black male identity in a racist society. His is not a formalist aesthetic: rather, Eady's lines are rhythmic, as if spoken or sung, and storytelling narratives predominate in his poems. Eady relies not so much on imagery or symbolism, but rather on a direct, grounded lyricism. He places his poetry in a lineage from Etheridge Knight.

Despite a host of enthusiastic reviews of his books, literary criticism has neglected to investigate Eady's work, with only one critical analysis published to date, perhaps because his poetry is accessible and doesn't appear to need interpretation to aid the reader's understanding. Yet his work is powerful and honest. The volume *Brutal Imagination*, which contains two poem cycles, one on the fictitious black male who Susan Smith claimed kidnapped her sons, and the other on a persona called Running Man, represent Eady's art at its height. In particular, Eady's construction of black masculinities merits critical analysis. With the publication of a collection of new and selected poems in 2008, perhaps critical attention to Eady's work is just around the corner. Useful frames for understanding Eady's poetry are the jazz/blues poetic tradition and the Black Arts Movement. Eady's most recent poetry, however, appears removed from the social protest of the Black Arts Movement in its reflective stance and highly personal themes, and his affinities with black musical traditions and performance are leading some of his current work toward drama.

The interview with Eady occurred at two different times and in two different formats: I first met with him on October 13, 2006, at Cave Canem's tenth anniversary celebration in New York City, where we found an empty meeting room and talked for over an hour and a half; nineteen months later, I spoke with him by phone on May 19, 2008. We focused our first conversation on Cave Canem and the second on Eady's poetry.

Selected Works by Cornelius Eady

POETRY

Kartunes, Warthog Press, 1980.

Victims of the Latest Dance Craze, Ommation Press, 1986; repr. Carnegie Mellon University Press, 1997.

The Gathering of My Name, Carnegie Mellon University Press, 1991.

You Don't Miss Your Water, Henry Holt, 1995; repr. Carnegie Mellon University Press, 2004.

The Autobiography of a Jukebox, Carnegie Mellon University Press, 1997.

Brutal Imagination, Putnam, 2001.

Hardheaded Weather: New and Selected Poems, Putnam, 2008.

OTHER

You Don't Miss Your Water (musical theater), with Deirdre Murray, produced at the Vineyard Theater, New York, 1997.

Running Man (jazz opera), with Deirdre Murray and Diane Paulus, produced at the Here Arts Center, New York, 1998, and the Prince Music Theater, Philadelphia, 1999.

Brutal Imagination (musical theater) with Deirdre Murray, produced at the Vineyard Theatre, New York, 2001–2.

Fangs (musical theater), with Deirdre Murray, produced at the Vox and Friends Festival with the New York City Opera and Thalia Theater at Symphony Space, New York, 2004.

Gathering Ground, coedited with Toi Derricotte, University of Michigan Press, 2006.

MALIN PEREIRA: I have really enjoyed getting to know your work. I promised you that today we would talk more about Cave Canem, and another time we will talk about your poetry. This weekend in New York City, we are celebrating the historic tenth anniversary of Cave Canem. On my invitation, it said Cave Canem is "A home for black poetry." The whole metaphor of home is so resonant, but it's also very literal. Can you talk to me about the necessity of a home for black poetry and how that relates to Cave Canem?

CORNELIUS EADY: We're not the only home for black poetry and not the only organization that has taken responsibility in that job. There are lots of other places, such as the Dark Room Collective, that came before Cave Canem. Cave Canem is trying to address what has been going on for a very long time. For whatever reason, you as a writer get into this moment where you decide you want to be a writer and you want to find out what it means. You ask yourself, "How do I best develop my ability?" If you want any space where you're seen as who you are or where you're from is taken as a given instead of a mysterious exotic thing, your options are limited.

In MFA or other creative writing programs, you find very quickly that you're a minority in many ways — in the physical sense, but also the cultural. Part of it is due to what we're dealing with — to use an old 1960s term — American language and American experience. African American experience gets categorized, and it's problematic because they don't know how to deal with you or they don't know whether what you're saying is relevant or has enough gravitas. There is an unspoken understanding that you're there to become someone better than who you are already — which means where you come from is bad. You find yourself in a situation where suddenly you're feeling that in order to be accepted into this other group, you have to change or transform yourself. You realize no one else is expected to transform or change in the way you are expected to change, and you become guarded and question why you're there. You hear all kinds of un-spoken pronouncements about who you are, why you're there, where you come from and where you're supposed to be, and you end up in discussions you feel have little to do with you as a poet. To be quite blunt, you realize some people — not all, but some — will resent the fact that you're there or think you're a charity case.

MP: On scholarship.

CE: Right. They think the only reason you're there is because somebody feels guilty. Take, for instance, language. Sometimes the only language that's available to you is the street. If you work with language that comes from your neighborhood, that's one thing, but they believe it's not intel-lectual enough. If you try to appropriate it, that seems suspicious because you're aping it. It's very often not seen as authentic voice. I've always carried this feeling that we really should be someplace where we could do the work we need to do without having to feel like we have to explain ourselves. The work should be about poetry. It should be about the work and nothing else. My MFA experience was not a good one. I carried that experience with me and my feeling was if I ever had an opportunity to do something like this, I would. I want to make sure that it never happens to somebody else again. That nobody else has to be put in a position where they have to question their existence or feel they have to be defensive about who they are. I want it to be about their development as a writer and nothing else.

MP: One of the things I hear you saying is that this is about identity — who you are. In contemporary African American poetry, the lyric po-etry in particular, it's about defining a black identity from the individual's point of view but in relation to a larger context. I think, too, about bell hooks's definition of the *homeplace* (42), and it sounds to me like what Cave Canem has set out to do is create "a homeplace." Not *the* homeplace, but *a* homeplace.

I heard you saying that black poets in MFA programs are expected to transform themselves, while the non-black students in the room don't feel they have to transform themselves in relationship to the black students sit-ting in the room. Whiteness doesn't have to change.

CE: It's simply a given.

MP: This home, then, is very much a metaphor or a symbol for identity. It's also a literal homeplace where you can have that identity flourish.

CE: Right, and having Cave Canem as a physical location — even for a week — is very important. I wish it was long. In fact, when Cave Canem was proposed, it was a real physical location. One of the earliest conversations I had was with Charles Rowell, the editor of *Callaloo*. We talked about the need to have a place to compose. I had this same discussion with another Cave Canem alumnus, Herman Beavers. This had always been at the back of my mind, and it's what a lot of others thought about, too — anyone who went through the system — sooner or later, you start thinking, *Wouldn't it be nice to have a place like this?* When I started talking about this with Toi Derricotte, it all started to happen. She's the one who suggested it should be a physical, permanent location. Later, we came to a point where we were talking about it and wondering if we actually did it, would anybody actually come? Is there really a need for this?

MP: There's a saying, "If you build it, they will come."

CE: At first, it was just us bitching and moaning about it, but we actually said that if we're building a school for African American poets, would anybody bother to come? We wanted to have the accreditation and we wondered if it would seem legitimate. My contribution was to suggest we do this as a test, as a retreat. One summer, print some ads and if anybody shows up, we know there's an audience. If no one shows up, we know there isn't. One thing led to another, and here we are ten years later. It's now a physical and kind of abstracted location at the same time. In the prize winners' reading yesterday, Kyle Dargan asked all the Cave Canem fellows to stand up, because Cave Canem is sort of an abstraction. It happens far, far away from an urban center for one week every summer, and then it disappears again. There's no permanent physical location, so by asking all the fellows to stand up, there was an actual physical representation of Cave Canem and the audience could see how big it really was — and that was really good. Cave Canem is physical, but it isn't. You can't *go* there.

MP: I'm recalling that Toni Morrison said she wrote *Beloved* because there wasn't even a bench by the road to mark slavery. There wasn't a physical, institutional, or documented thing. I'm thinking, too, of Audre Lorde's "The Master's Tools Will Never Dismantle the Master's House." With these resonances, you could argue perhaps it's a tradition of black America to have that sort of house that doesn't necessarily have a physical house. It's in the people. It's in the history.

CE: Right.

MP: At the same time, though, referencing Lorde, you have to consider that institutionalizing things is one of the ways you get power or dominance and repeat the worst of the system. I wonder if that ever bothers anybody on the board or if anybody's trying to resist codifying Cave Canem? You could start having the kind of dominance that would dictate things.

CE: It's something we try to be aware of and try to avoid. One of the things that worries me is the way our culture operates. When one black person or one black organization becomes highly successful, they become *the* person, the only organization — the bully on the block. It was never our intention to do that. Part of the reason we've survived so long is we were invisible for so long. Nobody cared. When we started to accumulate fellows who had their first and second books and were winning prizes and the recognition that started coming out of that, people said, "Who is this Cave Canem?" Then people saw it and we have become seen as an authority.

MP: Then people act differently toward you when you start to have power and authority.

CE: Which is totally understandable. This is part of the dues you pay for surviving. We intentionally had a small size and a small budget. There were numerous reasons for that. First of all, when we had workshops with around fifty-five people each summer, it started to lose cohesion. We could go through the whole weekend and there would be people who would come in and we wouldn't even know who they were. We wanted to know who these people were; we wanted that kind of intimacy. It's part of the power of Cave Canem; it's why it works.

The second element is we have a small budget. If we could do more programming, we would — but that costs more money. We've always been lean. Back in the early ages, we had only one full-time staff member, my mother-in-law, Carolyn Micklem. Now we have two to three people on the staff. To do more programming, you have to have more money, and we don't have a budget that will support more than one workshop a year. So because of that, there used to be a perception of "Who cares?" People could have cared less to get into a Cave Canem workshop. Now, they see it as more of a career move because so few people are invited. We didn't set it up as a career track in African American poetry, but people have made it into that. Suddenly, it makes you special. You're seen as something different than the rest of the bunch out there.

MP: Something to put on the resume.

CE: That's because the fellows started putting it on their resumes, started putting it in their books, and started mentioning it to different people. People then started asking what was Cave Canem and how do they get in, and they suddenly find out they can't get in because we only take a limited number of people every summer. Then it becomes, "I've tried to get into Cave Canem five times and I can't."

MP: Someone might say, "I'm not their kind of poet."

CE: What's wrong is there isn't enough space, and those who don't get in might question the idea of the program. There's also a suspicion that comes with how you negotiate this kind of situation with this kind of power. Some people see poetry writing programs as a sign of leaving your culture — you are traitors. On the other hand, the MFA degree — in this era — becomes a professional credential. So, why shouldn't African Americans have a credential? I have been ambivalent about the MFA program my entire adult life.

MP: Now you're directing one! You're clearly a traitor.

CE: There is always the fear of becoming your enemy. This is something I worry about. Do you inadvertently take on the trappings of the people you are fighting against? What I'm trying to do is find a way that you can be who you are but also recognize where other people come from. It's still poetry. If not coming from a middle-class Caucasian male position, it can still be considered poetry. When somebody like Major Jackson writes in sonnets, like in "Letter to Gwendolyn Brooks," you don't see it as aping or pretending. He's taking African American material and integrating it through that tradition. Nobody owns tradition. Nobody has a permanent claim on it.

The idea that poetry is static is really the most ridiculous stance you could have. History laughs in your face when you take that position. People still adhere to that idea — that poetry only belongs to certain people and not others. My whole deal has been to break that down as much as I can. The idea here for me is that the mission for Cave Canem isn't trying to train MFA students. I'm proud that most of the students who come to Cave Canem are not traditional MFA students.

MP: I heard the statistic that only about 37 percent have an MFA degree.

CE: We are not MFA top-heavy. It's a perception. Also, if you did a survey of the socioeconomic class these people come from, you'd realize this was not upper class at all.

MP: That seems to be the other thing people might be throwing at Cave

Canem right now, that it is East Coast or elite or for the privileged. Nobody is directly accusing anybody, but raising the question.

CE: And they should.

MP: We need to support the resources we have for black poetry. I was thinking about the wonderful work Joanne Gabbin has done with Furious Flower. In North Carolina, Trudier Harris started the George Moss Horton Society for the Study of African American Poetry. It was going well. But the question arose, just how many resources and how much energy do the folks who care about African American poetry have, and how many of us are there? Eventually, what Harris did when Furious Flower was going gangbusters was she threw her support to Gabbin. Why not think that way about Cave Canem? The other response people can have is that it's *a* home for black poetry, and people can go create other homes. That would be truly Johnny Appleseed.

CE: That is one of my true disappointments about Cave Canem, or more so about the reaction to Cave Canem. You're right. We are the one private organization out there doing this without a university affiliation.

MP: Because Joanne's affiliated with James Madison University.

CE: The problem with affiliating with a university is that it becomes *their* organization, and autonomy is something I want to fight for with my last breath for Cave Canem. It goes back to funding. I truly believed in my heart of hearts that we would be circumvented and taken over in a few years. I really thought two to three years after we started there would be ten to fifteen programs like this across the country, and Toi and I wouldn't even be doing this. When Cave Canem started, the concept was if you can get a volunteer faculty, keep the cost low by not charging tuition, find a retreat center with really low upkeep, then all the students have to do is pay as if you're going to a conference. You all agree that this is what you're going to do and no money changes hands. You can do this. I felt there was a kind of "duh" factor. You don't realize you can do it until you do it. I really believed that at a certain point people were going to see, "Oh, they can do that, I can do that. We'll do it here." What I found out is that they want *you* to do it.

MP: That's funny, because I was wondering, was there anything that surprised you? You are telling me you were surprised about that.

CE: There has been some response to Cave Canem in terms of other groups who are starting similar workshops. I'm aware of a conference on the West Coast called The Voices. Junot Díaz and some of the people teach there, as well as Quincy Troupe. That conference is more generally for writers of color, not just for African Americans. There's an Asian American workshop that happened about eight years into Cave Canem. I ran into someone who was thinking about doing a Latino version of Cave Canem.

This brings up an important point — different elements all have to be in place in order to make something like this happen. If I hadn't met Toi, who gave us the idea of doing this for no money, it might not have happened. Money was the Gordian knot for us. Most times when we had the conversation prior to that, it fell apart because of the money. The Latino Cave Canem is at that point right now. They're thinking about what they have to do to amass all that money. Part of me is saying that if they're really serious about it, do it without money. We did our first three years without money. I don't know if the atmosphere now will allow others to do what we did.

MP: I'm thinking of Virginia Woolf's claim that all a woman needs is money and a room to write in. Those are the two issues. You need a place — not necessarily a building, but a place to gather — and for that you need money. I wonder, if other groups came together and tried to come up with some of these in other locations, if they would run into funding problems because if they write for grants, the response might be, "Well, there's already Cave Canem."

CE: They say that now. When we were applying for early grants, we were invisible and too small. Our budgets were too small to pay attention to. The group out in Minnesota was one of our best funders. They were the first group to come to us and tell us they were going to fund us, though they were only funding in New York and Minnesota.

MP: The panel I just attended before this was asking the question, is there a Cave Canem aesthetic? Let's pursue that a little bit. Can you talk about the range of aesthetics you perceive among the fellows and faculty? The faculty signal a program's aesthetic bent. For example, if you brought in Wanda Coleman this summer, how would that change things?

CE: There are a number of things to say about that. One is that the aesthetic is sort of set by Toi and me because we read all the manuscripts and let people in. Unfortunately or fortunately, we're both lyric narrative poets, so that's where our interests lie. The way we try to counter that is to hire faculty who aren't like us. Like Harryette Mullen, for example. This will attract people, and they will feel safe applying, and once they're here they won't feel as strange. It's also complicated by the fact that we're not a beginners workshop and never set ourselves up as a beginners workshop. We don't operate on a first come, first served basis. It takes more to get in than just mailing us a check. It wouldn't be Cave Canem if it was open to all comers.

MP: There are others who've done that. That's what Gwendolyn Brooks's project was in Chicago. She took neighborhood kids and everyone. But Cave Canem's different.

CE: There are two ways of doing it. One way is to think of it as a big house and anybody can walk in and we'll try to accommodate as many people as we can get. That's a legitimate way of doing it. Toi and I weren't thinking about it in those terms. We're looking for people who are at a certain point in their writing, and it's really hard to explain what that might be. There has to be something registering in the manuscript that we attach ourselves to, that we notice. It doesn't mean it's a perfect manuscript because few of the manuscripts are actual knockouts. But, they always have some sort of element someplace where they can grow. Something where we think, "They could use talking to Elizabeth Alexander or Harryette Mullen." We assume certain things, and we also try to mix it up. By that, I mean we will pick people who are a little rougher, or a little less certain, but people who might have a good chance of developing or taking a step forward. For these kind of people, hanging out at Cave Canem might be something that lets that coalesce.

But, having said that, we have a limited amount of space — maybe eight or ten people, depending on how many people turn over. There can be criticism because the majority of Cave Canem's poets are lyric poets, and many of us are lyric poets. We have a lot of people who identify themselves as performance poets come through Cave Canem, and having gone through Cave Canem, they have gone on to MFA programs. A lot of performance poets have nothing to apologize for; in fact they do better than we do. They get on Def Jam poetry and get venues that can get them millions of viewers. Their books sell like hotcakes for every single performance poet. Every poet that I know personally that came from performance has gone through a program or is going through a program. Patricia Smith just joined a low-residency program. Tracie Morris has her PhD. Every performance poet I've had some contact with has gone through this transformation because, from their point of view, they're not legitimate poets until they're seen and recognized by us print poets.

MP: That's so interesting to hear.

CE: I've had this conversation with enough of them that I feel comfortable saying that. Pat Smith, for example, is going through it right now. She doesn't have to apologize to anybody. She can mop up the floor with anybody, on any terms. She can do it, but she really feels that she needs to be legitimized by going through a low-residency program and getting her degree.

MP: That's a very generous attitude on their part. There is something harder about print poetry because you can't use other tools to help the audience understand. You're stuck with the page, the print. You can do some things with italics, font, and some spacing, but these performance poets, they could just go and ignore the print poets, frankly. They're getting the attention and they're seen as the culture carriers — they're the coin of the realm.

CE: Exactly. They could live without the university.

MP: At the same time, I think their desire to get recognition from print poets is important. Print poetry is like doing a headstand in the middle of the room versus performance poetry being like doing a headstand against the wall. One could argue that it's harder, print poetry, because you don't have a wall to lean against and your tools and your supportive devices are limited.

CE: I don't want to minimize the question. There's always the need for a writer to grow, right? Some of these people are really good and can do things that I couldn't do on the best day of my life. From their point of view, they are thinking of what else they can do. It's also enacting a kind of interesting change in poetry — what are you going to do when they all have degrees? They'll have a foot in both worlds, and they're not denouncing their performance backgrounds to do it. What do you get when you have all these writers? They'll say, "You can't tell me about print. I've learned about it and I have proof because I have a degree." So what are you going to do?

MP: It's transformative for the field. It gets rid of that binary, the split between page and stage poets, right?

CE: Let's hope it refreshes the mix. It strikes me as curious that people who could live without the academy because they don't need it and have full careers without it feel there's this need to go back and absorb that as well.

MP: This is where I get overly optimistic and a little sentimental, but I would hope that this would bring about some real transformation in the academy, which tends to be so print based and so boring.

CE: Exactly — boring and stuck.

MP: Like knowledge with a capital *K*, and it's warehoused in these places. Ownership of knowledge and means of transmitting knowledge and styles of knowledge can then really be transformed. That would be great.

CE: I think you're right. That's my hope, too, that that's the way it ends up. We're at the point where most universities I've worked at acknowledge that there's something called performance poetry out there. I don't think they know what to do with it, and they're a little suspicious about what it is. They see it as more of a marketing tool at this point than anything else.

Part of the reason I'm at Notre Dame, for example, is it provided me with the possibility of integrating performance theater while having a performance theater center for African American poets at Notre Dame. I've gotten good support for that. Notre Dame opened up to the idea and really wanted it. But there's still a little part of me that says, do they really know what they want? Do they really want to see a performance of Amiri Baraka's "The Twilight" in their black box? Do they really want that kind of hard-edged stuff when they see what African Americans study in performance theater? I don't know.

Maybe I'm too pessimistic about it. I've always felt that there's a moment when you're confronted with the fact that black life is different. Black experience is different. There are a lot of similarities with the rest of the culture, but there's something that's very unique about black experience. Sometimes that reality is an ugly reality and if you're going to be true about it, you have to do it. You have to go there. There's this little recoil when you realize whose responsibility it is to do the work. People think that by saying we're going to let this in, that's all the work we're going to have to do, without thinking about how this is actually going to affect them, how it's actually going to transform their reality.

MP: It has to be incorporated. In my experience with the academy, when I've done controversial things or said controversial things in teaching African American poetry, there have been disruptions. There have been students who get upset — white and black.

CE: Absolutely.

MP: I will never forget one American Literature survey course where I had a black female student who was so livid that I was going to teach *The Adventures of Huckleberry Finn*. She was worried about the "n" word in the book. Trying to have that conversation and her filing a grievance while I was doing everything I could to teach this from a perspective that is propelled by black experience, literature, and culture was challenging. Then the question is, because this is always the question in the institution, is your dean behind you?

CE: That's the question I'm going to find when I go back to Notre Dame. That's the real test. A little part of me was thinking I'm really kind of excited but a little wary. Is it the African American students themselves who are questioning it, because sometimes it strikes a nerve? Cave Canem is special for me because there's a kind of egalitarian spirit about it. You can be poor and be in Cave Canem, or you can be bourgeois and be in Cave Canem. You can be from the street or from the middle class and be in Cave Canem, whereas African American students who go through college to become upper-middle class, or who have climbed up to middle class — there are sometimes complications with that. I taught an African American literature class last spring at Notre Dame, my first one there. Because I'm a new black faculty member, I have five or six African American students in my class, which is wonderful. We did Elizabeth Alexander's book *The Black Interior*, which they really loved. I kept thinking that there were times when the black students would read things and wouldn't want to identify with them. They didn't want to be seen as different from their other classmates, or have their white classmates see them as different.

MP: They didn't want this to be the first time their classmates saw them as black.

CE: Exactly, which is interesting. It really doesn't seem for you guys to be resisting, because you don't want to say *this is what my experience really is*, or *I know this is where my family comes from. I want to make sure you guys don't think of me as only a black person, but as a human.*

MP: As a fellow student who can analyze the piece.

CE: Yes. Once you start thinking about me as "ethnic," it's over. I didn't realize it then in the way I've seen it in other places since. How much of a threat that is, and how much of a risk that is when you stick your neck out. It's easier to do it here in New York because here there are no repercussions. Doing it someplace in Indiana is really tricky, but I didn't realize that. It didn't strike me in the way that it did, teaching in other places. I saw how fragile and tricky that existence has to be for them. The pressures on them are not the pressures I've put up with. I've had my share, but not the same.

MP: I've been fortunate to have majority black classes where I teach. Yet students who are African American often come in with narrow notions of what blackness is or can be. For them, it can be upsetting to have that shifted. Cyrus Cassells came a couple of years ago, and it was great because I saw some students' faces with shock in them because he's fluent in four languages and he's gay. For some of them, the preachers have taught them that this is hellfire and brimstone. First, they had to read his poetry, and we all agreed as a class that it was fabulous. Then, to meet him and see he was a good person and smart and all, it was transformative for them.

CE: One of the miraculous things about Cave Canem is that at least for a week people can let go of that and be really intellectual or gay or lesbian. There isn't one thing called "black poetry." A lot of people think black poetry is just for dissent — protest poetry. They think that's all you need, protest and dissent, because there's nothing else. You see Cyrus Cassells and he blows your mind because you're not expecting it. You see Harryette Mullen and she blows your mind because you see how she can mess with language. It's not illegal. You mess with the definition — I'm deeply into messing with the definition. Sometimes, we know what we see but we don't acknowledge it. Cave Canem pushes that button a little. People go in political and come out doing literature. They think it's all about one thing but find out it's not. They find out they can relax, it's okay. They can take a chance and write poems they wouldn't have thought of writing before had they not been exposed to Cave Canem. The other trick about Cave Canem is that we mix faculty and the students. We rotate the faculty the entire week so there isn't one approach — it's not a monolithic kind of *black* or one way of writing poetry. And it can still be cultural and all those things.

MP: Tell me, what happens over the course of the week? What kind of experiences are there? Do they get a different poet every day, another workshop?

CE: The structure works as a workshop model in that they have to write a new poem every day. They can't bring old material to Cave Canem — they have to generate it here. The most important day of Cave Canem is the opening circle. We have dinner and everyone gets into a big circle and we introduce ourselves and talk. The people who are veterans mingle with the new members. This is a time to reconnect and to learn why you're here, what Cave Canem is about. This sets the tone for the rest of the week. The workshops consist of five groups. The groups remain stationary and the faculty rotates among the groups during the week. The group might get me on Monday, Toi on Tuesday, Harryette on Wednesday, Cyrus on Thursday, and so on. When I come into a workshop, I don't give them any exercises. I come in and have them talk about their poems — what they want to do with the poems and the nuts and bolts of them. Toi has a different approach: she will come in and tell them to get in touch with their pain. They may have been workshopping with me on Monday, but on Tuesday they're all crying because Toi's got them. Then when Elizabeth comes in, she makes them think about something else.

MP: Do they eat their meals together?

CE: Yes, all their meals. They live in dormitories together, not as a group, but all in the same location. These groups are only broken up by the readings. Faculty readings come first, then fellows reading the next two or three days after that. In the last few years we've had an off-campus day where we go to the Andy Warhol Museum or another museum and do part of the faculty reading in a public location. You're being immersed in this universe for about seven days, and then we have a big reading at the end.

MP: Do they get to read any of their old poems?

CE: They're allowed to read old poems if they want to, but a lot of times they choose to read anything that was happening at the moment. The group bonds quickly, and it's not something you know you're going to do until you get there. There are some traditions too, like giving the groups signatures or making special signs, fake names, things like that. We've only been around a few years, but there are already traditions, like second years doing specific things, third years doing other things — and they're the ones that figured this out, not us. Every year, graduation is different, too. Everyone has to invent a different graduation ceremony.

MP: That's great. That's empowerment and getting people to be really committed to it — owning it.

CE: They own it, and that's the strength of Cave Canem — they really feel that they're invested in that space. I'm very happy about that.

MP: You're creating more and more black poets — or at least enabling more of them.

CE: We're enabling them in a way that isn't competitive, which is surprising to me. There are sharp, bright poets who are hungry for careers, but it's not like Iowa, where the lesson learned was that life is short so hit the ground running and stab everyone in the back who gets in your way.

MP: A lot of people say there's an Iowa poem. Do you want there to be a Cave Canem poem?

CE: There is an Iowa poem, and I hope to God there won't ever be a Cave Canem poem. I'd love to think that when you pick up the anthology *Gathering Ground*, of Cave Canem poets, what you're seeing is a whole range of poets. You should see poets who blow you away and it should occur to you that there isn't one particular cookie-cutter Cave Canem poem. We have different people who come with different styles, different locations, different experiences — and this is all black poetry. If our book gets reviewed, you'll never see that in any review. You will never see that it's all African American and all black poetry.

MP: Why wouldn't they put that in a review?

CE: First, because literally it's so obvious, so right in front of your face that you don't see it. And second, because if you do that, you're acknowledging something. You might see "We like it," or "It's too black," or "It's not black enough," but you're not going to see, "It's all black poetry." And you won't see, "Look what they pulled off." I would love to read that, but I doubt I'm going to read it.

MP: What my friend Shanna says is that blackness is getting bigger all the time. That's what the anthology *Gathering Ground* is all about, isn't it? It's gathering together the bigness of black poetry and all the directions it can go.

CE: Right, all the directions it has been going all along. It goes back to what we were talking about earlier. You don't have to go beyond black. You don't have to give up anything in order to be who you are. That's somebody else controlling who you are.

MP: So in ten years, what you would like to see is a little bit more of the dissemination of this model, but it doesn't sound like you're suggesting that it needs to be under the authority of yourself and Toi. What you're hoping for is that it spreads in the informal free way and that the model be a model that is simply a gathering ground.

CE: My hope is exactly that, yes. I don't want disciples. I'd like to think that we don't own this, and I don't think we should own it. I really feel what would be of most use culturally would be the idea of Cave Canem, not the physicality of it. I want Cave Canem to survive me and Toi. I want people to go with the idea of Cave Canem — the concept — and that people would support the concept and not us. The danger in a lot of African American groups and these organizations is there is focus on one person.

My lesson in life has come from following June Jordan. I followed June as the director of the poetry center at Stonybrook. I learned the hard way what it means when you have someone who's really dynamic and centered in charge. They were honoring June instead of the concept of the center. She left to set up Poetry for the People, and Stonybrook died a slow death. When June died, they paid attention to her, not her organization. Poetry for the People is an astonishing idea. That's not going to happen to Cave Canem. We can keep enough of it up and running so people will see that the idea is really good. The idea of cooperation, the idea of finding places where we actually end up helping one another, as opposed to tearing each other down. There's enough out there; there's enough for everyone.

MP: You don't have to fight over scraps.

CE: Right, there are enough for everybody. It helps more people, and it really effects change not only in yourself, but also in the way people perceive who you are. The idea is really worth defending and is important, whether or not Toi and I are there.

MP: I like the nonownership idea, too. The idea of owning land, owning ideas, owning people, all of those sorts of ownership things are problematic in obvious ways. Extending that to poetry, then, it's important to create a poetry community. It comes straight out of the poetry tradition.

CE: I definitely agree with that. That's all we're doing here. It's our take on that tradition, or picking up where that tradition has left off. We're informed by so much that goes before us. We have to think we're having a signal moment, and I'm really enjoying it. I believe that even if we weren't doing this, someone else would. When we're done, when people perceive that our usefulness is over and done, somebody else is going to pick it up and learn from our mistakes.

MP: The reason to take a leadership role in anything is because you can see what needs to be done next. What I liked in the panel I listened to before sitting down with you is that I heard so many people who are clearly fellows or currently involved in some way, and they all really want to contribute to Cave Canem's evolution. That's going to help it evolve into whatever it needs to be.

CE: I have different ideas about what the evolution's going to be, but I believe that it's all due to those folks. They are really invested in it. I've seen changes in those participants and the faculty, and it readjusts the way you look at things. You start to realize that things you thought were impossible could be possible. It's also beset me with a kind of deep impatience. I'm no longer patient to sit and wait and listen to polite conversations about how things can't work. I know better now, and I have faith that Cave Canem poets are the best poets in the country right now. I don't think there's any poet who can hold a candle to what these guys do. It's one of the hidden benefits, one of the boons that came out of Toi and I just starting this thing. We had no idea who would come through the door, but these people are really the sharpest, most adventurous and brilliant writers to come along recently.

MP: That's great.

CE: I try not to say these things, because I'm cofounder of Cave Canem — I'm not trying to toot my own horn. The fact of the matter is when people start asking me who my favorite poets are, I tell them A. Van Jordan, Terrance Hayes, Honorée Fanonne Jeffers. Having read all the other poets in other contests, the Cave Canem poets are really the top of the line. Major Jackson's work was absolutely amazing. It's a confluence of a lot of different elements.

At this particular moment, this bunch of poets is all together at the same time going through their era together. This is their era, this really is their time. I have a feeling these are the young poets you'll be talking about for the next fifty years. I get to see young Terrance Hayes and young Major Jackson, get to see the paths they are carving out — and it's amazing to watch.

MP: It's been an explosion. In 2004, four Cave Canem poets went on to win grants from the National Endowments for the Arts.

CE: It was news-making. That's also part of the downside of Cave Canem. Everyone assumes good things happen to them because they're in a club.

MP: That they have an "in."

CE: But they don't have an "in." They're simply the best. It's this confluence of things that happen. They happened to be around at the same time we started to put out our baby steps for Cave Canem. It's all a symbiotic moment, and you can't plan for that.

MP: It's like you found each other.

CE: That's what it feels like to me.

[2006]

MP: I want to talk about you as a poet now. You have *Hardheaded Weather: New and Selected Poems* coming out, and that's a major event because a selected poems is the kind of thing where you take stock of yourself as a poet. How do you choose from among your children — your poems? You emphasize some poems over others, but you also include some new poems. Rita Dove said in one of her essays that, in a new and selected poems volume, the new poems show that the poet hasn't become dead wood yet. Did you come away from that process with a particular sense of who you are as a poet? Did you confirm any major themes or discern any key shifts in your style or technique?

CE: I wish I could say there was a great revelation that came to me from organizing the poems a certain way, but I didn't really learn anything new. I already knew I was writing about certain themes. I'm a very restless sort of poet and I don't really stick to one consistent style from book to book. I'm not doing metered, structured rhyme, but other than that, it's pretty much what I thought.

The book could have been organized a lot of ways. One way was chronologically — *Victims of the Latest Dance Craze, Gratitude, You Don't Miss Your Water*, then *Brutal Imagination* — thinking of them like long poems. Or, I could have organized the book starting with the book-length poems, and then the looser poems.

MP: That's interesting, because I hadn't even thought about the question of organization or of the length of the poems. So, you perceive that you have two major modes you write in? Some are longer, more series poems or sequences, and others are more occasional poems?

CE: Right.

MP: If I remember correctly, you also inserted your unpublished volume into the chronological line up.

CE: Yes. I put in what I tend to think of as my second book, in order. I also returned a lot of the poems that I cannibalized and used in other books back to the way they were originally written.

MP: You get to put your history back the way it should have been if that book had been published. So this way, you get to foreground your development as the primary narrative of this collection.

CE: That's the basic argument. The "why" of the book. It gives the reader a sense of how I developed as a writer and what the arc of my writing has been, at least up to this point, up to *Brutal Imagination*.

MP: The new poems in the collection focus on a house, "Lucky House." Can you talk a little bit about that? The house is often symbolic of identity.

CE: The house is a number of things. It's a sense of identity and a sense of body. I discovered that when I was diagnosed with prostate cancer and have been trying to work it out.

The house was bought a little before the start of the Iraq war, so we have that idea of just what *home* would be, and what that means nationally as well as personally. All those different threads are behind the metaphor of *house*. It's also just being in another location. My wife and I bought the house as a place to get away on weekends so we both have a place to write — my wife is a novelist.

MP: I'm thinking now of Adrienne Rich's essay called "Notes toward a Politics of Location." Perhaps you mean it on all those different levels.

CE: When people think about a summer house, they usually think about it as a grandiose kind of thing, but ours is very modest. It's on the wrong side of the Catskills, a very depressed part of the Catskills, which was the only real estate that we could afford to buy. It's not touristy at all. It's not like Woodstock or Red Hook on the other side of the river. Our house is in a working-class neighborhood. This plays to the idea of just where you are, write the poetry where you are. Because it's not touristy, you can see the Catskills in a certain kind of way that you don't get if you're simply going up there to hang out.

MP: You're resisting some of those assumptions that can go with the ivory tower poet who goes to his summer home. We knew you would resist this, of course.

CE: It is a vacation property, don't get me wrong. I'm not trying to delude myself about what the purpose of that house actually is. At the same time, it's not like visiting me if I was living in Woodstock. There's a totally different vibe there. The town is very depressed and there aren't a lot of shops open on the main street.

MP: It's not high class or privileged?

CE: No, not at all. Of course, there's always that danger because this is how it all starts, right? Folks like us go looking for inexpensive property and we buy it, and then other people start buying it. There's more resistance because the housing market is so depressed right now; people aren't buying a lot of property — so it's good and bad with us. People who live there might be very resistant to having people with more income coming in because of course that means that the residents who are there usually get priced out. Having lived in New York for so long, I'm very conscious of that. You have to deal with those issues, and that's what I've done in the poetry. "Cairo, New York" is one of the new poems that's trying to deal with that issue.

MP: It also suggests that you've reached a certain point in your career where you can make these kinds of choices. You can create a space where you can go to, and it's privileged in that sense. You're privileging your poetry and yourself in ways that will help your creativity.

CE: That's exactly right. What money is good for, I've said many times, is that it gives you time. This all turns on the idea of privilege. It's from writing, something that isn't necessarily seen as something honored in this country. *Unless* you're a very, very rich novelist or screenplay writer or you've sold to the movies or something like that. There is that sense of it being a privilege to have time to sit back and write — but it's a kind of earned privilege as well. It isn't that it was given to you. It's also a generational thing. I don't think younger writers deal with this or even care about it on the same level.

When I was being interviewed a couple weeks ago by Terry Gross for *Fresh Air* on NPR, she asked, "How does it feel to move out of the neighborhood? You're African American." I gave her the best answer I could at that moment. Later, I thought, well, I'm a successful writer — so? You want to be successful as a writer, and I come from a certain generation where the emphasis was to get out of the neighborhood. The idea was that you were *supposed* to; it was sort of an imperative to kids to do better than their parents. I chose my own path to do that, but inevitably and eventually that is where I landed. The implication is that when you succeed you forget. That's the fear, that you leave a neighborhood behind and in a sense forget who you are. I suddenly realized that people don't ask that question of Phil Levine, for example. They don't ask that question of other working-class people who come out of the same conditions we did. It's something uniquely connected to race.

MP: From the beginning your poetry is similar in philosophy to what Audre Lorde says: "Poetry is not a luxury" (37). You don't see this as an elite, privileged practice.

CE: Poetry, in my perception, is a tool. It wasn't meant to be something that was going to open a door for you. It was an instrument for change. This is how I've always looked at poetry. I wasn't looking at it as an accumulation of books, and that books would be a kind of success — or that I'd be able to teach at the university. I wasn't thinking on those levels. I come from a generation where poetry was seen as a political tool. When Terry Gross asked me that question about leaving the neighborhood, it drew me up sharp because it's not the way I was looking at poetry, but it was how she was looking at me now as a poet.

MP: Very interesting.

CE: You don't change your perspective of who you think you are — someone else tells you. It's like growing old. You get to a certain age and you don't feel like you're fifty-five years old, but suddenly somebody tells you or looks at you and reads you as fifty-five — and there it is. I realized that was that kind of moment with Terry. She was trying to say, "You're a very successful poet."

MP: And you thought "Who? Me?"

CE: Right. Deep down, I don't feel different. Normally I don't think of myself as separated from the neighborhood where I grew up.

MP: How much of your poetry do these people know? I don't want to cast aspersions on my predecessor interviewers.

CE: Let's go back to the idea of perception. I emerged at a certain point. For Terry, she discovered my work in an anthology. A lot of people said, "Who is this guy Cornelius Eady? I've never heard of him." That started to get them — and Terry — curious. She realized she had to come and read the poems for herself. But there's so much that got me to that moment that she didn't see.

MP: I tend to be incredibly linear in the way I prepare for these interviews. I buy all the books and I read them *in order*. I read all the previous print interviews. I pay attention to the development as it unfolds before me and I draw all these conclusions or make a lot of hypotheses based on that chronological reading. It's been helpful, mostly. I suppose I'm probably limiting myself in some way that I haven't figured out, but for me, it helps me see poets the way they might see themselves — as they unfold into who they become as writers.

CE: Exactly. Then you're at a certain point. Usually, wherever people come in at and intersect that storyline is all they know about.

MP: And you can't control that, can you?

CE: No — like being fifty-five years old and not thinking of yourself that way until someone points it out. Suddenly, there you have it. Poets who come out of my generation definitely see poetry as a societal tool. It's meant to have a certain kind of connection to a certain kind of group that you identify yourself with. It's also meant to be a bit of an argument. There needs to be space for this kind of story. These kinds of experiences need to be documented and be considered in the same breath as everything else. Cave Canem is the ultimate reflection of the idea that you give back and encourage other people, and give back to the population.

MP: Let's talk about some of your earlier volumes. In both *The Gathering of My Name* and *The Autobiography of a Jukebox* — both of which I see as identity volumes — music figures prominently. There's blues, jazz, poems about musical figures, and a CD of your own music and autobiography. This thread is interwoven in the volumes with poems depicting brutally racist incidents. Could you talk about how you see the relationship between black music and racism? How does that understanding infuse your identity and aesthetic as a black male poet?

CE: It's about black creativity — that's the fastest way of explaining it. It's the idea that we have the ability and the skills for creativity, and jazz was one of the venues we had because there was no other way of expressing it. In the ghetto, you can't do what you want to do. It's an expression of African American creativity into the world and influencing the culture the musicians live in. I took that as a jumping-off point and as an inspiration. Sports are another option — music and sports were the two realms that were left open for African Americans who want to be creative. I know it's more complex than this — there are dancers and painters and all sorts of other ways that African Americans have been creating themselves — but music seemed to me the most immediate and direct way.

MP: It's interesting that it's tied so much in your poetry to the trauma of racism. That's the theme that comes back again and again in the poems interspersed throughout those volumes. Do you see racism as a wellspring of creativity or a source?

CE: It's a number of things. When you talk about it in terms of the music, it's one of those things where basically you're dealing with a certain kind of silence or a kind of disinclination to listen or to acknowledge. That's what racism really does. In some ways the response is clandestine in the sense of where you find the creating going on — it's in the urban neighborhoods, in the ghettos, in the small towns and clubs. It's in the networking of jazz clubs and the passing of knowledge between musicians. Then, it reaches another audience that starts to listen to all this wonderful stuff that's coming out, wondering where it is, where it's coming from. Still, it's like shouting at silence.

MP: Yes, and like you were saying before — I don't think you used this word, but you are *documenting* it — telling the story in your poems.

CE: *Documenting* — that's it. That's what I was looking for. I felt that, as a poet, that this is the story and this is what you hear when you're hearing a jazz musician. I have a story I've told many times. It's when Michael Harper came to town when I was in my early twenties and living in Rochester. He came to do a workshop, and he played a tape of John Coltrane doing "A Love Supreme," singing his "I am a black man. I'm a black man," and I suddenly realized that what he's doing, what he's telling me, is that there is a connection between the lyric on the page that he is reading and the music. They're telling a story that is being overlooked.

It's the imperative in the lines "I am a black man, I am, I am," that kind of shout that he chronicles and puts down on the page. When you hear a jazz musician doing this, that's what that musician is doing. You have to make a declaration against this big silence that says, "We don't want to hear" or "We don't have to hear and take you seriously." All that is the truth of the voice.

MP: It reminds me of several of your poems. I wonder if that moment with Harper was a defining moment for you, because it fused with your poetic identity?

CE: It wasn't exactly the *eureka* moment. I got it kind of subconsciously. I started to slowly integrate that into my work. The early work is doing other things. It's being almost surrealist in some ways. I was reading some of those poems the other day and I suddenly realized that a great deal of this work is about me dealing with the poets I was reading at the time. You find your touchstone poets. You find yourself in conversation with those writers.

Going back to your first question, what did I find out organizing the newest selections in my *New and Selected Poems*? Maybe one of the things I found was the fingerprints of all those other poets. For example, in the early poems I see a lot of talking to Niconar Parra, the Chilean poet who was writing what he calls anti-poems. I started reading him in the late sixties, early seventies. For some reason, that really gripped my imagination. When I'm reading things like "White Fox," for example, or "Living with Genius," I really see Niconar's hand in there. I'm not saying this is a Niconar poem, but I'm talking to him — kind of a conversation that I'm having. It's like writing a letter to Niconar.

So this goes back to Michael Harper and jazz. I wasn't consciously reacting to what Michael did with that poem, but unconsciously I was talking back to that point where you start to see certain kinds of consciousness, some kind of music. That's me talking back to Michael Harper.

MP: This question goes back into the past because I hadn't seen this detail anywhere before, but I came across it on the Notre Dame Web site. I read that you earned your MFA at Warren Wilson. Is that true? This school is revered down in North Carolina where I work. It's in the mountains in a pretty isolated area. It doesn't match my idea of you as a poet. Can you talk about Warren Wilson and its impact on you as a poet?

CE: It's complicated. First of all, I did *not* get an MFA. I was in the program but I didn't finish the degree. If they're listing me as getting an MFA from Warren Wilson, it's inaccurate and it didn't come from me.

MP: It might have said you *attended* the program there, so I could have drawn my own conclusions.

CE: They knew when I came in that I didn't hold an MFA degree, so I'm kind of surprised if that's what they did. Warren Wilson — this is complicated. Their MFA program was new. It's a very good program in a lot of ways. It's a very small program — at least when I was there — and a really strong faculty.

I studied with Stephen Dobyns and Heather McHugh, and I learned a lot there. This was back in the early 1980s and I had just finished teaching at my first college teaching job at Sweet Briar College as a writer in residence. I got to a point where I felt I had gone as far as I could go. I didn't have any degrees. I had one book and was struggling to get my second book out. I thought it might be a good time to go back to school and get a degree. I tried to get into the University of Virginia, but I couldn't do that. I did a workshop at the University of Virginia with Grey Gar and Charles Wright — it was a fabulous workshop. At the end of it, Grey told me there was a program he was teaching in at Warren Wilson, and we thought their program might be perfect for me.

I'll try to tell this in a fair way because I don't want this to sound like this was a victim's story or that they were evil. Looking back after all these years, it was a mismatch about who I was as a writer and who they were at that particular time as a program. I didn't fit the typical profile for an MFA student at that time. First, I was African American. I was also older, married, had one book out, and I had done some teaching. I had a certain idea about what poetry was about. I wasn't a blank slate. After I had registered at Warren Wilson, lighting struck, which is what happens sometimes in a career. I won a National Endowment for the Arts grant before I got there. I arrived with an NEA and left there with a Lamont prize.

There was an odd reaction from the people at Warren Wilson. That's the best way I can put it. Having taught all these years since, and having run a creative writing program now at Notre Dame, it mystifies me that there was a lack of support and enthusiasm for earning these awards, to tell the truth. At any other of the places I've taught, if you had a first-year student who came in and had won an NEA and then a Lamont prize the second year, that person would be your poster child from then on. That wasn't the case. In fact, there was a lack of enthusiasm and people were — on the surface — saying yes, but I got the feeling that there was something awful. They were thinking, *What the hell happened, who's this kid? He's one step away from the ghetto. No one knows who he is.* It bent everyone's nose out of joint when I won the Lamont prize. Not everybody, to be fair. It wasn't the entire faculty, but there was this vibe.

MP: That explains several things to me. One is the way you talked earlier in this interview about Cave Canem and some of the reasons why you feel there is a need for it. Obviously many people agree with you. This puts the little puzzle piece into place. Also, my reaction to seeing Warren Wilson in your biography was surprise. I knew it didn't fit. That was just my instinct. The Cornelius Eady who's in my head and the Warren Wilson that's in my head — I couldn't make those two go together.

CE: They didn't go together, you're right.

MP: I love it when intuition pays off. I understand, too, why you are trying not to turn it into a victim story or say they were all bad. It sounds like they were used to a certain kind of student who would come in as an apprentice and would be nurtured and created by them — and you were already half-formed.

CE: Exactly. I was not an apprentice. I wasn't a star in any sense of the word, but I wasn't an apprentice either. They couldn't read me well. I got this weird kind of vibe out of it, and it's one of those things that — as I get distanced from it more — I come to realize was really odd.

MP: I think *odd* is a very generous way of putting it.

CE: I just want to be as fair as I can. I was young and headstrong in a lot of ways. I had a certain kind of attitude, and I'm sure that came across as well. I'm saying that I wasn't totally blameless in this. I did expect a certain kind of response. I started to hear things about certain faculty that were sort of disturbing — about me being there. Then, a couple of things happened that convinced me that going back was not the smartest thing in the world for me to do. It didn't feel safe.

MP: I'd agree that it was time to "get out of Dodge" at that point.

CE: It felt that way to me. There are many ways of dealing with this. There was another student from Warren Wilson who was telling me the story about this happening to him, and he went to Rita Dove. Rita told him to "suck it up" and get through it — you're going to find bad people everywhere. Now this person has Cave Canem, right? At that time, they had a Rita Dove to go to, but I didn't have a Rita Dove, and I was on my own. I knew half of the African American poets, and if they had known what was going on they probably would have wanted to burn the place down. Sometimes, your gut instinct tells you that distance is the only thing that's going to solve the problem. That's what it felt like to me. The joke I've been making lately about how to deal with racial situations is to be like Arnold Schwarzenegger in *Terminator*. He's in some sleazy hotel and a guy is yelling at him, and you see a grid behind his eyes with all these different responses — one is shoot him, another is to beat him up, and then there's the option of saying, "Screw you, asshole." Sometimes you're in a moment and you blow it off, or you get angry, and sometimes you fight. Other times you might flee. I had to make a choice. Whatever the problem was with me, whatever the complication, it didn't seem healthy to me. I dropped out.

MP: You obviously had some indications that you'd be able to go ahead and keep making a living as a poet even without an MFA, so it seems like your choice made a lot of sense.

CE: Yes. If you asked them, they would probably say something along the lines of, "He peaked in the program," or "He didn't need the program." To a certain extent, that's exactly true. When I won the Lamont prize I realized it had made my career. It gave me the foundation for everything else. The experience with Warren Wilson wasn't a bad experience in the sense that it made me conscious of just what was lacking out there. It started this *itch* that only got scratched when I met Toi and we started Cave Canem. Without that experience I'd have been a lot more serene. I might have been one of those poets saying I don't see a need for a program like Cave Canem. Adversity is sometimes a good thing for you — if it doesn't kill you! It puts you on a different path. The path it put me on started me toward what would become Cave Canem. There are no losers here. At the moment when I was in it, it was a very uncomfortable place to be. One regret I do have is that I wish it had gone differently. I also realize it wasn't up to me to make that situation worth doing. For that situation to work it had to be the world we're living in right now.

MP: Let's talk about a few specific poems because I always like to dip into the poems a bit. Of course, there are a lot. I could talk about "Gratitude," or have you talk about it, as it's such an important poem.

CE: "Gratitude" was one of the reactions from Warren Wilson. I'm basically working out my time at Warren Wilson.

MP: That's helpful to know because it is such an identity poem. What about "Sherbet"? One of the things I thought of when I first read it is that it's kind of an anti–ars poetica. Have you thought about it in that way?

CE: I don't know what you mean by anti–ars poetica.

MP: In an ars poetica, oftentimes the poet is defining their poetic or commenting on what poetry is. You seem to be defining what poetry *is not*, at least for your purposes.

CE: You know what it is? It's not about my poetic, but it's about one of the things I picked up at Warren Wilson — the idea of the epiphany, which was really big when I was there. They wanted the epiphany, and the epiphany was going to be a sort of magic wand that will *boiiing* and everything will move from disorder into order. I realized that, sometimes, epiphany is not a pleasant experience. Sometimes it is learning, the breakthrough — a painful thing. That's what "Sherbet" is actually about.

MP: So it's an anti-epiphany poem?

CE: It's not even anti-epiphany. Not anti–ars poetica, not anti-epiphany, but simply saying that epiphany can also be this. You can sit in the moment and suddenly realize, "Wow," there you are. There is a kind of cautious reasoning there, but sometimes the epiphany is not a good thing. Sometimes the revelation isn't a revelation — but it is an epiphany. That's pretty much what it was. I was fueled by the idea of what everyone seemed to be very hot to put to the page.

MP: There's also *The Autobiography of a Jukebox* with the poem "Hard Times," where you place yourself in a poetic genealogy with Etheridge Knight — although you don't explicitly say that.

CE: Absolutely. There are a few poets out there that we work under the shadow of — Gwendolyn Brooks, Langston Hughes, Amiri Baraka. I feel that way. And Etheridge definitely.

MP: What continuities do you feel with him and what divergences?

CE: He's a little before me, but he's also not modern. He's sort of like a go-between, even though he was there in it. He's definitely Black Arts Movement with Sonia Sanchez. The stuff he's writing is slightly different. It isn't all polemic, it isn't all about the struggle or the problems. He does claim that territory, but you see these other kinds of poems coming out that are slightly different. Some of his poems are apart from whatever else he is agreeing makes up the aesthetic of an African American poet at that moment.

MP: I found his poems to be very sensitive.

CE: *Tender* is the word I was thinking of.

MP: Yes, and I'm thinking particularly of "The Idea of Ancestry." Every time I teach it I want to cry. I think he put his finger on an emotional truth, and that's why it's not polemic.

CE: Absolutely. There's a slight stepping toward where we are now. He is one of those poets who opened that possibility, or pushed it a little bit. I was trying to make a claim that I'm part of that because I — and the other poets of my age, too — have been influenced by those poems. There are very few *eureka* moments in writing poetry. You have to realize that a lot of people set the road open for you. Sometimes you're conscious of who preceded you, and sometimes you're not. It changes the atmosphere and allows you to breathe. Before, there was no air at all. Etheridge Knight is definitely one of those poets who made it possible for someone like me to go on and be tender. There's a bit of male tenderness in his work that I don't see in the other poets to the same degree. I was trying to acknowledge that in that poem.

I also regret that I never got to meet him. We came close to meeting once. We were both on the same campus but not on the same day — the same semester but not the same day. Etheridge left a note in my mailbox, something like "Hey, I hear you're here." I thought that the poetry world was small and sooner or later our paths would cross at a conference or a reading. I wasn't that concerned about it. I didn't make an effort to go and see him, and I regret that. I didn't realize that would be my only chance to meet him. He was gone soon after that. So, maybe the poem is also me talking to Etheridge. Besides being a poem, it's also a letter to Etheridge.

MP: Because he gave you permission in some ways to be the kind of poet you became. That's neat. You have a series of poems about your father in *You Don't Miss Your Water*. I noticed that most of those are prose poems. Is there any particular reason for that shift?

CE: Yes, because that's the only form that worked for me. I tried a lot of different approaches to the subject matter, and in the end, a prose poem was the best way for me to trick myself into writing what I needed to write. The standard-line verse construction wasn't working for me. There was so much I wanted to say, and trying to put it into that container wasn't satisfying. I wrote some poems in that form, but they're not published. It just didn't seem *done*.

MP: That's interesting. There are two different directions I could take that. One is that the prose poem allowed more narrative . . .

CE: Absolutely.

MP: It was the narrative imperative. So you think that's it?

CE: Yes. I think it needed more narrative than [the container] was actually allowing me to have in the conventional way I write.

MP: I also wonder if the formalism would seem a foreign container for those experiences.

CE: Yes. I'm not a formalist, but I subscribe to the idea that there's no such thing as free verse, in the sense that the poet has to organize the poem somehow. The prose poem to me was the organizational structure I needed.

MP: Then just two years later, you have this series of poems about your mother in *The Autobiography of a Jukebox*. In that series, the poem "The House" seems to be about the central idea of inheritances.

CE: I wasn't thinking of it along those lines, but you're right. I'm thinking of this in terms of my relationship with my parents and how property wasn't really that big of a deal for me. My parents came from a generation for which property was a big deal. My father was thought of as affluent in a totally working-class neighborhood because owning a house was a big deal. You could get a job — they weren't going to stop you from getting a job — and you could get a house in the neighborhood. It was a neighborhood where everyone owned their house, but it wasn't a rich neighborhood. It broke down for my parents because my mother never owned anything. People judged you by how much money you had — if you didn't have money, who were you? My dad never thought far enough ahead to think to leave the property to my mother, and that was the sad part about her situation. It was also tough that she was a schizophrenic at that time. In some ways, it was a blessing that she didn't get the property, because that would have made things even more complicated after he died.

MP: All of this circles around the figure of the house and the inheritance — or not — of the house. It's interesting when we circle back to the current volume of poetry and these houses. You made a point when we were first talking about "Lucky House" that it was *earned*; it wasn't given.

CE: It's funny to use that terminology because it ties back to that working-class ethos. I've always considered myself one of those people who escaped all of that, but actually it pops up in moments like this. I regurgitate something that is deeply ingrained in me — and hidden. I wasn't even conscious of it. Where do I use it? *Earned*, just like my parents would have used it, right?

MP: Exactly.

CE: It's funny you end up thinking about it, the idea of that house again. It's also kind of sad because I have a house, but I don't have my family. I have *a* family in the sense that I have my wife and we have a life together, but my parents never knew about this house.

MP: Just two years separate the publications of the series about your father and the series about your mother. It's often the case that there's a male lineage for inheritance of the house or the property. But for you, the house figures much more prominently in the mother's series of poems. In terms of an identity matrix emanating from that house, it's really not about the house at that point. It's more about the identity that you inherit — and that's through the mother, at least in those poems.

CE: I totally agree with that. It's kind of a tragedy, of course. It really wasn't much of a house, especially by the time my mom was living there. We had to give it up and force my mother out of the house because she was in such bad shape. We were really starting to worry about her living by herself, and we felt she needed to be safe. In order to do that, we had to lose the house. It was a traumatic thing — not only dealing with an ailing mother, but the house, too. She couldn't take care of herself. We had fantasies of course that when my dad was gone my mother would have her life restored.

That the things she wasn't able to do, she'd find the strength to do. I suddenly realized that time had run out for her. When a parent dies your life becomes *your* life. It becomes the kid's world finally. This isn't about grief or mourning, which I went through plenty of, but it was about the realization that now is the rest of your life. I was hoping to have the same thing for my mom. I was hoping she'd be able to get out of the house, drive, that she'd be able to take the house over. That didn't happen. In fact, the opposite happened. We had to kick her out of the house. Losing the house, even though it wasn't a great house, was a really traumatic experience.

MP: You think back to the house or houses of your childhood and it's your identity. You put your mind's eye in that house, and your whole identity formation is taking place in those spaces.

CE: It's where I grew up. If there's any place that's a central location to my life, it's that. The situation also seemed to be duplicated — it started a long decline, I felt. A lot of her friends started dying off, so people who I saw as surrogate moms were gone, too. I still had friends' places where I could crash, but it's not the same idea. I didn't even live in my parents' home after seventeen or eighteen, but I kept returning there to visit. A second surrogate home was my mentor's. I studied poetry with her as an undergraduate, and my wife and I had an apartment in her basement. That's gone, too. Most of my friends, they're all gone. Those physical locations are no longer there. I have a space, but the friends that I wanted to have in that space are no longer there. I put all that in the title poem "Hard Weather."

MP: In *Brutal Imagination* I see everything coming together for you poetically with those two black male personae — the fictitious black male who Susan Smith said took her boys, and then also Running Man. The long poem "Brutal Imagination" is just brilliant. I wish I could call up my students from those harrowing days down in North Carolina when the Smith case was unfolding. I was teaching two different Black Literature classes, and I wish we could have a week in which we read these poems. We spent all that time talking about this crisis in class instead of the stuff on the syllabus. One part you get so accurately is Susan Smith's point of view. What was it like to write those poems and enter her mindset? I confess, I try not to go there.

CE: You have to understand this was a fictional Susan. I'm not only constructing the African American guy, I was also constructing Susan Smith. That really isn't her.

MP: I know, but you get it so right.

CE: Thank you. The point is you want that person to feel authentic. You want the rightness of it to resonate and to feel like the real thing. I'm very glad to hear you say that because it makes me feel that the work I put into it paid off. I did a lot of research on this when I was writing. I knew what people were saying about Susan Smith, and I tried to incorporate that into the piece. Even though it's not autobiographical in any way shape or form, that vibe is there. The Susan I'm making is a fictional Susan. You'll never know what she was really thinking. I don't think she really understood what she was doing and why she did what she did. I do know that there were certain things she was drawing upon. The material for the boogie man is out there, and she knew this. It was almost as if there's a communal understanding about the role of African Americans — especially guys. We're dangerous, we're highly sexualized, and we're violent. It's a common thread that she was trying to run so she could make enough distraction to get away with it. If she could construct that guy the way I constructed her, she could get away with it.

MP: You could have tried to make her a flat character, so to speak, and the fictitious black man as a fully fleshed-out character because of what you're saying about the consensus understanding of black men. Instead, you insisted that she be rounded out, too. It reminds me of how Toni Morrison would often have a character that she could have made flat — like Cholly in *The Bluest Eye*. He's a rapist, but she gives him all this background and makes you enter the pain of his mind. That's what you did with Susan Smith. You had to figure her out to a pretty large extent and to some extent, know her. You're very nice to claim that it's not her and it's fictitious, yet there are things about a young white female southern mindset that you put in a good perspective.

CE: How that dread or that fear feels is something I know myself. I had to tap into that. There are also certain things we know about her from the story in the newspapers — the idea that she was trying to climb the social ladder by hooking up with some rich accountant. There's a fantasy about who she is and what the world's supposed to be about for her. There's a hunger there. It comes from the idea that she wants to have a world where she's acknowledged. She wants this new life for herself. She's trying to cobble together a story and a character that would be sort of like Frankenstein. No physicality, but the idea. She makes up this person who has some kind of gait, and she probably gets this from driving back and forth and seeing these guys on the street. People said that her path from her house to her job would have passed this area in town and she was focusing subconsciously on one or two people that actually got pulled in and questioned. These little details are all put together and that's where she's getting this information — this is how she started to think about it. She's trying to cobble together this monster made out of *real people.*

The miracle part of this is that the police, the sheriff, and the FBI wouldn't buy her story. It's an interesting thing because you realize if you change the scenario a little bit, put a different person in, it could have gone a different way. People were thirsting for resolution. They wanted to find somebody. If they couldn't find the kids, they had to find somebody to blame. But change the character of the players just a little bit, and you could have found the wrong guy in the wrong place. The wrong FBI director or field agent, or the sheriff who was looking to be reelected, or a new sheriff, or if there was an election going on for sheriff. You thank God it didn't go that way, but it could have gone that way, and we would have been having a conversation about this guy on death row right now.

MP: It reminded me, too — the way you enter her mindset — of the Gwendolyn Brooks poem "A Bronzeville Mother Loiters in Mississippi. Meanwhile a Mississippi Mother Burns Bacon." Your poem isn't a ballad, but it's the same in the sense of getting into the mindset of the white southern female. There's a narrative that the speaker wants to follow: "I want to be a princess."

CE: Yes. They want to be great and have a different destiny — and they want it right now. That was definitely one thing motivating Susan Smith.

MP: In both cases, these white women are also seen as victims themselves of violence. They are perpetuating that in the way they are allowing other people to be victimized on their behalf.

CE: Absolutely. There was abuse in Susan Smith's background and there's this cycle that she's in the middle of.

MP: It would have been so easy for you to leave that out and then it could have been a poem that's a polemic and not more tender. We go back to Etheridge Knight and understanding the sensitivities of the situation — the emotional trauma that's behind her point of view as well.

CE: If you can't see that, then it doesn't work. I learned that from doing *You Don't Miss Your Water.* I suddenly realized that I couldn't portray my father as a monster in the book, even as complicated as my relationship was with him. It would have been intellectually and poetically dishonest for me to set this up with me as the hero of the book. It's the absolute worst move you could make as a writer — to pretend, or to ignore what's potentially on the page. If you don't see my dad as a three-dimensional, complicated character, then you're not going to enter the book. If you can't enter the book, then why write it at all.

MP: Now I'd like to talk about the "Running Man" cycle of poems — most of which were the libretto for a jazz opera. These seem to me to be your most experimental poetry because you create these archetypal figures and seemingly are not drawing upon autobiographical material.

CE: It's not *my* story. It's Deidre Murray's brother. I'm making a fictionalized version of Deidre's brother. That's really what Running Man is.

MP: Where's the story? Did she write a memoir?

CE: No. Deidre and I were working together and she had an idea for a story about a guy who goes bad. She was thinking in terms of where the location was going to be — she had it all worked out. She wanted it to be on the eastern shore of Virginia in a black town. I told her to tell me the story, and I realized the story she was really telling was asking, "Who is my brother? How could I not have known him? How could I not have known this guy who I loved and who turned me on to art and music?" I started asking Deidre questions — told her to tell me about her brother. Every so often I'd hear something and I'd say, "Ah! — there's a poem." Later, I'd show the poem to her and ask if I got it right. It would be either yes or no, and she started taking the poems and setting them to music. That's how we started to get the libretto and the score together. Deidre wanted to find out how she could have been so close to somebody and not know who he was. "Running Man" becomes a journey of exploration. If you saw "Running Man" as an opera, that's what you'd get.

What happens to Running Man is not what happened to Deidre's brother, but there are some real things in it. Like for example, the poem about the radio is a true story. Deidre is a musician because of her brother. He's the one who turned on the radio and told her to listen to all these jazz musicians. The poem about the parent who sticks the toothbrush up his anus, that's based on a true story. What happened with the brother — the dynamics between the mother and the father — are based on real things. The father didn't have people piss on him in the war in a ditch — I really like that one. After *Running Man* the opera was a hit, I had a drink with Kurt Vonnegut and his wife . . .

MP: Oh my.

CE: I know, I couldn't believe it! I was in a bar in Soho having drinks, and Kurt asks me if that really happened with the father — if he was really pissed on. I told him it wasn't [from life], but he thought it was plausible. In a really hostile world, the best thing [the father] could do was to keep his head down. That's what he learned about the world. And his mother wanted to be in the world but couldn't be in the world — a woman at that time couldn't be in the world. She was living vicariously through the son. She wanted him to go out and do anything he could. He could do no wrong. That's based on Deidre's family. Deidre's brother did not murder anybody — all that stuff there is made up. The other stuff that happened is based on real things.

MP: Interesting, because he does that arc — the trajectory does come off as a very archetypal sort of trajectory. I wonder if that isn't the highest compliment that could be paid to it, becoming a libretto. There's something about opera: it is always about these universal traumas. Somehow that story about her brother did become an archetypal, universal story.

CE: That was the absolute genius of Deidre — she sensed that this was something that could be blown up into an opera. This is her story, not mine. I didn't invent Running Man, I'm simply there as a writer. There was really the genius of her instinctively knowing that these are archetypes.

MP: They really are, even though the particulars as you've been talking can be tied directly to her family — and some of them not at all. The particulars add up to something very universal.

CE: She got it right. The more I started working on this, I realized she was on to something. You see some universality in the mother. We had this wonderful aria for the mother that's not in the book. It's when she finally realizes that the son is just no good.

MP: He's a sociopath!

CE: Right. That's what he is, who he really is, and thus we have that moment with the mother, and then one for the daughter, who basically has to turn her brother away. That is one of the best things I wrote because it pulled the scales away to reveal, "This is what you are."

MP: That's incredible. One of those sticky spots that I found myself in teaching that last year is that my students read "Running Man" very reductively. They immediately came to the conclusion that he's gay. Even more reductively, they said "Cornelius Eady is gay." I'll tell you, Cornelius, I don't know if I ever convinced them, and I really worked hard. I kept telling them how the character wasn't necessarily the poet's voice — that you create personae and on and on. That was one of the aspects that was difficult in teaching that.

CE: I know. The poem about the toothbrush is the one that students glom onto. It had nothing to do with me. It doesn't bother me for them to think I'm gay, but the fact of the matter is that they really believe that there is this story about this black guy who has a sexual thing and he's punished. It's very reductive. There's a lot going on. In the opera you'd get a little more clarity. There is a complicated thing going on with the mother and son, and yet there is this sexuality we're trying to get at. We're trying to avoid going, "Aha! You're gay!" The true Running Man was not in that sense.

MP: I found myself trying to explain to my students how one could have these sexual experiences or traumatic experiences as a child, and that might impact one's development and sexuality — and it was just too simplistic to then turn around and say he was gay. I found myself at a loss for vocabulary. We had read four poets that semester, and you were the last one. We had already read Cyrus Cassells, and there were some overtly gay poems in his work. I wondered why they couldn't tell the difference.

CE: I have had this moment, too, especially when I go to black colleges and they *really* want to know. I'm not Running Man. I've been married for thirty years, but I don't always come right out and say this — I get sort of mischievous.

The other thing that I think is that sometimes the students are talking about their own sexuality. I think there are students out there saying, "That's me." They don't feel comfortable actually coming out and saying, "I'm gay, too." I feel that's the scenario they would like to have happen. Maybe I disappoint them when I say this is a fictional character, when what they might really want to hear me say is, "Yes, I'm gay," so they can say, "And so am I." It's hard to read what the students are actually trying to tell you, or if what's going on is titillation — which I think they also go for.

MP: How do these two sequences — "Running Man" and "Brutal Imagination"— go together in the book? I'm sure you didn't just say they added up to a book because to you it's enough pages.

CE: To me, they're like cousins in the sense that one is the idea of a mythical guy, and then the other is a real guy who becomes mythical.

MP: The archetypal — that's true in a pair of volumes of Rita Dove's where she moves from the particular to the mythical and then back again.

CE To me, that's the arc of "Brutal Imagination." One of the poems in the new section of *Hardheaded Weather* — the poem is for Joe Wood — is an earlier version of what was going to be the first poem of "Brutal Imagination."

MP: I saw that there was going to be something similar going on with those poems, and I wonder a little bit about how they all fit.

CE: The poem for Joe Wood is about someone who disappears — who was there but not seen. Then, someone who was mythical who's real becomes mythical again. I thought of those poems talking to one another. That's when you get to the last section of the first poem — where is the young black man? That's the idea I want you to have in your head as you turn the page into "Brutal Imagination": a man who isn't there but is.

I thought of all three of those poems as talking to one another in that way and about mythology being in the particular. The "Brutal Imagination" and "Running Man" poems were definitively so close — talking to one another. I felt that they needed to be in the same place. The style is totally different, but even so, I felt that they needed to be together.

MP: Was I right in seeing that *Hardheaded Weather* originally had a different title? Was it supposed to be *The War against the Obvious*?

CE: Yes, that's the last line in "Jazz Dancer" in my book *Victims of the Latest Dance Craze*. I've had that title for decades, and I held onto it for a while, but it seemed that the book had changed. The range of the poems didn't feel like *The War against the Obvious* to me anymore — it didn't feel like a war at all.

MP: No, it doesn't fit the house poems.

CE: My point exactly. It felt different, so it needed a different title. I really felt that *Hardheaded Weather* was a much better and friendlier way into the book.

MP: What's next? What are you working on now, and where are you going?

CE: It's on to the next thing, which is the next book.

MP: Poets never know where they're going, right?

CE: No. Hopefully it will be a book, better sooner than later. I'm also working on some theater pieces with Deidre. I'd like to do more theater. I've really been feeling out of it for a few years. I need to get back to write some more — so hopefully in the next year or so there's going to be some movement on that.

MP: I have to thank you, Cornelius; this has been a delight.

CE: I enjoyed it, too. I hope I gave you something useful!

[2008]

CYRUS CASSELLS

Cyrus Cassells has wide-ranging interests: the author of four books of poetry, he is also an actor and translator and is writing his first novel. He travels extensively and speaks four languages. He is currently a professor of English at Texas State University at San Marcos.

Cassells was born May 16, 1957, in Dover, Delaware, and was raised in Southern California. His mother was a tutor and homemaker, and his father was a graduate of West Point and career military officer who pursued a master's degree in engineering at the University of Washington and became an aerospace engineer. Cassells's childhood was shaped by the civil rights movement's desegregation of institutions such as the military and the public schools, and a home environment that nurtured the arts and reading. His father's stories of travel fueled Cassells's interest in other countries and inculcated in him a global perspective; early exposure to Spanish initiated a lifelong multilinguality that enabled his transnationalism, leading to his fluency in Spanish, Italian, and French. A study-abroad year in Japan in 1978 contributed another dimension to his international interests and provided the experiences undergirding the third section of his first book of poetry, *The Mud Actor* (1982). Cassells graduated from Stanford University with a BA in 1979; he studied poetry with Linda Gregerson and also trained extensively in the drama department. He was a fellow at the Fine Arts Work Center in Provincetown, Massachusetts, in 1982–83; while he was there, *The Mud Actor* was named a 1982 National Poetry Series selection. During this time he met Terry Pitzner, who was his partner for a decade; in 1986 they moved to Boston, where Cassells worked on translations from the Catalan of Salvador Espriu, Catalonia's main candidate for the Nobel Prize in Literature. Cassells's teaching career began in 1987. He taught, variously, at Chamberlayne Junior College, College of the Holy Cross, Assumption College, Northeastern, and Emerson College until 1993; in that year, his relationship with Pitzner ended, and he moved to Rome until 1997, working in the film and theater industry as an actor and a dubber. While there, he studied acting with Carolynn de Fonseca. Cassells's father was diagnosed with lung cancer in 1997, so Cassells relocated to San Francisco to be closer to him; while there, he studied at Kurt Wagner's mystery school for the spiritual training of gay men. He joined the faculty at Texas State University at San Marcos as an assistant professor of English in the fall of 1998. While living in Texas from 1998 to 2007, Cassells pursued select acting opportunities in university and Austin, Texas, productions, including the role of Fielding in August Wilson's *Jitney* and a one-man show on Frederick Douglass. He also served as dramaturge for a production of Lorca's *Blood Wedding* in 2004. Cassells began teaching at Cave Canem in 1996.

Cyrus Cassells's poetry has a lushly sensual and spiritual quality unique among his contemporaries. His work is perhaps the most insistently transnational of this generation, with poems set in Afghanistan, America, Japan, and Spain, among many other countries. His themes often revolve around the relationship between trauma and beauty and trace lineages back to the troubadours, the American civil rights movement, and prophetic traditions. He has consistently explored black gay sexuality and aesthetics.

Cassells's poetry can be viewed in the lineage of Robert Duncan (of the San Francisco school), who saw the poet as a seer and whose work is considered Romantic. (Duncan was himself influenced by the modernist H. D., whose poetry Cassells admires.) Cassells sees his poetic stance as empathetic toward other people and cultures, perhaps due to his training as a mystic in the late 1990s in San Francisco. One theme across his work is finding insight amid horror. Many of his poems follow a poet-seer who traverses a landscape of hardship and discovers meaning. His poems, while highly crafted and not particularly free-ranging, present a meditative open form unfolding revelation. Cassells himself sees his work as influenced by Federico Garcia Lorca, whose passionate lyricism and intense themes resonate with Cassells; he functions as a gay spiritual father and poetic mentor in Cassells's *More than Peace and Cypresses*.

While Cassells's poetry has received mostly positive reviews and his poem "Soul Make a Path through Shouting" has been widely anthologized, scholarly attention to his work has been minimal, with two interviews and one journal article on his post-soul cosmopolitanism. Fruitful areas for critical attention include a queer analysis of *Beautiful Signor*, the geography of *More than Peace and Cypresses*, and *Soul Make a Path through Shouting* as a millennial text. A comparativist study of his work alongside that of

Reginald Shepherd and Carl Phillips could contribute considerably to an understanding of contemporary black gay poetry. Awards Cassells has won include the Poetry Society of America's William Carlos Williams Award and finalist nod for the Lenore Marshall Prize for outstanding book of the year for *Soul Make a Path through Shouting*, which was also named one of the Best Books of 1994 by *Publishers Weekly*. *Beautiful Signor* won a 1997 Lambda Literary Award. Cassells is currently seeking a publisher for his new manuscript, "The Crossed-Out Swastika."

I interviewed Cassells on March 30, 2001, at University of North Carolina, Charlotte with several students in attendance. He had visited my African American Poetry class earlier in the day.

Selected Poetry by Cyrus Cassells

The Mud Actor, Holt, Rinehart and Winston, 1982.
Soul Make a Path through Shouting, Copper Canyon Press, 1994.
Beautiful Signor, Copper Canyon Press, 1997.
More than Peace and Cypresses, Copper Canyon Press, 2004.

MALIN PEREIRA: So much of one's art begins with childhood experiences and ways of living. How does your upbringing relate to your becoming a poet?

CYRUS CASSELLS: From the beginning, I knew that I was going to be a writer. Often, one waits for an adult to give permission to go ahead, but I was already writing. I got the assignment of doing the class prophesy in fourth or fifth grade. I was very excited about that. Also, my father had bought a set of encyclopedias when I was born — which really wasn't a very practical thing, because by the time I was old enough to use them they were out of date — and I remember going to the *N* volume to read about the history of the novel because I thought, "This is what I want to do." I began collecting stories from my relatives and my family when I was young — I had both sets of grandparents and my paternal great-grandparents — and I was fascinated with their history because I figured that I was going to use it later on in my writing. I was always remembering the titles of novels and wondering what kind of book I was going to write.

My mother was a big reader, so there were always books and magazines around. I read all the ladies' magazines; that is how I got introduced to Toni

Morrison's work because there was an excerpt of *Sula* in one magazine. My mother was also a lover of literature, so there was a lot of support for books in the house. My parents are an interesting mixture of the old-fashioned and the very progressive. Even without saying a lot, they created an environment where my brothers and I felt we were free to express our interest in the arts. My brothers are both musicians, and we used to pretend that we were the Monkees. I did all of the arts growing up: I did visual art really well and was drawn to watercolors; I started learning to play the clarinet when I was in fourth grade; I started acting in seventh grade and got a lot of support and awards for that. So I think it was just a family atmosphere of acceptance. Even though my dad was in the military and it was a little disturbing to him at first, when it was apparent I was going to become an artist, my dad gave up and said, "This child isn't one who's going to follow my way," so that gave me permission.

MP: It sounds like a pretty privileged childhood in the sense of a lot of opportunity, educationally and artistically.

CC: Yes, I was exposed to a lot. Because we traveled every summer, I got a sense of the whole country, and I think that was also one of the really important things in my life. My father was a person who had been all over the world, and we traveled a lot together as a family, so it just seemed natural to move around the world and feel like it belonged to me. That was part of my dad's legacy. As an adult, I would mention a place I was going to my dad, and it always turned out, of course, that he had already been there. One problem my father had with me was that I desperately wanted to travel all the time when I was a kid and we never got stationed overseas. I had friends in my class who had come from Germany or Paris, and I would think, "Why are we living here?" But my father had lost the enjoyment of travel because it was always related to work. So by the time I was growing up, he didn't really want to travel abroad. I was always fantasizing about Europe, and my family would comment, "Cyrus wants to go to Paris; Cyrus is making chocolate mousse and coq au vin." I was pretty eccentric as a kid — I was the kid who orders gelato or something. I got a birthday card for a friend of mine that shows this little girl telling her mother how to stock her lunch box, and I laugh because I was exactly like that as a kid: 'And mommy, don't forget the crème brûlée." I drove my father nuts that way.

MP: He probably was more practical.

CC: He was from Detroit, and he grew up in the Depression. Money was an intense issue for him, and here I was always ordering the most expensive thing. I was a funny kid that way, but always really clear inside about the writer identity. That has been a constant for me.

MP: You've had an incredible range of travels, and I see that coming up a lot in your poetry. I am thinking, of course, of the wide range of references that you employ in *Soul Make a Path through Shouting*. Beyond the wide range of references, how does your international perspective influence your work?

CC: The issue of empathy is key to my life and work. I feel that you don't belong to just your home place or your country. I have always been fascinated with history and have this sense of the history of the world, not just American history; I feel very identified with ancient times too. America is a very young country, comparatively speaking, and so I also identify with ancient beliefs and ancient people from a lot of different countries.

MP: It sounds like a broader view and not a regionalized sense of identity or self.

CC: I parallel it to being an actor: your sense of self is flexible. Part of what an actor is demonstrating is that the boundaries we think are so embedded into our identities are actually imposed or self-created; the actor is demonstrating that the self is actually malleable and that things can be shifted around inside of yourself so that you can portray a different person in a different culture in a different time. In literature, it may be more on an intellectual level, but I know with acting it is mostly an emotional realm. You are seeing yourself mirrored in someone through various cultures and languages. I learn by pushing myself into the unknown, so my life cannot be about security at all. I have to be a pioneer person in some way. Now that my father is dead and I am looking back on his life, I see that my father had the same kind of spirit, in the sense that he was one of the first generations of blacks to leave the black community. It happened through the military — as adults, they had to move into a white world for the first time. That was quite pioneering.

MP: You said to me yesterday that your dad was one of the key figures in desegregating the housing at West Point when he went there.

CC: Yes, my father was there in 1950 or so. There were about six or seven black cadets; they decided that they didn't want to room with just each other, that they were going to protest it, and it was effective. My father claimed that before Rosa Parks, he had done the same thing. Because some of the stories are so painful, my parents don't tell them often. One time my dad was in the South, and he was set up for a blind date, and he arrived at the blind date and the girl was white. But interestingly enough, her parents weren't freaked out. They said to go ahead and have a good time. But they went to this officers' club where the officers were ready to throw him into jail. So I think my father was very much a pioneer that way. Now I understand how lonely it must have been for my parents to be separated from what they grew up in. That was really a hard experience, I realize now. They didn't talk about it in those terms, but it must have been very isolating.

MP: When you look at your own position now, as a next-generation person in relation to various literary or cultural traditions, how do you see yourself operating in these differing cultures and traditions as a writer?

CC: When I went to Stanford, I realized that I had grown up in a distinctive way. I had a different perspective because I had grown up within the black community *and* the white community. I decided to take the same tack that the poet Ai had taken: like her, I came from a multiracial, multicultural background, and I wanted to pay allegiance to these different parts of myself and to say that I pledge allegiance to *all* of them in some way.

My poetry is really about my own sort of spiritual journey. And what I am discovering about myself is that *I* prefer to write about my connection to the African American experience in genres other than poetry. There is an intensely lyrical strain in my poetry; I want to pursue the complex issues of race in fiction or drama. In working on my selected poems collection, I find I am participating more in the African American literary tradition by including the poems that have African American themes, but I haven't really consistently addressed that part of my life in my poetry. You cannot really control your poetry, in my experience. You can guide it intellectually. I can express a multiracial perspective, but other people can perhaps write about elements of African American experience that are more familiar to them, such as oppression and fighting daily forms of racism, some of the extremely important issues.

In terms of expressing a gay identity, I, like many others, got upset as a result of the AIDS crisis and the persecution of gays and gay art and decided that I was going to be as bold as I can be because I was tired of people trampling on things that are central or sacred to me. That was part of the impulse behind *Beautiful Signor*. Like some people, I have been a little bit ambivalent about my gay identity, because I know that it is really controversial within the African American community. Of course, I want to be liked or appreciated. But there is that fear.

In all, one has to resist the simplistic notion that one must write some kind of representative poetry, that I have a representative black experience. When I was growing up, my parents refused to limit my ideas about being African American. I remember my mother saying to me, "When I was growing up, Cyrus, I would look in the mirror, and all I would see was a black person. I don't want you to grow up thinking that is the only thing you are going to see about yourself." At the same time, it helps you to understand where you came from. I don't think that you ever feel more American than when you live abroad; you realize, "I really am an American, I really am an African American." You feel the specifics more intensely when you are away from the dynamics that we take for granted. What happened to me in Rome, interestingly enough, is that my closest friends were African American.

I can't forget that I was born in 1957, just as the civil rights movement and desegregation were beginning to happen. From what I know, I was born in a segregated hospital. My mother is not sure — it was either me or my brother. We were both born in Dover, Delaware. As the only black child in the hospital he/I had to be put in a separate room. So when my mother came out to look at the baby and it wasn't there, she freaked out and said, "Where's my baby?!" That's what we were born into: apartheid. People think that it's so far away, and it isn't.

MP: That's right. One theme that I have really enjoyed in your three published volumes is transcendent love, a belief in an ideal love that transcends not only the material and the individual but also horrors in the world. You can see this, for example, in *The Mud Actor*, where you write, "what the soul remembers / is love." And in *Beautiful Signor*, where love is seen as healing wounds, and of course in your spiritual narrative of healing in *Soul Make a Path through Shouting*. Could you comment on this ongoing theme of love in your work?

CC: It's not something that I have thought about much consciously. I am one of those people who has never had a moment of doubt about a creator. I so strongly felt the presence of the creator and so strongly believe in the sense of love that comes from what created us, and that has permeated my life. When I was growing up, people thought I was going to be a priest. My mother's family was a part of the Episcopal Church, and I was fascinated with religion from the beginning. I realized later on that it was spirituality more than religion. I came into the world as what people would call an old-soul person, feeling that living is a very multidimensional experience. Everyone seems to be fearful about that, but the more you are willing to experience various levels of reality and feel connected to humanity's different things, the better. Part of what goes on within the black community *is* that we are supposed to insist that we are only interested in the African American experience, which is nonsense because we are also Americans, and we are also citizens of the world. We should be interested in everything and everyone, ideally. When someone like me comes along and demonstrates that, people wonder, "Is it really OK to identify with everyone? What does that really mean?" In *Soul*, I wanted to have a panoramic perspective, to see everything from that mountaintop vantage point. That's the view in "Down from the House of Magic," the opening poem. In terms of transcendent love, that view is just a part of my life and nature. I did it also in *Beautiful Signor*, which is about the idea that there are many paths to God, including the path of love and sexuality, which has been discounted by Judeo-Christian culture. I was looking for different traditions, and what I found in Judeo-Christian culture was that the troubadour culture had some of those elements of what I was trying to get at, but I finally had to go to the Sufi tradition in Rumi. I tried to include some elements of Western tradition because I am writing out of that tradition: I am not living in India or those places; I am coming from this culture and I have to give my audience connections to Western tradition. For me, it was going to Dante and going to the troubadours, but the Sufi tradition comes closer to what I was really getting at.

It is love that allows disaster as a schoolroom, as a place of learning. I have evolved a sense of the world as a place beyond the binary of good and evil. I feel like all of the really horrible things are inseparable from the really good things.

MP: What do you think of the reception of *Soul Make a Path through Shouting*?

CC: It got a lot of praise, but it was also attacked. Gary Soto's review of the book dismissed it and said it was banal. I don't really feel that's an attack. I heard of one man who wrote a really intense attack on the book and then evidently sent it out to many different editors and it was rejected.

People who were looking for a particular kind of political consciousness in the book had a really hard time with it.

Interestingly, at first I could hardly get the poems published. It took a long time. I believe there comes a time, culturally, when people can embrace things that they couldn't before. By the time *Soul* came out in 1994, people were ready for a different take. Perhaps we are not willing to settle for the paradigm of victim and perpetrator in the same way that we used to. There was a period where people were into talking about their wounds as a way of connecting to other people, and now we are looking at tragedy from all the different perspectives and seeing that there is no easy solution. We keep evolving a more sophisticated sense of what is happening in the world. Artists like Toni Morrison are contributing to this more sophisticated perspective. In *The Bluest Eye* and *Jazz* you have a crime, and she is able to put you inside the mind of the criminal and help you understand that often what they are doing is related to what is happening inside of them. For example, Joe Trace stalks Dorcas. It has everything to do with the way he was raised as a hunter — tracking is instinctive to him — and his mother was this wild child. Perhaps now we are willing to look at situations in terms of this new paradigm and not willing to have this victim/perpetrator binary view. Part of what I was trying to do in *Soul* was to move beyond that paradigm and say, "What does it mean to be a victim and refuse that tag?" If someone oppresses you, do you have to accept that as being the truth about you? My spiritual teacher — I studied in a mystic school in San Francisco in 1997–98 — was sexually abused by both his parents as a child. He said there was a point he reached when he realized that his life had to be about some other story than that. I thought that was really interesting language. He consciously had to decide that his life was more than just this one story. That's the idea I was trying to get at in *Soul*: I am not just a victim, I am not just black, I am not just one thing. Just changing your interpretation of events can lead one spiritually in a creative direction.

MP: I am thinking of the lines quoting Etty Hillesum that you placed in "Life Indestructible": "We were never in anyone's 'clutches'; / Always, always, / We were in the arms of God." She is referring to Holocaust victims.

CC: I think that, culturally, we are at a moment where we understand that. As a mystic, my training is that we create our own reality, and that's not an idea that is usually endorsed in our culture because then you are less controllable, right? Part of what Etty was arguing—and what I feel *Soul* is showing—is that everything that happens in life is totally meaningful. Part of what happened in post–World War I and post–World War II thinking was that the world was absurd and things were happening in a random way, but my own life experience and training is that it's really the opposite—that everything is full of meaning if we are willing to take the time to find out what it might mean to us. Even extreme negatives. Of course, this can make people who are invested in being seen as victims very angry.

MP: Of course. It's hard to believe that brutal experience can be viewed in that larger frame, with those outside the experience seeing it as having meaning and positive dimensions from that meaning.

CC: Actually, I was thinking about you as a white professor of black literature: it signifies that black culture belongs to everyone in some way that's real. That's very upsetting for people, because they want pride of ownership.

MP: And they should be proud.

CC: Of course they should be proud. And they should be angry if they feel that it is appropriated without ordinary black people being respected. But black culture itself belongs to the world.

MP: It will only benefit black culture, I would argue, to have white people know it, because that respect comes with that knowledge, I think.

CC: It has to do with intimacy, too. It is a way for people outside of the black community to have some intimacy and potential empathy. You know I believe in reincarnation. I was thinking about this today in your African American Poetry class. I seem to remember being a white person; I seem to remember being a black person; I seem to remember being an Asian person. So what does that mean about racial identities?

Part of what I was arguing in *The Mud Actor*, maybe too directly with the memory of Hiroshima in part 3, was that perhaps the truth is that we literally *are* each other in some way, but we don't want to accept it. I remember when I was really young I felt distant from Asian experience, and then as an undergraduate I had a superdramatic experience of going to Japan and seeming to relive the bombing of Hiroshima. I felt, "I don't belong just to the African American community." I have also had, since I was a top Spanish student in my high school, heavy doses of the Hispanic community. I had really positive feelings about Hispanic culture and felt that as a black kid I could read Garcia Lorca.

I have been reluctant to focus too much on reincarnation publicly because I know people are very resistant to that. So every now and then I just throw it out there, saying, "Oh, by the way, I am a black person, but perhaps once upon a time I was a white person or an Asian person or a woman or . . ."

MP: Some of what you are saying right now reminds me of H. D.; a lot of times in your work, especially in *Soul*, you remind me of H. D., particularly her World War II epic *Trilogy*. Is that something conscious in your mind, or an affiliation you feel?

CC: I came to H. D. at the end of *Beautiful Signor*. I had heard about her, but I came to H. D. later. The descriptions of Christ in *Trilogy* are so beautiful — that is my favorite part.

MP: There is a lot of empathy between your work and hers, such as the spiritual dimensions and the way that horror can lead to insight and love.

CC: Illumination.

MP: Yes, illumination. So there is a real empathy there, maybe just spiritually. Speaking of trilogies, one thing I also noticed in your volumes is that you like thirds.

CC: I am Cyrus Curtis Cassells III. Lots of thirds there. There is just something about that vibration. In terms of the traditional biblical story, three represents creation on the third day. So maybe that has something to do with it. It's just a pleasing vibration for me.

MP: All three of your poetry volumes have thirds, although you manage it slightly differently in each. In *The Mud Actor* it was more equivalent, balanced thirds.

CC: It was a very conscious thing in *The Mud Actor*. I wanted to have a multilevel art.

MP: In contrast to this — and I suspect your answer will be "no," but I have to ask — do you ever, as an artist, set yourself technical challenges when you're writing poetry?

CC: Rarely, but I am a structure freak, and I haven't been able to write occasional poetry ever; I always seem to have to have a theme. I'm trying to do that now for my new poems. I'm starting to give myself permission. I haven't completely decided yet whether I should even do a volume of selected poems, because it is a misrepresentation of what I've done. Part of my impulse is that I want to keep those poems in print as books because I really created them as books. So I'm in a little bit of a quandary. I also feel now, looking at the work, that it's valuable to [select] what I think are the high points, and that's not really damaging, but I did create them as books.

With *The Mud Actor*, I worked on all the sections at the same time, and that's the only way I've been able to do these poems, is to have a theme. I also prefer to choose the art for the cover — I chose the cover of *Beautiful Signor*. I use that as part of my process to inspire me; that was a piece of visual art that helped me get closer to what I was trying to express. For me, it was this layered feeling of living in contemporary Rome, which is a place where you can literally see the layers of history and humanity. That's one of the rich parts of living in Rome. If you're not into history and multilevels in life, why live there? You step out of your house and there's a pillar coming out of the pavement. I like saying, "Look at all these layers, and which one do I want to pay attention to?" The result with *Beautiful Signor* is that it feels contemporary and yet it belongs to other time periods. And that's exactly what I wanted it to be.

MP: So as with H. D.'s work, it's a palimpsest, with multiple layers?

CC: I was a little more conscious of that with *Beautiful Signor*. With *Soul Make a Path through Shouting* it was a long process, and I didn't really know what I was doing. I didn't know what the theme was. It's clear now. I finally got it when Eric Kahn [a Holocaust survivor] handed me his poem from Terezin [a way station to Auschwitz]. I realized I was a witness for this; I came to the understanding that as this generation dies, there have to be people who are the repository of those experiences. Even if we didn't go through that experience, the story has to be told because it has everything to do with our humanity. If we don't learn some of these lessons, we'll just keep stumbling.

MP: When I was reading *Beautiful Signor*, I wondered if it was a deliberate technical challenge you had set yourself: you use all these words that end in *-able*, like *embraceable* and *riskable*, and they really stand out for the reader. Was this something conscious?

CC: It's a more elegant kind of diction. Another dimension of my political and moral education has been a sensitivity to language that became acute because going to another culture and learning another language from scratch sensitized me to particular words and the feeling of the words. It's a reality of constantly having to shift levels of language, especially if you know two or more languages. We can get very peevish about that, but if you want to communicate with people, you have to be cognizant of where they're at and be willing to adjust and work to be precise and clear in communication. I insist on the beauty of language and on creating what I think are new and beautiful combinations within the language — a mixture of words that we do not use so often. I didn't know that my vocabulary was unusual until *Soul Make a Path through Shouting* came out and people kept talking about the words.

MP: You mix discourses. For example, in the first poetic sequence you use *razzmatazz* at one point. But then you also use *muezzin*, from another discourse, and then military discourse like *marshal*, so you mix words from different discourses and different cultures. Furthermore, *razzmatazz* might be seen as a colloquialism, as opposed to words that are seen as erudite. It's the mixing that strikes me.

CC: The main quality I wanted to portray with *Beautiful Signor* was being passionate and peaceful at the same time, not qualities that are often linked, and I had to find music that had those qualities. The music I found was that of the Portuguese group Madredeus. I thought it had the quality I wanted to convey — love and passion creating self-knowledge and aware-ness of peace and healing. That was important.

I have a musical sense of language, and I feel my way through language. Sometimes I go to the dictionary to check if I'm using a particular word ex-actly the way I think I want to use it, and it's not quite as precise as I think. Part of my project as a writer is to take periods and language from the past and make them alive in the present because they're relevant now. I have this sense of the past as being usable all the time and not to be ignored.

In *Beautiful Signor*, I wanted to create a book that was all tenderness. In terms of this culture it's a very risky project, because of the whole question of sentimentality. There's also the problem of a love poem: how do you create intimacy that allows the reader to enter that realm of the intimate without feeling left outside? The question is, can you create ecstatic poetry without showing the shadow side? I felt it was important to let a little bit of the shadow side of love come into the book.

MP: You also show awareness in *Beautiful Signor* of how gay love is out-law still. While it's risky because the poetry could be seen as sentimental, it's also risky because you're writing in a tradition that has always celebrated heterosexual love, and you are celebrating gay love.

CC: And using the same tropes — which is what threw reviewers. For example, the *Publishers Weekly* piece said I was effective at conveying a sense of ecstasy, but didn't seem to know that those tropes hadn't been used in a gay perspective before. Part of what I was saying was that we have lovey stuff too. I wanted to take a little bit of all that, even though it is tried and true and perhaps clichéd. Why can't we dip into Western romantic tradition, too?

MP: Do you think this volume is itself a political act?

CC: Definitely. It was in response to Jesse Helms, who thinks homosexuality is all about sex. I had a monogamous relationship with another man that lasted ten years; people like Helms think that almost never happens. There are even gay men who don't believe these relationships exist: there's no model. It's meant to be very much political in that way. I felt as if parts of my deepest experience were being trampled on by this "respectable" ideology, and that I, as a person, wanted to bear witness to something else, to say, "No, my experience has been this." When the book came out, I used special strategies: I wouldn't have my picture on it, and I wouldn't have a naked man on the cover. What happens in the gay community is that the advertising reinforces the sexuality in a provocative kind of way. Sex is always used to manipulate. Gay men have this catch-22 going on where sexuality is extremely important because the politics swirl around the fear of the sexuality itself, and it's so easy to end up overemphasizing sex even if you don't mean to. Part of what I was trying to do with *Beautiful Signor* was to bring the sexuality and the eroticism in, but put it in some kind of perspective, so that the sexuality didn't feel compartmentalized from the rest of one's life experience. I feel that's a major part of where the suffering for gay people is, particularly for men. Many lesbians have been more able to integrate their sexuality into the rest of their lives. For gay men, some shadow-world stuff goes on, a fleeing from the emotional life. A lot of lying has to happen to pretend that sex is just a mechanical thing. I see spiritual dimensions here that are lessons we need to understand. One of the lessons of the AIDS crisis for me is that, when you participate with people sexually, it's not just on a physical or sensual level, it's also about energy. Mystics strive to keep the integrity of one's own energy and not use others'. You can't live with the illusion that people are like Kleenex, to be used and dispensed with when you're done. That's a huge lesson about sexuality. I don't think any morality is really attached to that, but what you hear in the public discourse is that it's all about morality.

My own views about sexuality have changed. I was a pretty moralistic person growing up. Even when I lived in San Francisco, I was very judgmental about what was happening with other people. What was thrilling for me about *Beautiful Signor* was winning the Lambda Literary Award and having the gay community get what I was writing. Because it took a while. I thought the book would be ignored — it wasn't packaged in a way I thought the gay community would be drawn to. So when the book won the Lambda, I thought, "Oh, this is really great!" There were something like seventy judges. It seemed that people really understood what I was doing: I was trying to bear witness that as a man I had this experience of loving another man deeply.

[2001]

Elizabeth Alexander

Elizabeth Alexander represents the youngest edge of this generation of poets following the Black Arts Movement. Her work is deeply engaged with black history and culture, inseparable from America at large. She has published five books of poetry, a play, two collections of essays, and a children's book (coauthored with Marilyn Nelson). She is currently professor and chair of African American Studies at Yale University. In 2008, she was asked to read an original poem at the inauguration of Barack Obama as president of the United States on January 20, 2009, pulling her into national and international prominence. The poem, "Praise Song for the Day," typifies her themes and aesthetics, mediating national and African American tropes through individual details and experiences in an accessible lyric voice.

Alexander was born on May 30, 1962, in Harlem, New York, and raised in Washington, D.C. Her parents were among the black professional elite; as such, her childhood included education, travel, and involvement in civil rights issues. Her poems and essays depict an upbringing in a loving family with an abiding belief in racial affiliation. She earned a BA from Yale University in 1984, an MA from Boston University in 1987, and a PhD from the University of Pennsylvania in 1992. At Boston University, she studied with Derek Walcott. She was an assistant professor of English at the University of Chicago from 1991 to 1997. Alexander married Ficre Ghebreyesus, a native of Eritrea, in 1997, and they have two sons. She was a poet in residence and the director of Smith College's Poetry Center from 1997 to 1999, moving to Yale's African American Studies department as an adjunct associate professor in 1999.

Alexander's earlier work charts the experiences of girlhood and young womanhood, yet always within broader contexts of race, class, and national issues (such as AIDS). Her interest in history is apparent from her first book of poetry, *The Venus Hottentot*, written from the perspective of Sartje Baartman, the young Xhosa woman who was lured to Europe and then displayed as a sideshow freak and scientific curiosity. History has become an extended focal point in her later work, including an extended sequence on Muhammad Ali and, in *American Sublime*, an epic sequence of poems on the *Amistad* story, written in individual lyric poems that each feature their own persona. Motherhood and family life have emerged as recurring themes since her marriage and two pregnancies. Alexander's poems rely on a degree of formal restraint, detailed images, exact diction, and a plainspoken rhythm. Art and aesthetics are the subjects of poems across her oeuvre. Her ars poetica "This I Believe" expresses her belief that poetry is found in the everyday and is a tool for connecting the individual voice and the group: it ends, "Are we not of interest to one another?"

Alexander's poetry strongly identifies with African American poetic precursors such as Gwendolyn Brooks and Countee Cullen and with the African American literary tradition more generally, nodding to iconic writers such as Ralph Ellison and Toni Morrison. Brooks's formalism, modernist poetic, and ongoing involvement in the black community function as a model for Alexander. Called a "romanticist of race" by reviewer Maureen McLane, Alexander writes poetry that posits race and racial identity as lived — although not static or reductive — realities, and that celebrates black traditions and history.

Alexander's poetry is deeply influenced by the poetics of Elizabeth Bishop, who, like Brooks, wrote within the modernist/postmodernist continuum and whose formalism is well known. Many of Alexander's poems read like a Bishop poem, in which details build to a moment of intense realization and insight. The confessional dimensions of Alexander's poetry, by which she draws upon personal information such as her marriage to an Eritrean national and the births of her children, distinguish her poetry from Bishop's, affiliating more closely with Sylvia Plath's later poetic, although far more from a positive perspective — Alexander's confessional dimensions are constructive rather than self-destructive. Alexander discusses her views of both poets in the interview. Alexander also considers herself as writing women's poetry within a feminist poetic tradition, although she seeks to revise that tradition to include supposedly "unfeminist" expressions such as liking the idea of being rescued by men.

Critical reception of Alexander has been relatively slight, although largely positive, and will most likely increase as a result of her reading at the Obama presidential inauguration. She was one of five black female writers featured in a *Callaloo* special issue that featured her play, *Diva Girls*, and she has several substantial interviews in print. In my analysis of Alexander, published in *African American Review* in 2008, I focus on Alexander's (and Cassells's) "post-soul cosmopolitanism," a frame that delineates her wide range of cultural references as a prominent feature of the post-soul era (post–Black Arts Movement), which I trace through a close reading of the trope of movement in her poetry. Key areas in her poetry that deserve further exploration include her adaptation of the genres of epic and ars poetica, a developmental study of her work, the relation of history and biography in her portraits of African Americans, and the turn toward Africa in her midcareer work. Alexander's contributions across poetry, criticism, academia, and community building position her as an emerging leader.

I interviewed Alexander in the book-lined living room of her home in New Haven, Connecticut, in the spring of 2005. She even drove me to and from my hotel for the interview.

Selected Works by Elizabeth Alexander

POETRY

The Venus Hottentot, University Press of Virginia, 1990.
Body of Life, Tia Chucha Press, 1996.
Antebellum Dream Book, Graywolf Press, 2001.
American Sublime, Graywolf Press, 2005.
Crave Radiance: New and Selected Poems 1990–2010, Graywolf Press, 2010.

OTHER

Diva Studies (play), excerpted in *Callaloo* 19.2 (Spring 1996): 474–92; produced by the Yale School of Drama, 1996.
The Black Interior (essays), Graywolf Press, 2004.
Power and Possibility (essays), University of Michigan Press, 2007.
Miss Crandall's School for Young Ladies and Little Misses of Color, coauthored with Marilyn Nelson (children's book), Wordsong / Boyd's Mill Press, 2008.
"Praise Song for the Day: A Poem for Barack Obama's Presidential Inauguration, January 20, 2009." Graywolf Press, 2009.

MALIN PEREIRA: One of the ways I have come to have an interest in your work is through our shared appreciation of Rita Dove and her poetry. You've identified her elsewhere as being a big sister in your poetic lineage. Big sisters can do a lot of things for us: they can loosen up our parents so we can stay out later, lend us clothes, and they can give us advice. What did Dove's work, past or present, do for you as a big sister? What issues are you glad she dealt with before you?

ELIZABETH ALEXANDER: Yes, that's a great question. Well, I came to her work on my own. I have a distinct memory of reading it in 1985–86 — this was pre-*Thomas and Beulah* — when I was in Boston getting my master's degree in creative writing. I just somehow happened onto it. I knew she was exactly ten years older than I was to the year, and I knew that she was a contemporary black poet who was writing about quote-unquote "un-black" things. I would describe that differently now, but at the time it felt like this was fresh, this was not doctrinaire, and I could somehow be included in it. Although it wasn't as though she was describing a childhood exactly like mine. Her first three books are about the life of the mind and a young girl's intellectual development, curiosities, and obsessions. Those three books taken together, especially *Museum*, could be described best by the metaphor "a cabinet of curiosities." The first two books really rocked my world, and being able to write about thinking and knowing was terribly important to me and there she was doing it in an absolutely remarkable, strange way. Her strangeness — people don't talk about this a lot — her strangeness really spoke to me. I thought, *Wow*, so even if her galaxy wasn't my galaxy, it didn't matter because she honored her galaxy.

When I was in Philadelphia getting my PhD, Dove was giving a university reading. I went across town with my finished manuscript for *The Venus Hottentot*. I went up to her after the reading and did something I've never done before — I pressed my manuscript into her hands. Afterwards, she wrote me a really lovely letter saying, "This happens to me a lot, but I'm really excited about what I see here." It felt like such a big deal because she was youngish, and I had been reading her work and she had been putting her work out in a very discernable way. When the Pulitzer came for *Thomas and Beulah* in 1987, I found her number through information in Arizona. I called her and left a message on her answering machine, saying, "This is probably inappropriate, but I take pride in your award; I'm so excited, and you don't know me but this means a lot to me." She was an icon who wasn't in my midst, but close enough that the Pulitzer meant a lot.

I thought I was trying to do the same thing as her, though her work has more decorum than mine. I think that this sort of breaking away from the big sister has to do with breaking with decorum. Part of her brilliance is the way she is able to do so much, and signify so much, from within that incredible decorum. Her new little sister is Natasha Trethewey; she has this incredible formal, tight control, but there's a lot that's really raw. I think of myself as the more wildly coiffed of the three sisters. Over the years Dove has been very kind and attentive, and has given me very useful pieces of advice. I feel like she's out there for me. She nominates me for Pushcart Prizes, and probably does other things I don't even know about. I feel I could ask her big, discreet questions I wouldn't want to ask a lot of other people.

MP: It's interesting that you bring up the issue of her decorum in contrast to your own. I'm immediately thinking of her poem "After Reading *Mickey in the Night Kitchen* for the Third Time Before Bed"; it stands out so much because it is opposed to her usual decorum. You've consistently depicted the female body very graphically and unsentimentally in your work, and I've been struck by that and respected it, too. I sensed there was a project going on for you about how to represent the female body. I wonder if you feel, in writing about those details of childbirth, or writing in one poem about your "titties" or being "finger-fucked," you're deliberately trying to write against some of the decorum about the black female body Gwendolyn Brooks might have had, and that's all in response historically to the hypersexualization of black female bodies. Is this a project you have consciously had?

EA: It's not a conscious project, but as I look back on it, it's very much generational and reflective of the way I've come of age through feminisms, and the explosion of blacks studying in the academy. These have been very, very formative influences on me, and it dovetails with thinking specifically about black women. *The Venus Hottentot* marked a particular moment in terms of my saying, "Okay, I'm reading about this woman and she has been put on display, she has been hypersexualized, and what she doesn't have in the historical record is voice." That's what the poet can do; the poet can give the Venus Hottentot voice. In my prose work and more so in my teaching, I call it a project of thinking about black women coming to voice, about submerged historical voices of black women. What does it mean to reclaim the body after it's been objectified and terrorized in so many ways? What does it mean to break away from all of the injunctions that say we have to keep ourselves under wraps? How does that repress? I think of Hazel Carby's important essay on black women blues singers, and how you can think about that against all of that tight formality of the bourgeois black women's novels that needed to be that way in order to get their hearing. Being a child of later times, I feel there's more to explore, more that's really necessary to explore, because if we're not able to give voice to that huge part of our experience, then there's so much that's unexamined.

MP: So it's a question of female agency. To you, it seems like aspects of a fully rounded, fully manifested female agency are articulated in these dimensions.

EA: I think so, as well as a coming of age either after or in the sexual revolution. *Our Bodies, Ourselves* was an early bible of mine. I remember what it felt like among my girlfriends to break those silences of our sexuality — of what we were doing, what we desired, for people to talk about abortions — it was powerful. I think Brooks was more explosive and frank than she's often given credit for in that regard.

MP: I'm thinking of *Maud Martha*, specifically of the childbirth scene, and I suppose it's revolutionary it's mentioned at all. The revelation for Maud Martha seems to be, "Having a baby is *nothing*" (240). Then there's this cheery little moment where she's looking out the window or the doorway and she's happy — and that's it. It's very different than more graphic details about childbirth. That's the type of contrast I'm thinking of. So which ones do you think about?

EA: "Rites for Cousin Vit" and "Jesse Mitchell's Mother," for instance — if you're asking just about embodied black women. What a surprise, her frankness after the bath scene in "Jesse Mitchell's Mother"; you just don't expect it from Brooks.

MP: One part of the *Antebellum Dream Book* that makes me smile is the poem you have about sexual encounters with Jack Nicholson, Michael Jordan, and even Mick Jagger (whom you forgive for his singing). Tell me, what were you thinking about, writing those poems — did you ever have a moment when you wondered what people might think? That this is a dream book, these are your personal fantasies?

EA: I think dreams are quite distinct from fantasies. People love those poems, especially the Mick Jagger and Michael Jordan ones, and they always ask me to read them. I think it's their fantasy, too. I think play is important in poetry; I wouldn't want play to seem evacuated from seriousness. What was interesting about writing those poems is the extent to which I allowed dream logic to govern, and dream illogic to govern. They continually surprised me, and I wanted the surprises to stand and be something I couldn't explain. It's something I enjoy.

MP: That's good. Generally speaking, in your poetry the body matters, and it matters whether it's male or female. I'm thinking of your collection of essays, *The Black Interior* — you write about the histories our bodies know. Why is it so important for you to repeatedly return to the body as the source of knowledge and truth, as opposed to knowledge and truth being in the mind?

EA: Well, for a couple of reasons. First of all, the brain lives in the body and that's very important. We often dichotomize those two, but it's terribly important to realize we're creatures. One of the amazing things we do in our creature-ness is think, and imagine — but it's all in that organism. I've given talks on writing *The Venus Hottentot*, and I've talked about what it really means to have so much told about our bodily experiences as black women that is simply not true. What does it mean to exist at first in the national consciousness as an impossibility — as three-fifths of a person? I'm fascinated with rape laws: "You weren't raped, maybe someone trespassed against your master's property, but you weren't raped." All you know up to the present moment is what our bodies know, is we are denied, and we are not given the same kind of weight and credence as intellectually acquired information. It's about correcting the imbalance and then hopefully bringing it all together. It's interesting living in a female body — the cycles, pregnancy and childbirth, aging — it's fascinating. I couldn't imagine not writing about it, and it has to do with my coming of age in the 1970s and 1980s, and having some sexual freedom. Can I — as the rhetoric would have it — separate this sexual pleasure from all of the other things that do or don't bring two human beings together? In this stage of life, at the end, the answer is "no," but the journey was an interesting one. There are a lot of stories in there, and so many times when women tell the stories of what their bodies know, there's revelation involved, and revelation always interests me.

MP: One pattern in your volumes of poetry that has always interested me is oftentimes you have a section — typically it's in the second section — that charts an artistic genealogy of sorts. You might even think of it as a portrait gallery of artists. These appreciative portraits are not only in your first, apprentice-like volume, but they've continued in your other volumes. You keep returning to artists and artist figures — why?

EA: I think artists are amazing people. I've always felt that way. My great-uncle was an artist — Charles Ballston. When I was a kid, the life he and my great-aunt had was perfectly bourgeois. It seemed their apartment was always jazz, and action, and lots of food being prepared, and a certain kind of talk and freedom and swirl and fabulousness — and I very clearly wanted that life, I wanted to make this kind of life for myself.

MP: So you're surrounding yourself with artists in every volume?

EA: I just live in it, but also, what artists give us is a vision of what we've been constrained against imagining as black people. What artists do for us is to go elsewhere, and I really need that.

MP: I've also been struck with the wide range of cultures those artists come from: Pablo Neruda, Frida Kahlo, Claude Monet, Ralph Ellison, Fats Waller, Igor Stravinsky, Josephine Baker. It seems you draw from the artistic impulse wherever you find it. Dare we say you are cosmopolitan in your sensibility?

EA: My grandmother was my first cosmopolitan, and she was anachronistically cosmopolitan. She had a vision of the world far beyond her world and some people just have that quality. We were very close when I was growing up, and I had her until I was about thirty years old. She was, other than my parents, the most important grown up to me, and she was quite insistent that you see yourself as part of the world. She was extremely unparochial, she made you fight against it. She didn't talk about black this and black that, she thought it was inappropriate, but yet she had all those worlds in her. She told me that when she was in college she got a notion about Denmark. She had always told me she had read about the statue of the Little Mermaid that had been unveiled in 1913. She wanted to see it, so she wrote to a university in Denmark and said, "I suppose you've never had a colored American student. I would like to be your first." And they said, "Come!" They gave her a scholarship to study in Denmark. It's crazy, this was around 1926. In the old fashioned way she believed in "exposure," as she would have called it. She was a social worker, so she believed you could be civilized.

MP: My Nella Larsen bells are going off. Larsen was published in some of the black periodicals in the 1930s.

EA: Yes, and I've often wondered if they might have known each other, because they were in Harlem at the same time in the early 1930s. I'm sure my grandmother read her work.

MP: So that might have helped with the spark to go to Denmark.

EA: Well that's interesting, but "Passing" is 1929, which is after she went.

MP: Then she anticipates Larsen!

EA: She anticipates Larsen, that's right.

MP: I do love your poem "Manhattan Elegy," where you're visiting your grandmother and there are all those experiences. I hear echoes of Elizabeth Bishop in your poems.

EA: Thank you for noticing. As important as Elizabeth Bishop has been, has her influence on any black poet ever been discussed? I don't think she's been a huge influence on black poets in general, but I haven't liked the way she's seen as the province of white people, especially in contemporary poetry.

MP: It seems to me she's particularly important to you with travel poems — I'm remembering "For Miriam" and "Visitor" — and your interests in Brazil and the cultures of Latin America. What has she done for you? Has she offered you a template for some of these issues?

EA: Not being thematic, but more stylistic. It's part of what I value in Dove, and value even more in Bishop. First of all, she represents the young woman intellectual. She has that Joseph Cornell box in her poem, which says, "Let's look inside your brain for a little while, because what you're thinking about is fascinating." I came to Bishop when I started reading poetry in a really focused way when I was in Boston. Her poems were so meticulous, and were so beautiful but not fussily so. They're absolutely exquisitely made, but they are never being ornamental for their own sake. That's what I'm trying to do in a very scrupulous way as well. I believe in the amazing-ness of a word, and the beauty of language, and the possibility of praising in lines. I want them to be gorgeous objects, but I never want them to love the sound of their own voices too much. She's never cute, but always beautiful. I have a bigger published body of work than she does; she was so much like Hayden — just a few perfect poems and they won't go out until they're absolute masterpieces. I'm not like her to the same extent, but I admire her work. It's a reminder you should try to be perfect.

MP: I remember in the interview with Christine Philip in 1996, you talked about poetry being "scrupulous," and having "emotional rigor." Taking these terms in relation to what you're saying about Bishop, she must have helped you value that or at least helped you find a way to achieve what you already valued.

EA: Absolutely! I think also we have a shared visuality in the poems, but there's a way her visual attention and powers of description are so much an aspect of what she does well, and that's something I've tried to do well, too.

MP: That's a good reminder for me, because I guess that's the first time I realized I can picture all your poems. I'm not talking about the words but the picture, the scene. It probably has to do with the visual artwork you talked about in your parents' home, and the importance of paintings to you. You must be working on rendering a visual landscape. Bishop helped you do that?

EA: I think so, yes. I'm half an artist. I'm an artist without the skills to actually paint, but I see everything. I once went to speak with Alice Quinn who was teaching a graduate class at Columbia, and she has poets in to talk about other poets. We got into a conversation about Bishop and I was going on and on and I realized, it was a really a funny, oddly important thing, but those lines, "You are an Elizabeth," from "In the Waiting Room"— those lines spoke to me. That is a poem I love, though I often wonder how I felt when I first read it; about those *National Geographic* women being described as grotesqueries, and if it spoiled anything for me.

MP: One poem surprised me in *Antebellum Dream Book* — the one on Sylvia Plath, "The Female Seer Will Burn upon this Pyre." First of all, I was surprised you have a Plath poem . . .

EA: Why?

MP: I don't see many people writing back to Plath, and I can't think of but one other black woman poet who's written back to Plath. There seems to be a source of kinship in the poem between Plath and your persona in the poem: she's setting your hair, she shares a word and a prophecy with you, but then she's also distinguished by the flat American belly and all that perfection of the domestic scene, like things are a little too perfect. The title suggests there's a common ground here between two female seers, women with prophetic dimensions in their work. What do you think about Plath's work?

EA: Plath's been very important to me, more as a figure than as a poet. It's the life. I read *The Bell Jar* when I was thirteen or fourteen. I thought it was fascinating, a young woman coming of age. She was complicated and intense and I found her fascinating. In my apprentice year in Boston I remember reading her journals and letters to her mother. I felt total identification with Plath's ambition. The poems typed to go by the door, that sense of duty, of self-laceration and perfectionist's standards; I definitely have all of that. It's a kind of ferocity about ambition. I think Plath said I want to be *this*, and I have a vision of what it is to be a *this*. I, too, have been expected to achieve; my poem that deals with that perhaps most explicitly is "Blues," about the radio always tuned to the station that says line up your summer job months in advance, follow your duty to the race, your people, and all of that. I understood Plath's high expectation, and I also understood the joy of that.

MP: Perfection is a very rewarding goal if you can achieve it again and again.

EA: I never experienced it. It's funny, you mentioned the "flat American belly," and I think of all that discipline, maybe the body was less disciplined space. I think of her as being anorexic, even though I know she wasn't, but I think of it as being an anorexic mentality, and that was not my issue. I certainly admire her poems, but are they absolutely in my bones and my blood the way some other people's are? No, but I've read her carefully and she was a fiercely dedicated professional woman poet, and that was really important to me. Also, maybe there was something about the example of her craziness and the inability to sustain the domestic that makes the poem an act of counter-definition, a "That's not me. I won't go down that road."

MP: The Plath poem follows the sequence of the Toni Morrison dreams in *Antebellum Dream Book*. Those poems capture something very distinctive about Morrison, which is how awestriking and intimidating she can be to many of us. I've met her two or three times, and every time, I can barely speak. She appears god-like in these poems and those might be the first poems written about Morrison. What are those poems about to you?

EA: I don't think she's appeared in a poem, that's true. They're next to Plath for a reason, because they're about ambition, and they're about imagining something I never had, which is the great female queenly mentor. Imagine what it would be like to seek the blessing of the queen, and the difference there would have been to have the blessing of someone like Morrison. Then to get knocked down, being told having babies is what you're supposed to be doing, to have your ass kicked. That's the thing I love about the hard work of it.

MP: Oh, and "the work is hard," to quote your poem.

EA: "The work is hard." I like that part. Those are very tongue-in-cheek poems. I certainly laughed writing them, although I wanted that poem to end in just the rich heft of Morrison's work. It's just a monument.

MP: Yes, and we feel there's so much behind the monumental body of work, and the texts written in response to her work have created an industry.

EA: That's right. Her whole career has happened in my adulthood. I have a hard copy original of *The Bluest Eye*, one of only a few thousand published in the beginning. After it was published, I waited for every novel to come out, and then read every article written about her, and tracked her career. I tried to keep track for a while, and then just couldn't anymore. Her career is so unprecedented. There's peace in imagining what it is to come of age as a writer, and how ultimately, you can't wait for the queen to bless you. Now, the apprentice has to make her own work.

MP: You can look back at her work as an inspiration and be grateful it's there. But you make it clear it wouldn't necessarily have been a positive experience to have had that queen. The scenario in the poem is you running out and getting her coffee, and your poetic persona doesn't seem to laud this role.

EA: That's right. After I read that poem to audiences, I always say it's a dream poem, because people take it literally and ask me "What was it really like to work for Mrs. Morrison?" I have to tell them I don't know Mrs. Morrison.

MP: You'd probably have to say the same thing before all of those dream poems, which is a good lead in to my next question. Do you see dreams as prophecy? How do you see your dream poems working?

EA: In so many cultures, especially Judeo-Christian culture, there's an idea that extraordinary things happen in dreams, they're prophetic, they show you things — things you know and don't understand in your conscious life, but your subconscious life can put together. Dreams are remarkable, powerful and amazing machines, because of what can be processed in a dream, and the speed and richness of them. I feel a real need to be unmoored from my rational daily thoughts, because my life is now about duties and responsibilities, so I don't live a bohemian life. Dreams are my bohemian space, and they keep me connected to the not knowing, the uncertainty, and the surprise — without which, I would have no writing.

MP: The mundanity of daily life can drive the writing out. In *Antebellum Dream Book* I admire how instead of trying to be functional and left-brained during your pregnancy and in the time after, you went with it, you went with the life and the bodily experiences and the hormones. You have this vivid dream life when you allow yourself to become immersed in that life. You mined it rather than trying to overcome it.

EA: That was my first son's gift to me. I prepared myself to put everything on hold for many years because I didn't know what it was going to be like. *I was a poet then, and I will be a poet again later,* I thought. I was okay with this, because caring for this child was what I chose for myself. But it was in the middle the night nursing him that the first notes for "Neonatology" came to me on little scraps of paper towel. I thought how he, in this experience, is telling me there's just another way of being a poet — and that was really, really great.

MP: Kids teach you so much. I'm thinking of things twenty years ago, like "The Birth Project" by Judy Chicago, which is an artistic rendering of the fullness of childbirth, not just showing birth but the whole maternal process. Your work goes beyond what she was attempting to do because you're not only rendering the experience, but also allowing yourself to go down all of the emotional, artistic, and imaginative paths.

You are now in the stage of your life where you're a mentor rather than being mentored. I'm thinking of Cave Canem, but you have other workshops, and have your role as a teacher. What ideas do you have about mentoring? In an early essay that now appears in *Power and Possibility*, you expressed concern about the mentoring in which the female poet becomes the "glittering girl" who shines light onto her male mentor (129). Is this something that happened in your mentoring with Derek Walcott? What is your style of mentoring? And how do gender and race play roles in mentoring?

EA: No, that was not Walcott. He was really great. He once talked beautifully about mentoring women, because he has a daughter who is a writer, and a PhD, and a mother. He has an understanding and respect for what it means to have all those demands. He took the women very seriously, and he took the men very seriously, and he took the poems seriously. With Derek Walcott, it was his devotion to the poem and to the word. He was unwavering and lauded. It was about greater poems written before, and the blank page he will face at five o'clock the next morning. It was never about self-satisfaction, not even for a second. It's about taking your own work seriously; the example of seriousness is something not every student can take something from. I like the word *devotion*, not just to making poems, but to the greatness of black culture and history. It's a very precious thing I've been entrusted with, so I need people to take it seriously.

I take my mentoring really seriously. The students I love, I really love. I feel so lucky to have a job where they pass through and then go off and do interesting things. They're so full of life and possibility. On my husband's side, we have a huge extended family, and lots of young, college-age nieces, so the mentoring is always going on. I believe in process mentoring. It's getting harder and harder as there's more and more pressure for students to get As, and they ask me "How do I get an A?" and it drives me crazy. I expect they'll get an A if we do our work together well, but I wonder if they're working hard, if they're only doing things because they know it will earn them an A. I have students in our home because I've found it means a tremendous amount to them to see a home, to see food prepared, and kids and a marriage. Part of what good mentoring is, is what I experienced with my grandmother when I was growing up — going with her to the corner store, seeing how she talked to strangers or wrote a letter to the editor, watching her dress — these things taught me a whole lot. It's important as a grownup to share your life with young people, because how else will they see how to make a life? They're always watching. I don't bring them into my home all the time — it definitely has to be earned because I'm very private in that regard.

MP: Do you find you have issues with race or gender in mentoring? Very often, male students gravitate towards male professors for mentoring, but female students seem to take male professors more seriously. Black colleagues are not sought out as mentors as often, and very often the only students who seek them out are black students. What do you think about these patterns?

EA: This was my experience as well. Recently I attended a reading that was part of a larger ceremony. There were seats set up with pieces of paper with names on them, and everyone was *professor* and I was *Mrs.* They had invited me, they had my CV and knew who they had invited, and I thought, *Wow.* They can't in their subconscious and conscious space get their head around it. When they see a professor, they don't see me. It comes down to how much energy I want to expend thinking about this. Mostly, I try to let it go and turn to the work, and conduct myself the way I'm supposed to and work with the students who are interested. I won't allow students to make me prove something to them, I can't enter that space because it's hideous. It doesn't bring out the best in me.

MP: One thing distinctive about you is you're both an MFA and a PhD, and it's not a creative-dissertation PhD — it's in literary criticism. How does having training in literary criticism and literary analysis help you as a poet, and then conversely, how does the poetic point of view help you as a critic?

EA: When I'm writing poetry, I really experience myself and want to keep myself in an uncritical space. Otherwise, it would be too schematic and the death of the creation of the poem. My greatest strength is not necessarily seeing the bigger patterns, but seeing localized patterns and then making references. I've tried to do a kind of a critical writing that is somehow my own — you know conventional argument is very hard — and I don't feel I do it very well. I have an associative mind, which is a strength in poetry, and it's a strength in my critical writing. As a teacher, I'm always interested in the idea that "someone made this." One of the classes I inaugurated and have taught for five years at Yale is African American Literature from 1970 to the present. I bring writers into the class, which makes it a living writers class, though this is something even a professor who isn't a writer could do — but this brings my world into the classroom. I can be the professor and literary critic but the writer side comes out, too. I find myself chitchatting with the writers and it shows students another context I can bring to the discussion.

MP: My students who are practicing poets have been the freshest contributors to my seminars on poetry, because they're inside the poem from the beginning. They're inside the poem in a way I can't get into it. I'll write down the things they talk about because they don't break it up and categorize things.

EA: There's a way in which writing poems is fundamentally addictive. Writing a poem is about creating more options, whereas coming up with an analysis for a poem is about zeroing in. You need this play from students because you learn something, and it's how you get a good conversation.

MP: One of the classes you were teaching at Yale shows that kind of play. You looked at the changing canon in African American literature, looking at the previous ways in which texts were interpreted and comparing to new ways — revisionist interpretations. What can you tell me about this class?

EA: It was a fun class. For years there was a class called "Problems in the Interpretation of African American Literature," and this type of class would be the kind of first graduate literature class in black literature. For a while it was the only one offered and was the canon class. I taught it for a while in several different ways, and something wasn't working in the definition; it felt like it was working with too rigid a notion of what the canon encompasses. What's frustrating is at the end of the day, you're arguing with your syllabus, thinking "I could have done this," and then students are arguing with the syllabus — which can be productive — but ultimately, if felt as if I had to change the shape of the class and acknowledge here we are, almost thirty-some years into African American studies, and there have been a lot of conversations, and so much critical work to draw upon, and there are children of the canonical texts. I came up with a plausible canon. I'm always going to teach Frederick Douglass and Harriet Jacobs (Linda Brent), but I want to try to surround them with really challenging types of critical and literary texts that could not have existed without these previous texts. For example, we talked about Phillis Wheatley and Robert Hayden's "A Letter to Phillis Wheatley," and this year I'm teaching a course on August Wilson.

MP: I found how you conceptualized the class to be very fresh. Switching gears a bit, many of us understand through your poems, essays, and interviews how important New York and Washington, D.C. have been to you, and I'm not going to ask you about those two cities. But more generally, cities and places matter tremendously in your poetry — most of what you write is situated in a place. The uncle who passes for white out in Oregon, your year in Boston, the poem for Nelson Mandela written from Philadelphia, poems referencing Birmingham — I could go on and on. In *American Sublime* you focus on New Haven from the *Amistad* story. How and why does place matter so much, not just for you personally, but in a poem, which is often understood as a sort of atemporal abstract idea?

EA: Place just matters. There's something I can't put my finger on about African Americans saying where we're from, and having this sense of, "Well, I'm a Detroit Negro," or "I'm from D.C."— it carries a lot along with it. How can we not talk about our experience in terms of place? First, there's the fundamental displacement of the Middle Passage and making ourselves new in new places, and then the voluntary but still violent and disheartening displacement of the Great Migration. It seems so fundamental to the black experience in those cities, including the realities of segregation and what it meant as far as how we narrate our largest experiences. I understand people better when I understand where they come from. Think about *A Raisin in the Sun*; it doesn't say Chicago, 1959, but you know you're in a place where there are covenants dictating who can and cannot buy houses. The fundamental drama of this family is where they are going to live, and what are their dreams, and whose dream gets to live.

MP: You answer makes me think you are mapping blackness in the sense of the way you started, such as "Detroit Negro," "Chicago Negro"— the experience is different in all those different places.

EA: I think so. My mom's a historian and has always been a "mapper." You could give her the tiniest scrap of information and she would put it together and it would yield a lot more information. Part of me is like her and is interested in history.

MP: One of the most interesting generative creative tensions in your work is between a sort of diasporic migrating or ever-moving sense of blackness, and yet there's the sense of blackness as a home. I don't mean there's tension as a bad thing, but as interplay. How do you see this working?

EA: I guess if blackness is a home, it should be a complicated home — a contradictory home. It should be an "I am large, I contain multitudes" or a "Many things are true at once" kind of home. This is where I find myself aware of my resistance to being pegged as sentimental in my work. Coming through the academy during a time when antiessentialism was on the rise, I suffered because of my attention to history and to how culture functions. These things were seen as being naive and reactionary, which is not how I see it at all. Those kinds of characterizations penalized me in my own formation.

MP: There is one poem, "Haircut," which is important for articulating how you see and don't see the ideas of the migrating, moving blackness and blackness as a home as being incompatible. You figure it as building more stately mansions, and you imagine this blackness in this super, really big home — which is what a mansion is, right? It moves around and things come in and out of it, but there's a structure and shape, and an entity that exists. You try to bridge the two with that sort of image.

EA: We have been confined to, and circumscribed in Harlem, USA — the literal space of Harlem, and therefore everything can be in Harlem. It's culturally accessible and you know the political, cultural, and historical life of Harlem. In the poem, there's the fantasy and the wish for a black Valhalla, and at the same time there's the question of what's reality. It's many things: it's all the history, the haircut, people asking me for money. It's everything, but it's not an indiscriminate and undifferentiated everything. I was trying to paint a very precise portrait, a street scene.

MP: You understand people can be constructed and constituted by place or in their interaction with a place, and it can change if they go to another place, like in the poem "Visitor," about going to Belo Horizonte, Brazil. The poem focuses on the question of, "Who am I here?" You don't see these migrations as threatening or as a loss, but more of an openness to changing constructions, and it's a shared experience, an experience people can tap into.

You dedicated your third volume to your husband, Ficre Ghebreyesus, who's from Eritrea, Africa. You've had poems about your African relatives, but what has it meant for you having Africans in your life, and what has it opened up for your in imaginative possibilities?

EA: That's a great question, because it's huge, life changing, and it's perspective changing. Every year, the magazine *Pen* hosts an international festival. Last year, they asked me to be on a panel put together by Breyten Breytenbach called "Africa and the World." There were a lot of African writers and me, and I was flipped out! I kept thinking, "What am I doing here, what do they want me to talk about?" And asking myself, "Why am I on this panel, exactly?" I really just wanted to do a good job, and Kassalhoun Shacole from the Africa World Press was there, and he's sort of the American dean of East African literature. Being on the panel was a great opportunity to start thinking about that question — how has having an African husband shaped my life? In some ways, it has sharpened my focus on a question I see for young black Americans — the challenge of seeing themselves as international and the challenge of really thinking through their relationship to Africans and people from the Caribbean as well. On campus I get to see all this drama playing out, and not only at Yale but with my Eritrean nieces. They have to decide whether to be part of the Black Student Union or not, for example. One of my nieces at Earlham University told me there was an African American student who wanted to be a part of the African American Students' Union, and she said "You are all making me feel left out." I had such race shame, and wanted to call this child whom I don't know, and tell her, "Why don't you go and learn something about their lives?" and "It's not about you." So I think about this type of broadening, but also I've really been thinking about what I think the next generation of African American writing and culture is going to be like. I tell this story about my little boy, who once said, "So Daddy's African?" and then to me he said, "And you're African American," then "So we're *Aaaa*frican American." So what's that going to look like, what is that literature going to be? I feel great anticipation about this, because it's the interesting and great part about being in this country. Despite everything that's wretched, there is so much that is happening. I was never much of a "Back to Africa" or "Afrocentric" type, but this has made me much less sentimental about thinking about what kind of connection an African American has to the African past. I've become more and more interested in thinking and writing about the idea of "Africa" for black writers. It's an idea, and it's not a good thing or a bad thing. It bears repeating: we have no pipeline, and it's something we need to think about as well.

I have never been to Asmara, Eritrea. I think a great deal about what travel can mean for black people; there are many reasons we get either devoted to or mired down in the local and in the American scene and situation. The possibility of living elsewhere or just experiencing yourself elsewhere, and understanding the ways in which you are an American — and how some of that needs to be challenged — has been really wonderful. Getting to know any other culture is a really lucky thing. In the case of Eritrean culture — which I think is a very noble culture with a noble struggle in their thirty-year independence war — I see it in the character of the people I now know. It makes me think about immigrant experience and it's been very humbling.

MP: Oftentimes, the immigrant doesn't feel like he or she has a home. There's a line in your poem "Stray," spoken I'm assuming by Ficre, "*I was a stray man before I met [you].*" This line circles back in a way to blackness as a home, but differently — it's playing in a different key there.

EA: I really love that poem. I read it once at a reading and I made myself cry and I was so embarrassed. It makes the relationship to home and the relationship to language much more complicated. My husband speaks seven languages, and he speaks them because of colonialism, migration, and forced migration. I always thought it was important to be bilingual, but it's more about pushing yourself out of a comfort zone, and letting yourself shift and learn more — having more facets. This is not altogether about Africanness. I was very lucky to have time to know my mother-in-law because she was a product of place. They were Eritrean Christian Coptic

Highlanders for generations upon generations upon generations. It's also a small group of people — three million people, that's it. And they have a purer language than English: there is something hefty in the way proverbs are transmitted, for example. The information is transmitted in straight language without a lot of other things coming into it.

MP: Does it have a presence?

EA: Yes. My kids don't speak it; they know some words — we all know some words. When my mother-in-law was here, she didn't speak English. A lot of people of her generation would come to visit her because she was really quite a matriarch. There could be a whole day of not speaking English except for us, but this doesn't happen as much anymore. My husband's extended family speaks a kind of hybrid. They speak Tigrinya, Italian, English, Amharic, or they go in and out with certain purposes. For example, when my husband is being avuncular with his nieces, it's always in Tigrinya, so there's a tone that comes along with it. He does this also when he wants to be absolutely, breathtakingly succinct. There's something about not only being good with language, but about the concentration of a language that's one strain — that's out of one place. Often when he translates it for me, there'll be one word and he'll give me an English paragraph translation — but I still can't distill it back to one English word. There is just that much complexity in single words. It's interesting just trying to see myself in a broader context even though I realized, especially in my last book: I am so American. This is one of the sublimities I explore in *American Sublime* — is what I think is sublime about American English and the vernacular.

MP: We're all really basic on some level — that we define in opposition. Having a whole life with someone who is not American highlights your Americanness. And I love what you say about travel. Cyrus Cassells came to my last Black Poetry class and it was the biggest gift he gave to my students, many of whom are so invested in the local and what one might call local definitions of blackness. He was there talking about living in Italy or travelling through Spain, and he started speaking Spanish to one of my students who's a Spanish major — and it was clear he could be black and go anywhere in the world and he was not giving up his blackness. Blackness is everywhere, as you said in your poem "Today's News": "I called / home to say it was colored on channel three . . ." It's such a gift for students to see, "Have blackness, will travel."

EA: That's right. We have our own graduation for black students with their own ceremony. You see students in their everyday clothes like blue jeans and a T-shirt and their student garb, and their parents are all decked out — representing the race because they're in their best; it's fantastic. Not all Africans are happy about some of the African Americans' ideas about Africa, and productive dialogues get started this way. I feel sad because I want black people who find themselves in the United States to be able to see each other. There are instances where I've heard comments like, "The black Americans resent the West Indians because . . ." and "The West Africans look down on black Americans . . ." and I just think we need to explore who we all are — and eat each other's food!

MP: One of the things I wonder about in your poetry is the trope of the Middle Passage. Has it been reopened for you? I see in your poems about your mother-in-law or the *Amistad* how it's a rescripting of passages. Have you thought about this at all?

EA: I haven't, no, but it's interesting. I was recently looking at a poem written by Kamau Brathwaite called "Passages," which I hadn't looked at in about fifteen years. He's talking about a lot of New World journeys. I glanced at it and thought, "Oh, I can't just glance at it, I have to really, seriously read it all the way through." We have different African ancestors and he's coming from someplace where they were not enslaved. It's interesting — and I don't know . . .

MP: You used the trope in the childbirth poems, too. There are some ideas of passages or journeys, so I wonder if you are doing it creatively in your work. You keep coming back to the *Amistad*? I was wondering if, like Rita Dove and her incest motif, yours will be this journey or passage motif?

EA: Maybe I am. I'm not done with it yet. I thought I was done. I knew I didn't want it to be a book-length poem, and I questioned myself, "Why don't you be a part of something large? Be a part of other things, work with other things?" Somehow I felt like even if I wrote the greatest book-length poem in the world, there would be something complicating its reception. I am waiting for someone to point out that there was ambition behind writing the *Amistad* sequence, and at least to use the word *epic* behind it. Someone needs to ask, "Who else is telling these big American stories?" Writing that sequence was not ambitious for the sake of ambition, but you know that if a white man wrote this, if a white writer wrote this, it would get talked about in a different way. There would be a whole different language for recognizing what I was trying to do, whether it was successful or not.

MP: Are you deliberately moving into epic now? You have longer and longer narrative sequences such as "Neonatology" and the Toni Morrison dreams — although that was pretty short — but also the *Amistad* poems. I wondered if you're feeling that you are a mature poet now and can move into the epic?

EA: The *Amistad* is such a rich and amazing topic. When the sequence was published in *South Atlantic Quarterly*, there was a little article called "The Negro Digs Up Her Past: *Amistad*," telling about her past. I tell the story of coming to write that poem, and about walking New Haven, and thinking about what happened there, and thinking, "Where am I *really*?" I know where the university tells me I am every day, and I know where these buildings tell me I am now, but I still wonder about it all. I had just delivered the Phi Beta Kappa poem at Harvard's graduation, which was quite an auspicious occasion. I wrote an occasional poem. That's where I found that I hadn't exhausted the *Amistad*, because I was talking about that, and it took me into the African burial ground in New York, in lower Manhattan. I've always been completely obsessed with that place, and to think of what's underneath the ground we walk. I can't imagine not thinking that's important to explore, to know where the stories are, and that's where so much irony always is.

MP: The *Amistad* is so much now the thing you're digging up, so to speak. I'm fascinated by Covey, too — the translator. There's only one poem on Covey — "Translator." He's a *translator* — a better detail couldn't have dropped in your lap, and what a role for you. There's a moment when he has contact with the captives and he says, "Who am I now?" which echoes back to the Belo Horizante poem. It's what Hazel Carby talked about last time I heard her speak. She was talking about "the encounter." I wonder if there's then a corollary? In your poem the African American encounters the African — and it's being imagined through Covey, even though he's not African American, per se. He's the no-longer African because he's migrated, yet he's having the encounter with the Africans. The poem ends so beautifully: he sings his father's song from this specifically black body, so loudly he shakes the jail. How does he embody your own relations to Africanness, the Diaspora, to singing the father's song in the black body?

EA: You just said it all. It is beautiful, but in that poem, I love him most all. I always thought it was just my attachment to him, and that had to say something about me. That's the most important moment to me, and he's the most important figure, and the most interesting.

MP: You end with Cinque because he is the hero in the classic sense of the story, but for your telling it, Covey is the hero.

EA: Yes, Covey's the hero. It is interesting that his body must be black, because certainly this is about an anachronistic moment. It's an anachronistic yearning and declaration, and it isn't about my interest in black culture. "What is this thing called *blackness*? What is this thing called *black people*? Who are we? How do we hang together even if we diverge?" In my Phi Beta Kappa poem, I mention that in the African burial section, it says there are four hundred Africans buried here. In the poem I correct this and say they were Americans, and I say they were African New Yorkers. I was trying to be precise about who they were, but they're not the romantic version — they weren't Africans anymore because they lived and died in America. Nobody knows where these particular people were born, and they could have been born in New York City, or could have been born in the United States.

MP: For you, it always seems to come back to this question of self-definition. You're talking about black culture at large, but it always comes back through the personae as the "Who am I?" Even though the Ali poems are in *American Sublime*, they were originally published a good ten years ago, correct?

EA: They're old. They were published in a book edited by Elliot Goren. For the longest time, they were a part of the Dark Room Collective. Kevin Young and Thomas Alice had a press called Fisted Pick Press, and they were going to do it as a chapbook for a long time, so I held off on it.

MP: In the Ali poems, you're showing how the man made himself, a self-definition poem. Like in the essay where you talk about Anna Julia Cooper, who creates herself in writing, or the childbirth poems, where giving birth is all about yourself. You come back on the individual level to the self-defining again and again. That's where I think it goes back to Covey. You talk about the black culture at large in this whole project, but always come back to the individual, too.

EA: I do love people and their stories. At a simple level, this interests me. I want to know who people are, I want to know their stories and the quirks in their stories. In Anna Deavere Smith's work, she writes about how she gets people to talk in a way that's real. What she's trying to get from people when she interviews them is the moment where they are speaking in their own true voice. She said a linguist told her to ask one of three questions:

Have you ever come near death? What are the circumstances of your birth? Have you ever been accused of something you didn't do? The linguist said these are situations when you will get people to speak in their own unguarded language. After I had my first child, not only was that the story I had to tell, but I was interested in the same experience with other women. I love to hear birth stories, the whole package — because it's a whole story. There's great richness in these kinds of stories.

MP: One of the other things I've noticed in your poetic is you often are linking loss, art, trauma, and aesthetics. "American Blues" is about loss, you have a series of ars poeticas, and then you have the *Amistad* poems, which you follow with the "American Sublime" section. You did the same thing in *Body of Life*. You said earlier you're a poet about joy, and you believe in joy. How do you see trauma connected to art?

EA: I believe in trauma, too. I feel I've been entrusted with some of *The Terrible Stories*, to use Lucille Clifton's great title. I feel more and more kinship to her work as I move along, realizing not everyone can tell the terrible stories — but I can — and this started with *The Venus Hottentot*. It's just my job. Bearing witness is important, and it's something art must do, and can do. Of course, it's transformative, bearing witness. It's not only recording, although I am very interested in bring bits of the documentary into the poetry. It can be wonderful, and interesting, and exciting and fruitful. The African American experience has so many amazing stories that need to be witnessed, which need to be told and need to find their resting place.

Also, one of the things experiencing trauma does is it takes language away by suppressing it or by distorting it, or not giving it a place to be spoken. I'm interested in excavating and exploring and imagining this.

MP: This is a big part of the *Amistad* poems — the whole issue of them being able to speak, and not speaking in the other person's language but finding their own, their own voices. You end with Cinque speaking, and the first thing he does is testify to the painful horrific things which happened.

One of the things I found interesting, and this has come up a couple of different times in your interviews, is you have placed yourself in the lineage of Gwendolyn Brooks and Walt Whitman. You might be surprised that I've written an essay in which I place you as Emily Dickinson in comparison to Cyrus Cassells as Walt Whitman in the contemporary scene of African American poetry. I'm curious about why you might see yourself as

Whitmanesque, and what comes to mind if you can frame your work in Dickinsonian words instead?

EA: That's great. The Whitmanian part is "I am large, I contain multitudes," so it is about a complex self saying "This is who I am." It's also about the epic American prerogative, which I want to rewrite as female — to take long steps to cover that land, really just go for it in a large way. It's about me. There's that, and even in "Haircut," or "Harlem Birthday Party," which Marilyn Hacker published in the *Kenyon Review* — it felt like such a wonderful ratification of this new thing I was trying to do. When I first did it, it didn't feel like me but they needed to be long. I would put Dickinson in my theme of the peculiar girl intellectual, the most important, secret part of me. It's the part I feel like no one will ever totally know, and that I can only reexperience in my poetry. Dickinson doesn't sound remotely like anyone else. What one can learn from a Dickinson is wholesomeness with utter economy. Her poems don't feel parsimonious, they don't feel boney. They feel like attar, nectar, rock, tincture — it's like one of those Brooks things I said — tensile strength. Also, detailed without being fussy, which I think is so hard to achieve, and philosophical but elliptically so. As much as I'm very interested in narrative in a lot of the poems, I'm also interested in elliptical-ness. I have to force myself to that more, but I think there's great power in that, and it's important to do.

MP: Your poetry is very often internal. Maybe what you're identifying is a "being in over your head sort of being" in yourself. Cyrus Cassells's poetry roams all over the place now, and especially in his last two volumes. You're roaming, but you're roaming from within. In "Haircut," it's not like you roamed very far; you roamed back to another homeplace and there's all this migration and diaspora represented in that local.

EA: I got the idea for the poem "Krishna Denies Eating Mud," from a show "At the Age of Society." There were Mogul miniatures and by each one they had a little drawer with a magnifying glass, and they were so incredible. The titles were little poems, so that's where I saw that the mother looks inside and sees the universe in Krishna's mouth — in a little boy's mouth.

MP: The universe is within, it's localized. I know there's a phrase that gets batted around quite a bit, and it's *postmodern blackness*. How, to your mind, can blackness be postmodern? There's the idea in your work about having a home in blackness, and articulating or singing the black female body. There are many themes that might seem incompatible with the idea of postmodernism, in which there are no stable terms, nothing can be outside of play, and identity is ever-shifting subjectivity. Do you see your work as postmodern, and if so, how?

EA: We've had to redefine what modernism is when we put black creativity into the conversation, and the same must happen for postmodernism. For example, when I teach the "New Negro" or modernism, I discuss how this was supposed to be a period in literature all about detachment and envoi. Meanwhile, in African American literature in that era, there's all this looking to the past and not finding anything. It's looking to an African past, it's not looking to an evacuated European past, and looking to the future and seeing great promise. How do we put all that together? I would say, also, why must white postmodernism be separate? Let's talk about Harryette Mullen for a minute as an example. To me, *Sleeping with the Dictionary* is a really good example of how you can have a kind of language play — and a L=A=N=G=U=A=G=E play — that doesn't *not* have politics in it, that doesn't *not* have history in it, and is *not* about play for its own sake. It's about play that's coming out of something. If you put what black writers are doing into the larger conversation, you have to redefine the terms, or you have to say when the term *postmodernism* was coined we were only talking about white people, or white people from this particular part of the country. I feel like there's a way in which so many of the L=A=N=G=U=A=G=E poets haven't thought about black poets at all, or when they see black poets they see maybe two people. They don't see them in the complexity of what their work is doing at all, and they have a very, very limited understating of what falls or could fall under the sign of blackness. They don't know what innovation is, in terms of African American creativity. Maybe some of the things they are defining as innovations might not seem very interesting to a lot of us, or seem very fresh. Writing epics, for example, or telling history is maybe the far more radical break with the past, and it's the *more* important work some of us felt the need to do. So yes, in a rich and complicated conversation about postmodernism, it's more about saying, "How does my work change how we talk about what postmodernism is?"

MP: That's of course what postmodernism is supposed to do. This brings me to my final question. One of my favorite poems in *American Sublime* is also one of the shortest. "Ars Poetica #16: Lots": "the captives drew lots for everything / rations, labor, sleeping, space — / I drew a laminated card / that read 'Countee Cullen.' / Here I am." I love the laminated card. Where did this come from, and why Cullen? Why is he aligned with your poetic identity?

EA: This is where interviews are useful. We share a birthday — May 30. And, there's another little trick, a little clue, a funny little thing. The dedication to my first book is syntactically the same dedication that's in Cullen's first book. He says "To my mother and father, this first book." I've always liked that, even before I knew his work. I only learned about ten years ago we shared birthdays. Whitman's is a day after mine, and Brooks's is a few days after that, so we are all Geminis. Shirley Varrett the opera singer also shares my birthday. Because of this, I feel a close affinity. There weren't a lot of poetry books in my house growing up, but his poetry was around because my father said he lived in the neighborhood. He was a Harlemite who might have known my grandmother. We had one of his children's books, which had been my dad's — *Christopher Cat* — and we had *Color*. I read whatever poetry books were around, and Cullen was part of my idea of what a poet was. I find a great deal in his "Heritage" poem, "What is Africa to me." This is a big, huge, fascinating, important poem with a lot of applications and a lot of different directions.

MP: So this allusion to him in this volume is very significant because of that?

EA: Right. His career interested me, and W. E. B. DuBois and others really thought he would be our Negro ambassador in letters. That didn't work, so in some ways it's a cautionary tale; you can't think of yourself that way even if you get rewarded. You ultimately have to return every day to the work.

MP: The card is laminated then because it's protective?

EA: Yes.

MP: And it — you — won't get all beat up.

EA: That's right.

MP: Well, this has been great, Elizabeth. Thanks so much for your time.

[2005]

BIBLIOGRAPHY

Walking into the Light

Grewal, Inderpal. *Transnational America: Feminisms, Diasporas, Neoliberalisms*. Durham: Duke University Press, 2005.

Johnson, James Weldon. *The Book of American Negro Poetry*. New York: BiblioBazaar, 2006.

Mullen, Harryette. "Poetry and Identity." In *Telling It Slant: Avant-Garde Poetics of the 1990s*, edited by Mark Wallace and Steven Mark, 27–31. Tuscaloosa: University of Alabama Press, 2001.

Pereira, Malin. *Rita Dove's Cosmopolitanism*. Urbana: University of Illinois Press, 2003.

Young, Kevin. "Thieves of Paradise." *The Boston Review: A Political and Literary Forum*, April/May 1999. http://www.bostonreview.net/BR24.2/young.html (accessed March 11, 2010).

Wanda Coleman

Brown, Patricia. "What Saves Us: An Interview with Wanda Coleman." *Callaloo* 26.3 (2003): 635–61.

Coleman, Wanda. "Coulda, Shoulda, Woulda." Review of *A Song Flung Up to Heaven*, by Maya Angelou. *Los Angeles Times*, April 14, 2002, R3.

———. "On Theloniousism." *Caliban* 4 (August 1988): 67–79.

———. "Poetic Dynamics and the Meta-Lingo of the Manuscript." In *Ordering the Storm: How to Put Together a Book of Poems*, edited by Susan Grimm, 29–33. Cleveland: Cleveland State University Poetry Center, 2006.

Cormer, Krista. "Black Los Angeles and Wanda Coleman." In *Landscapes of the New West: Gender and Geography in Contemporary Women's Writing*, 88–103. Chapel Hill: University of North Carolina Press, 1999.

Magistrale, Tony. "Doing Battle with the Wolf: A Critical Introduction to Wanda Coleman's Poetry." *Black American Literature Forum* 23.3 (1989): 539–54.

Magistrale, Tony, and Patricia Ferreira. "Sweet Mama Wanda Tells Fortunes: An Interview with Wanda Coleman." *Black American Literature Forum* 24.3 (1990): 491–507.

Pereira, Malin. "Sister Seer and Scribe: Teaching Wanda Coleman's and Elizabeth Alexander's Poetic Responses to Sylvia Plath." *Plath Profiles* 1

(August 2008): 280–90. http://www.iun.edu/~plath/vol1/index.shtml (accessed March 22, 2010).

Pettis, Joyce. *African American Poets: Lives, Works and Sources*. Santa Barbara: Greenwood Press, 2002.

Review of *Mercurochrome*, by Wanda Coleman. *Publishers Weekly* 248.23 (June 2001): 76.

Ryan, Jennifer D. *Post-Jazz Poetics: A Social History*. New York: Palgrave Macmillan, 2010.

Skyes, Bobi. "An Interview: Wanda Coleman." *Callaloo* 24 (Spring/Summer 1985): 294–303.

Strand, Mark. *The Weather of Words*. New York: Random House, 2000.

"Truong Tran and Wanda Coleman." In *Letters to Poets: Conversations about Poetics, Politics, and Community*, edited by Jennifer Firestone and Dana Teen Lomax, 25–58. Philadelphia: Saturnalia Books, 2008.

Waniek, Marilyn Nelson. "Review: Sisters and Poets." *Callaloo* 16 (1982): 133–40.

Yusef Komunyakaa

Academy of American Poets. "Yusef Komunyakaa: An Argument Against Simplicity." http://www.poets.org/viewmedia.php/prmMID/5828 (accessed March 22, 2010).

Anderson, T.J. "A Finer Form: T. J. Anderson and Yusef Komunyakaa in Conversation." *Callaloo* 28.3 (2005): 585–91.

Asali, Muna. "An Interview with Yusef Komunyakaa." *New England Review* 16.1 (Winter 1994): 141–47.

Aubert, Alvin. "Rare Instances of Reconciliation." *Epoch* 28.1 (1989): 67–72.

——. "Stars and Gunbarrels." *African American Review* 28.4 (1994): 671–73.

——. "Yusef Komunyakaa: The Unified Vision — Canonization and Humanity." *African American Review* 27 (1993): 119–23.

Baer, William. "Still Negotiating with Images: An Interview with Yusef Komunyakaa." *Kenyon Review* 20.3–4 (1998): 5–29.

Blackburn, Alexander. "Komunyakaa in Colorado." *Callaloo* 28.3 (2005): 491–99.

Brice-Finch, Jacqueline. "Review: *Thieves of Paradise*." *World Literature Today* 73.1 (1991): 154–55.

Brown, Ashley. "Review: *Pleasure Dome: New and Collected Poems*." *World Literature Today* 76.1 (2002): 153–54.

Cartwright, Keith. "Weave a Circle around Him Thrice: Komunyakaa's Hoodoo Balancing Act." *Callaloo* 28.3 (2005): 851–63.

Collins, Michael. "Komunyakaa, Collaboration, and the Wishbone: An Interview." *Callaloo* 28.3 (2005): 620–34.

———. "Komunyakaa's Pictures of Choice: An Introduction." *Callaloo* 28.3 (2005): 467–71.

———. "Staying Human." *Parnassus: Poetry in Review* 18–19.1–2 (1993–94): 26–49.

———. "Yusef Komunyakaa: A Bibliography." *Callaloo* 28.3 (2005):883–86.

Cronk, Olivia: "*Taboo* by Yusef Komunyakaa." *Bookslut*, December 2004. http://www.bookslut.com/poetry/2004_12_003800.php (accessed March 22,2010).

Dargan, Kyle G. "Excursions: A Conversation with Yusef Komunyakaa." *Callaloo* 29.3 (2006): 741–50.

Datta, Goutam. "Komunyakaa and the Kolkata Book Fair: Entries from a Diary of a Journey to India." *Callaloo* 28.3 (2005): 734–47.

Davis, Anthony. *Wakonda's Dream*. Libretto by Yusef Komunyakaa. Opera Omaha, 2007.

Dawidoff, Sally. "An Interview with Yusef Komunyakaa." In *Page to Page: Retrospectives of Writers from the Seattle Review*, edited by Colleen J. McElroy, 181–86. Seattle and London: University of Washington Press, 2006.

Deming, Alison Hawthorne. "The Tension between Memory and Forgetting in the Poetry of Yusef Komunyakaa." *Kenyon Review* 15.4 (1993): 217–22.

Derricotte, Toi. "Seeing and Re-Seeing: An Exchange between Yusef Komunyakaa and Toi Derricotte." *Callaloo* 28.3 (2005): 513–18.

Dowdy, Michael C. "Working in the Space of Disaster: Yusef Komunyakaa's Dialogues with America." *Callaloo* 38.3 (2005): 812–23.

Fabre, Michel. "On Yusef Komunyakaa." *Southern Quarterly* 34.2 (1996): 5–8.

Feinstein, Sascha. "An Enormous Yes: Contemporary Jazz Poetry." In *Jazz Poetry: From the 1920s to the Present*, 163–82. Westport, Connecticut, and London: Praeger, 1997.

———. "Portrait of Gratitude." *Callaloo* 28.3 (2005): 488–90.

———. "Yusef Komunyakaa's 'Testimony' and the Humanity of Charlie Parker." *Callaloo* 28.3 (2005): 757–62.

———."Yusef Komunyakaa: Survival Masks." In *Ask Me Now: Conversations on Jazz and Literature*, edited by Sascha Feinstein, 190–211. Bloomington and Indianapolis: Indiana University Press, 2007.

Francini, Antonella. "Notes on Translating Yusef Komunyakaa's Poetry into Italian." *Callaloo* 28.3 (2005): 707–12.

Gilyard, Keith. Review of *Blues Notes: Essays, Interviews, and Commentaries*, by Yusef Komunyakaa. *African American Review* 35.4 (2001): 677–79.

Goldstein, Laurence. "Madame Nhu, Woman and Warrior: A Reading of 'Le Xuan, Beautiful Spring.'" *Callaloo* 28.3 (2005): 764–70.

Gonzalez, Dennis. "The Herido Project." *Callaloo* 28.3 (2005): 604–9.

Gotera, Vincente F. "Depending on the Light: Yusef Komunyakaa's *Dien Cai Dau.*" In *America Rediscovered: Critical Essays on Literature and Film of the Vietnam War*, edited by Owen W. Gilman and Lorrie Smith, 282–300. New York: Garland Publishers, 1990.

———. "Killer Imagination." *Callaloo* 13 (Spring 1990): 364–71.

———. "'Lines of Tempered Steel': An Interview with Yusef Komunyakaa." *Callaloo* 13 (1990): 215–29.

———. "Mentor and Friend: Yusef Komunyakaa as Teacher." *Callaloo* 28.3 (2005): 505–12.

———, ed. *Radical Visions: Poetry by Vietnam Veterans*. Athens and London: University of Georgia Press, 1994.

———. Review of *Dien Cai Dau*, by Yosef Komunyakaa. *Callaloo* 13.2 (Spring 1990): 364–71.

———. "Review: Synecdoche: Brief Poetry Notices." *The North American Review* 288.1 (2003): 53.

Gracia, Chad. "Collaborating with Komunyakaa: The Creation of Gilgamesh." *Callaloo* 28.3 (2005): 541–44.

Gwynn, R. S. "Review: What the Center Holds." *Hudson Review* 46.4 (1994): 741–50.

Jakubiak, Katarzyna. "Between Failure and a New Creation: (Re) reading Yusef Komunyakaa's 'The Beast and Burden' in the Light of Paul Gilroy's Black Atlantic." *Callaloo* 28.3 (2005): 865–81.

Jarab, Josef. "Translating Yusef Komunyakaa into Czech: A Personal Confession." *Callaloo* 28.3 (2005): 691–96.

Johnson, Thomas C. "Interview with Yusef Komunyakaa." *Worcester Review* 19.1–2 (1998): 119–27.

Jones, Kirkland C. "Folk Idiom in the Literary Expression of Two African American Authors: Rita Dove and Yusef Komunyakaa." In *Language and Literature in the African American Imagination*, edited by Carol Aisha Blackshire-Belay, 149–65. Westport, Connecticut: Greenwood Press, 1992.

Jones, Patricia Spears. "Yusef Komunyakaa — Blue Notes: Essays, Interviews and Commentaries." *Black Issues Book Review* (2000). http://findarticles. com/p/articles/mi_mOHST.is_4_2/ai_65805489 (accessed March 11, 2010).

Kelly, Robert. "Yusef Komunyakaa and William Matthews." *The Georgia Review* 46.4 (Winter 1992): 645–61.

Kirsch, Adam. "Verse Averse." *The New Republic* 224.4493 (2001): 38–41.

Knowles, Pamela. "Thirteen Kinds of Desire: A Collaboration." *Callaloo* 28.3 (2005): 578–81.

Komunyakaa, Yusef. "Dark Waters." In *The Color of Nature: Culture, Identity, and the Natural World*, edited by Alison H. Deming and Lauret E. Savoy, 98–112. Minneapolis: Milkweed Editions, 2002.

Komunyakaa, Yusef, and David Lehman, eds. *The Best American Poetry*. New York: Scribner, 2003.

Leonard, Keith D. "Yusef Komunyakaa's Blues: The Postmodern Music of *Neon Vernacular*." *Callaloo* 28.3 (2005): 825–49.

Lewis, Rudolph. "Interview with Pulitzer Prize-Winning Poet Yusef Komunyakaa, New Orleans, May 1985, Part 1." *ChickenBones: A Journal for Literary and Artistic African-American Themes*. http://www.nathanielturner.com/rudyinterviewsyusef.htm (accessed March 22, 2010).

Marshall, Tod. "Yusef Komunyakaa." In *Range of the Possible: Interviews by Tod Marshall*, 146–56. Spokane: Eastern Washington University Press, 2002.

Matejka, Adrian. "Off the Rim." *Callaloo* 28.3 (2005): 500–504.

Mejer, Valerie. "On Awareness." *Callaloo* 28.3 (2005): 716–17.

Mitrano, G. F. "A Conversation with Yusef Komunyakaa." *Callaloo* 28.3 (2005): 521–30.

Pavlić, Edward M. *Crossroads Modernism: Descent and Emergence in African-American Literary Culture*. London and Minneapolis: University of Minnesota Press, 2002.

———. "Open the Unusual Door: Visions from the Dark Window in Yusef Komunyakaa's Early Poems." *Callaloo* 28.3 (2005): 780–96.

Pettis, Joyce. *African American Poets: Lives, Works and Sources*. Santa Barbara: Greenwood Press, 2002.

Pinson, Hermine. "Yusef Komunyakaa's New Blues." *Callaloo* 28.3 (2005): 568–71.

"Princeton University's 'Jazz' Poet." *Journal of Blacks in Higher Education* 34 (2002): 38.

Ramsey, William M. "Knowing Their Place: Three Black Writers and the Postmodern South." *Southern Literary Journal* 37.2 (2005): 119–39.

Richards, David R. "Warrior Aligned with Beauty: A Visit with Bloomington's Pulitzer-Prize Winning Poet." *Arts Indiana* 18.1 (February 1996): 20–21.

Richter, Jennifer. "Review: *Magic City*." *Callaloo* 17.2 (1994): 650–52.

Ringlanda, Don. "Rejecting 'Sweet Geometry': Komunyakaa's *Duende*." *Journal of American Culture* 16 (1993): 21–28.

Rocha, Flavia. "Man Talking to a Mirror: On the Attempt to Translate Yusef

Komunyakaa's Vibrant Verbal Landscape into the Mild Undulations of Brazilian Portuguese." *Callaloo* 28.3 (2005): 725–27.

Salas, Angela M.. "'Flashback through the Heart': Yusef Komunyakaa and the Poetry of Self-Assertion." In *The Furious Flowering of African American Poetry*, edited by Joanne V. Gabbin, 298–309. Charlottesville: University Press of Virginia, 1999.

———. "Race, Human Empathy, and Negative Capability: The Poetry of Yusef Komunyakaa." *College Literature* 30.4 (2003): 32–53.

———. "*Talking Dirty to the Gods* and the Infinitude of Language: Or Mr. Komunyakaa's Cabinet of Wonder." *Callaloo* 28.3 (2005): 797–811.

Salas, Angela, Keith Leonard, and Sascha Feinstein. "Panel on the Poetry of Yusef Komunyakaa." The Internet Poetry Archive. http://www.ibiblio.org/ipa/komunyakaa.php (accessed March 11, 2010).

Samaras, Nicholas. Review of *Magic City*, by Yusef Komunyakaa. *Harvard Review* 6 (1994): 210–11.

Shaw, Andrea. Review of *Talking Dirty to the Gods*, by Yusef Komunyakaa. *World Literature Today* 75.3–4 (2001): 153.

Sherman, Susan. "Interview with Paul Muldoon and Yusef Komunyakaa." *Bomb* 65 (Fall 1998): 74–80.

Stein, Kevin. "Vietnam and the 'Voice Within': Public and Private History in Yusef Komunyakaa's *Dien Cai Dau*." *Massachusetts Review* 36.4 (1995–96): 541–61.

Suarez, Ernest, T. W. Stanford III, and Amy Verner. "Yusef Komunyakaa." In *Southbound: Interviews with Southern Poets*, 130–43. Columbia: University of Missouri Press, 1999.

Tabaczynski, Michal. "Rhythm that Survives, Rhythm that Saves." *Callaloo* 28.3 (2005): 701–2.

Trethewey, Natasha D. "On Close Reading: Yusef Komunyakaa's 'White Lady.'" *Callaloo* 28.3 (2005): 775–77.

Turner, Daniel C. "Yusef Komunyakaa." In *Southern Writers: A New Biographical Dictionary*, edited by Joseph M. Flora and Amber Vogel, 241. Baton Rouge: Louisiana State University Press, 2006.

Wallenstein, Barry. "JazzPoetry/jazz-poetry/'jazz poetry'???" *African American Review* 27.4 (1993): 665–71.

Waniek, Marilyn Nelson. "Review: Black Silence, Black Songs." *Callaloo* 17 (1983): 156–65.

Young, Andy. "Komunyakaa and the Launching of Meena." *Callaloo* 28.3 (2005): 750–51.

Young, Kevin. "*Thieves of Paradise*." *The Boston Review: A Political and Literary*

Forum, April/May 1999. http://www.bostonreview.net/BR24.2/young
.html (accessed March 11, 2010).

"Yusef Komunyakaa." In *Ecstatic Occasions, Expedient Forms: 85 Leading
Contemporary Poets Select and Comment on Their Poems*, edited by David
Lehman, 120–22. Ann Arbor: University of Michigan Press, 1996.

Rita Dove

Alexander, Elizabeth. "An Interview with Rita Dove." *The Writers Chronicle*
38.2 (2005): 163–68.

"At the Hands of Fate: Writer Rita Dove Reveals the Genesis and Evolution
of *The Darker Face of the Earth*." http://kennedy-center.org/interviews/
ritadove.html (accessed November 19, 1997).

Bada, Valerie. "'Dramatising the Verse': or Versifying the Drama: Rita
Dove's *The Darker Face of the Earth: A Verse Play*." In *Mechanics of the
Mirage: Postwar American Poetry*, edited by Michel Delville and Christine
Pagnouelle, 277–84. Liege, Beligium: Universite de Liege, 2000.

Baker, Houston A. "Rita Dove, *Grace Notes*." *Black American Literature Forum*
24 (1990): 574–77.

Bellin, Steven. "A Conversation with Rita Dove." *Mississippi Review* 23.3 (1995):
10–35.

Berger, Charles. "The Granddaughter's Archive: Rita Dove's *Thomas and
Beulah*." *Western Humanities Review* 50–51 (1996–97): 359–63.

Booth, Alison. "Abduction and Other Severe Pleasures: Rita Dove's *Mother
Love*." *Callaloo* 19.1 (1996): 125–30.

Carlisle, Theodora. "Reading the Scars: Rita Dove's *The Darker Face of the
Earth*." *African American Review* 34.1 (2000): 135–50.

Carroll, Rebecca. *I Know What the Red Clay Looks Like: The Voice and Vision
of Black American Women Writers*. New York: Carol Southern Books,
1994.

Cavalieri, Grace. "Rita Dove: An Interview with Grace Cavalieri." *American
Poetry Review* 24.2 (March–April 1995): 11–15.

Cook, Emily Walker. "'But She Won't Set Foot / In His Turtle-Dove Nash':
Gender Roles and Gender Symbolism in Rita Dove's *Thomas and Beulah*."
College Language Association Journal 38.3 (1995): 322–30.

Costello, Bonnie. "Scars and Wings: Rita Dove's *Grace Notes*." *Callaloo* 14.2
(1991): 434–38.

Cruz, Diana V. "Refuting Exile: Rita Dove Reading Melvin B. Tolson."
Callaloo 31.3 (2008): 789–802.

Cushman, Stephen. "And the Dove Returned." *Callaloo* 19.1 (1996): 131–34.

DuBois, W. E. B. *The Souls of Black Folk*. In *DuBois*, edited by Nathan Huggins, 357–548. New York: The Library of America, 1986.

Dungy, Camille T. "An Interview with Rita Dove." *Callaloo* 28.4 (2005): 1027–40.

Edmundson, Mark, ed. "Rita Dove's *Mother Love*: A Discussion." *Callaloo* 19.1 (1996): 123–42.

Erickson, Peter. "Rita Dove's Shakespeares." In *Transforming Shakespeare: Contemporary Women's Re-visions in Literature and Performance*, edited by Marianne Novy, 87–101. New York: St. Martin's Press, 1999.

———. "Rita Dove's Two Shakespeare Poems." *Shakespeare and the Classroom* 4.2 (1996): 53–55.

Georgoudaki, Ekaternini. *Race, Gender, and Class Perspectives in the Works of Maya Angelou, Gwendolyn Brooks, Nikki Giovanni, and Audre Lorde*. Greece: Aristotle University of Thessaloniki Press, 1991.

———. "Rita Dove: Crossing Boundaries." *Callaloo* 14.2 (1991): 419–33.

Gregerson, Linda. *Negative Capability: Contemporary American Poetry*. Ann Arbor: University of Michigan Press, 2001.

———. "Review: *The Yellow House on the Corner* and *Museum*. *Poetry* 145 (October 1984): 46–49.

Hammer, Mike, and Christina Daub. "Interview: Rita Dove." *Plum Review* 9 (1996): 27–41.

Hampton, Janet Jones. "Portraits of a Diasporean People: The Poetry of Shirley Campbell and Rita Dove." *Afro-Hispanic Review* 14.1 (1995): 262–76.

Harris, Peter. "Four Salvers Salvaging: New Work by Voigt, Olds, Dove, and McHugh." *Virginia Quarterly Review* 64.2 (1988): 262–76.

Hull, Akasha (Gloria). "Review: When Language is Everything." *Women's Review of Books* 11.8 (1994): 6–7.

Ingersoll, Earl G., ed. *Conversations with Rita Dove*. Jackson: University Press of Mississippi, 2002.

Jablon, Madelyn. "The African American *Kunstlerroman*." *Diversity: A Journal of Multicultural Issues* 2 (1994): 21–28.

Jones, Kirkland C. "Folk Idiom in the Literary Expression of Two African American Authors: Rita Dove and Yusef Komunyakaa." In *Language and Literature in the African American Imagination*, edited by Carol Aisha Blackshire-Belay, 149–65. Westport, Connecticut: Greenwood Press, 1992.

Keene, John. "Rita Dove's *The Darker Face of the Earth*: An Introductory Note." *Callaloo* 17.2 (1994): 371–73.

Keller, Lynn. *Forms of Expansion: Recent Long Poems by Women*. Chicago and London: University of Chicago Press, 1997.

Kirkpatrick, Patricia. "The Throne of Blues: An Interview with Rita Dove." *Hungry Mind Review* 35 (1995): 36–37.

Lloyd, Emily. "Navigating the Personal: An Interview with Poet Laureate Rita Dove." *Off Our Backs: A Woman's News Journal* 24.4 (April 1994): 1–22.

Lofgren, Lotta. "Partial Horror: Fragmentation and Healing in Rita Dove's *Mother Love*." *Callaloo* 19.1 (1996): 135–42.

McDowell, Robert. "The Assembling Vision of Rita Dove." *Callaloo* 9.1 (1986): 61–70.

———. "Rita Dove: Poet at the Dance." *American Poet* (2003): 32–38.

———. "This Life." *Callaloo* 26 (1986): 63–70.

Meitner, Erika. "On Rita Dove." *Callaloo* 31.3 (2008): 662–66.

Moyers, Bill. "Rita Dove." In *Language of Life: A Festival of Poets*, edited by James Haba and David Grubin, 109–28. New York: Doubleday, 1995.

Muske, C. "Breaking out of the Genre Ghetto (Sandra Cisneros, Rita Dove)." *Parnassus: Poetry in Review* 20 (1995): 409.

Nussbaum, Emily. "*American Smooth*: Dance Fever." Review of *American Smooth*, by Rita Dove. *New York Times Book Review*, November 21, 2004.

O'Connell, Erin. "Black Oedipus? Slavery in *Oedipus Tyrannus* and *The Darker Face of the Earth*." *Text and Presentation: The Journal of the Comparative Drama Conference* 24 (April 2003): 37–47.

Peabody, Richard, and Gretchen Johsen. "A Cage of Sound: An Interview with Rita Dove." *Gargoyle* 27 (1985): 2–13.

Pereira, Malin. "An Interview with Rita Dove." *Contemporary Literature* 40.2 (Summer 1999): 183–213.

———. *Rita Dove's Cosmopolitanism*. Chicago: University of Illinois Press, 2003.

———. "'When the pear blossoms / cast their pale faces on / the darker face of the earth': Miscegenation, the Primal Scene, and the Incest Motif in Rita Dove's Work." *African American Review* 36.2 (2002): 195–211.

Pettis, Joyce. *African American Poets: Lives, Works and Sources*. Santa Barbara: Greenwood Press, 2002.

Proitsaki, Maria. "Black Aesthetic and Beyond: Aesthetics and Ideology in the Poetry of Nikki Giovanni and Rita Dove." *Moderna Språk* 102:2 (2008): 15–23.

———. "A 'Circus-Freak' and 20,000 Other Migrants in Rita Dove's *Museum*." *Moderna Språk* 93.2 (1999): 149–56.

———. "Seasonal and Seasonable Motherhood in Dove's *Mother Love*." In *Women, Creators of Culture*, edited by Ekaterini Geogoudaki and Donna Pastourmatzi, 145–52. Greece: Hellenic Association of American Studies, 1997.

Ramakrishnan, P. "Wings of a Dove." *The Peninsula*, Spring 2007: 43–46.

Rampersand, Arnold. "The Poems of Rita Dove." *Callaloo* 9.1 (1986): 52–60.

Ratiner, Steven. *Giving Their Word: Conversations with Contemporary Poets.* Boston: University of Massachusetts Press, 2002.

Righelato, Pat. "Geometry and Music: Rita Dove's 'Fifth Sunday.'" *Yearbook of English Studies* 31 (2001): 62–73.

———. *Understanding Rita Dove*. Columbia: University of South Carolina Press, 2006.

"Rita Dove." In *Ecstatic Occasions, Expedient Forms: 85 Leading Contemporary Poets Select and Comment on Their Poems*, edited by David Lehman, 48–52. Ann Arbor: University of Michigan Press, 1996.

"Rita Dove Interview." Academy of Achievement. June 18, 1994. Las Vegas, Nevada. http://www.achievement.org (accessed February 22, 2010).

Rosenberg, Judith Pierce. "Rita Dove." *Belles Lettres* 9.2 (1993–94): 38–41.

Rowell, Charles Henry. "Interview with Rita Dove: Part 1." *Callaloo* 31.3 (2008): 695–706.

———. "Interview with Rita Dove: Part 2." *Callaloo* 31.3 (2008): 715–26.

Rubin, Stan Sanvel, and Judith Kitchen. "'The Underside of a Story': A Conversation with Rita Dove." In *The Post Confessionals: Conversations with American Poets of the Eighties*, edited by Earl Ingersoll, Judith Kitchen, and Stan Sanvel Rubin, 151–65. Teaneck, New Jersey: Farleigh Dickinson University Press, 1989.

Schneider, Steven. "Coming Home: An Interview with Rita Dove." *Iowa Review* 19.3 (1989): 112–23.

Sexton, Danny. "Lifting the Veil: Revision and Double-Consciousness in Rita Dove's *The Darker Face of the Earth*." *Callaloo* 31.3 (2008): 777–85.

Shaughnessy, Brenda. "Rita Dove: Taking the Heat." *Publishers Weekly* 246.15 (April 1999): 48–49.

Shea, Renee H. "'Irresistible Beauty': The Poetry and Person of Rita Dove." *Women in the Arts* Spring, 1999: 5–9.

———. "Review: *American Smooth*." *Poets and Writers* September/October 2004: 38–43.

Shoptaw, John. "Segregated Lives: Rita Dove's *Thomas and Beulah*." In *Reading Black, Reading Feminist: A Critical Anthology*, edited by Henry Louis Gates Jr., 374–81. London: Penguin, 1990.

Spiegelman, Willard. "Rita Dove, Dancing." *Virginia Quarterly Review* Winter (2005): 228–34.

St. Lawrence, Robb. "'Taking the Cards You're Dealt and Building a House': An Interview with Rita Dove." *Bellingham Review* 29.2 (2006): 77–84.

Steffen, Therese. "Beyond Ethnic Margin and Cultural Center: Rita Dove's 'Empire' of *Mother Love*." In *Empire*, edited by John G. Blair and Reinhold Wagnleitner, 10. Tübingen: Gunter Narr Verlag, 1997.

———. *Crossing Color: Transcultural Space and Place in Rita Dove's Poetry, Fiction, and Drama*. Oxford and New York: Oxford University Press, 2001.

———. "*The Darker Face of the Earth*: A Conversation with Rita Dove." *Transition: An International Review* 7.2.24 (1998): 104–23.

———. "Movements of a Marriage; or, Looking Awry at U.S. History: Rita Dove's *Thomas and Beulah*." In *Families*, edited by Werner Senn, 9. Tübingen: Gunter Narr Verlag, 1997.

———. "Rooted Displacement in Form: Rita Dove's Sonnet Cycle *Mother Love*." In *The Furious Flowering of African American Poetry*, edited by Joanne V. Gabbin, 60–76. Charlottesville: University Press of Virginia, 1999.

Stein, Kevin. "Lives in Motion: Multiple Perspectives in Rita Dove's Poetry." *Mississippi Review* 23.3 (1995): 51–79.

Steinman, Lisa M. "Dialogues between History and Dream." *Michigan Quarterly Review* 26.2 (1987): 428–38.

Taleb-Khyar, Mohamed B. "An Interview with Maryse Condé and Rita Dove." *Callaloo* 14.2 (1991): 347–66.

Van Dyne, Susan R. "Siting the Poet: Rita Dove's Refiguring of Traditions." In *Women Poets of the Americas: Toward a Pan-American Gathering*, edited by Jacqueline Vaught Brogan and Cordelia Candelaria, 68–87. Indiana: University of Notre Dame Press, 1999.

Vendler, Helen. "Blackness and Beyond Blackness." *New York Times Literary Supplement* (1994): 11–13.

———. "A Dissonant Triad." *Parnassus: Poetry in Review* 16.2 (1991): 391–404.

———. *The Given and the Made: Strategies of Poetic Redefinition*. Cambridge: Harvard University Press, 1995.

———. "An Interview with Rita Dove." In *Reading Black, Reading Feminist: A Critical Anthology*, edited by Henry Louis Gates Jr., 481–91. New York: Meridian, 1990.

———. "Rita Dove: Identity Markers." *Callaloo* 17.2 (1994): 381–98.

Viebahn, Fred. "Rita Dove: A Selective Bibliography." *Callaloo* 31.3 (2008): 804–5.

Vogel, Amber. "Rita Dove." In *Southern Writers: A New Biographical Dictionary*, edited by Joseph M. Flora and Amber Vogel, 109. Baton Rouge: Louisiana State University Press, 2006.

Wallace, Patricia. "Divided Loyalties: Literal and Literary in the Poetry of Lorna Dee Cervantes, Cathy Song and Rita Dove." *MELUS* 18.3 (1993): 3–19.

Waller, Gary. "I and Ideology: Demystifying the Self of Contemporary Poetry."
  Denver Quarterly 18.3 (1983): 123–38.

Walsh, William. "Isn't Reality Magic? An Interview with Rita Dove." *Kenyon
  Review* 16.3 (1994): 142–54.

Walters, Jennifer. "Nikki Giovanni and Rita Dove: Poets Redefining." *Journal
  of Negro History* 85.3 (2000): 210–17.

Walzer, Kevin. "Rita Dove's Ascent." *ELF: Eclectic Literary Forum* 6.3 (1996):
  142–54.

Ward, Scott. "No Vers Is Libre." *Shenandoah* 45.3 (1995): 107–19.

Wheeler, Leslie. "Rita Dove: The House Expands." In *Poetics of Enclosure:
  American Women Poets from Dickinson to Dove*, 138–57. Knoxville:
  University of Tennessee Press, 2002.

Wiseman, Laura Madeline. "Rita Dove: A Woman of Many Words."
  Empowerment4Women: The Online Magazine (2005). http://
  empowerment4women.com/culture/the_feminist_experience/rita_
  dove%3a_a_woman_of_many_words/ (accessed March 11, 2010).

Harryette Mullen

Beall, Emily P. "'As Reading as If': Harryette Mullen's 'Cognitive Similies.'"
  Journal of Literary Semantics 34.2 (2005): 125–37.

Bendall, Molly. Review of *Trimmings*, by Harryette Mullen. *Antioch Review* 51.1
  (1993): 154.

Bendient, Calvin. "The Solo Mysterioso Blues: An Interview with Harryette
  Mullen." *Callaloo* 19.3 (1996): 651–69.

Bettridge, J. "Harryette Mullen's *Sleeping with the Dictionary* and *Blues Baby:
  Early Poems*." *Chicago Review* 49.2 (2003): 160–64.

Crawford, Margo. "Preface: Erasing the Commas:
  RaceGenderClassSexualityRegion." *American Literature* 77.1 (2005): 1–5.

Crumpacker, Caroline. "Licked All Over by the English Tongue: An
  Interview with Harryette Mullen." *Double Change* 3 (2001). http:///www
  .doublechange.com/issue3/mullensint-eng.htm (accessed March 22, 2010).

Cummings, Allison. "Public Subjects: Race and the Critical Reception of
  Gwendolyn Brooks, Erica Hunt, and Harryette Mullen." *Frontiers: A Journal
  of Women Studies* 26.2 (2005): 3–36.

Dargan, Kyle. "Everything We Can Imagine: An Interview with Harryette
  Mullen." *Callaloo* 30.4 (2008): 1014–16.

Frost, Elisabeth. *The Feminist Avant-Garde in American Poetry*. Iowa City:
  University of Iowa Press, 2005.

———. "An Interview with Harryette Mullen." In *Innovative Women Poets:*

An Anthology of Contemporary Poetry, edited by Elisabeth Frost and Cynthia Hogue, 191–207. Iowa City: University of Iowa Press, 2006.

———. "Review: Breaking the Rules." *Women's Review of Books* 10.5 (1993): 11–12.

———. "'Ruses of the Lunatic Muse': Harryette Mullen and Lyric Hybridity." *Women's Studies: An Interdisciplinary Journal* 27.5 (1998): 465–81.

———. "Signifyin(g) on Stein: The Revisionist Poetics of Harryette Mullen and Leslie Scalapino." *Postmodern Culture: An Electronic Journal of Interdisciplinary Criticism* 5.3 (1995). http://muse.jhu.edu/journals/ postmodern_culture/v005/5.3frost.html (accessed March 10, 2010).

Griffin, Farah, Michael Magee, and Kristen Gallagher. "A Conversation with Harryette Mullen." Electronic Poetry Center, The State University of New York at Buffalo (1997). http://wings.buffalo.edu/epc/authors/mullen/ interview-new.html (accessed March 11, 2010).

Harris, Reginald. "Harryette Mullen's Abecedarian Dreams." *Oyster Boy Review* 17 (Fall 2003). http://www.oysterboyreview.com/issue/17/Harris R-Mullen.html (accessed March 11, 2010).

"Harryette Mullen." In *Ecstatic Occasions, Expedient Forms: 85 Leading Contemporary Poets Select and Comment on Their Poems*, edited by David Lehman, 162–67. Ann Arbor: University of Michigan Press, 1996.

Henning, Barbara. "Coast to Coast: An Interview with Harryette Mullen." *Poetry Project Newsletter* 161 (April–May 1996). http://myweb.brooklyn.liu .edu/bhenning/mullen.htm (accessed March 11, 2010).

Hinton, Laura, and Cynthia Hogue, eds. *We Who Love to Be Astonished: Experimental Women's Writing and Performance Poetics*. Tuscaloosa: University of Alabama Press, 2001.

Hogue, Cynthia. "Interview with Harryette Mullen." *Post-Modern Culture — An Electronic Journal of Interdisciplinary Criticism* 9.2 (January 1999). http://muse.jhu.edu/journals/postmodern_culture/v009/9.2hogue .html (accessed March 11, 2010).

Hoover, Paul. "Stark-Strangled Banjos: Linguistic Doubleness in the Work of David Hammons, Harryette Mullen, and Al Hibbler." *Lenox Avenue: A Journal of InterArts Inquiry* 5 (1999): 71–85.

Huels, Mitchum. "Spun Puns (And Anagrams): Exchange Economies, Subjectivity, and History in Harryette Mullen's *Muse & Drudge*." *Contemporary Literature* 44.1 (2003): 19–46.

Jordan, June. "The Difficult Miracle of Black Poetry in America, Or Something Like a Sonnet for Phillis Wheatley." In *Some of Us Did Not Die: New and Selected Essays*, 174–86. New York: Basic Books, 2002.

Kane, Daniel. "Interview with Harryette Mullen." In *What Is Poetry? Conversations with the American Avant-Garde*, 126–37. New York: Teachers and Writers Collaborative, 2003.

King, Rosamond S. "'Word Plays Well with Others.' Harryette Mullen's *Sleeping with the Dictionary*." *Callaloo* 26.2 (2003): 536–38.

Luck, Jessica Lewis. "Entries on a Post-Language Poetics in Harryette Mullen's *Dictionary*." *Contemporary Literature* 49.3 (2008): 357–82.

Mix, Deborah. "Tender Revisions: Harryette Mullen's *Trimmings* and *S*PeRM**K*T*." *American Literature* 77.1 (2005): 65–92.

Mullen, Harryette. "Drinking Mojitos in Cuba Libre." *Callaloo* 26.1 (2003): 89.

———. "Nine Syllables Label Sylvia: On Plath's 'Metaphors.'" *Chain*, 1997.

———. "Poetry and Identity: Harryette Mullen." In *Telling It Slant: Avant-Garde Poetics of the 1990s*, edited by Mark Wallace and Steven Marks, 27–31. Tuscaloosa: University of Alabama Press, 2001.

Myers, Christopher. "Harryette Mullen with Christopher Myers." *Index Magazine* September/October, 1999. http://www.indexmagazine.com/interviews/harryette_mullen.shtml (accessed March 11, 2010).

Rankine, Claudia, and Juliana Spahr, eds. "Harryette Mullen." *American Women Poets of the 21st Century: Where Lyric Meets Language*, 400–20. Middletown, Connecticut: Wesleyan University Press, 2002.

Rowell, Charles H. "Harryette Mullen: A Collective Force of Burning Ink." *Callaloo* 22.2 (1999): 417–26.

Spahr, Juliana. *Everybody's Autonomy: Connective Reading and Collective Identity*. Tuscaloosa and London: University of Alabama Press, 2001.

Thomas, Lorenzo. Review of *Sleeping With the Dictionary*, by Harryette Mullen. *African American Review* 36.4 (2002): 697–99.

Walker, Alice. "The Diary of an African Nun." In *Children of the Night: The Best Short Stories by Black Writers, 1967 to the Present*, edited by Gloria Naylor, 296–99. New York: Little, Brown, and Co., 1995.

Williams, Emily Allen. "Harryette Mullen: 'The Queen of Hip Hyperbole': An Interview." *African American Review* 34.4 (2000): 701–7.

Williams, Tyrone. "Review: *Recyclopedia* by Harryette Mullen and *a half-red sea* by Evie Shockley." *Callaloo* 30.4 (2008): 1122–26.

Zapf, Harald. "An Othering of Language: Harryette Mullen's Experiments in Transpoetry." In *Another Language: Poetic Experiments in Britain and North America*, edited by Kornelia Freitag and Katharina Vester, 173–86. Berlin: Lit Verlag, 2009.

Thylias Moss

Bunge, Nancy L. *Master Class: Lessons from Leading Writers.* Iowa City: University of of Iowa Press, 2005.

Campo, Rafael. "Sturdy Boxcars and Exploding Pickle Jars." *Parnassus: Poetry in Review* 21.1/2 (1996): 341–51.

Deming, Alison Hawthorne. "Review: Walking on Rough Water." *The Women's Review of Books* 21.10/11 (2004): 18–19.

Frost, Elisabeth. "Review: Countering Culture." *Women's Review of Books* 11.6 (1994): 11–12.

Jarman, Mark. "The Curse of Discursiveness." *The Hudson Review* 45.1 (1992): 158–66.

Moss, Thylias. "Bubbling." Oregon Literary Review 2.2 (2007). http://orelitrev .startlogic.com/v2n2/MossBubble.pdf; http://orelitrev.startlogic.com/v2n2/ OLR-moss.htm.

———. "Contemplating the Theft of the Sow: An Appreciation of Galway Kinnell's 'Saint Francis and the Sow.'" Modern American Poetry. http:// www.english.illinois.edu/maps/poets/m_r/moss/essays.htm (accessed March 11, 2010).

———. "Project Genealogy." *Countermeasures: A Magazine of Poetry and Ideas* 7 (2003).

Newson, Adele S. Review of *Last Chance for the Tarzan Holler,* by Thylias Moss. *World Literature Today* 72.4 (1998): 837.

Pettis, Joyce. *African American Poets: Lives, Works and Sources.* Santa Barbara: Greenwood Press, 2002.

Pope, Jacquelyn. "Review: *Red Summer* by Amaud Jamaul Johnson and *Tokyo Butter* by Thylias Moss." *Callaloo* 30.4 (2007): 1110–13.

Selinger, Eric Murphy. "This Personal Maze Is Not the Prize." *Parnassus: Poetry in Review* 24.2 (2000): 77–117.

Shapro, Dan. "The Raggedness of Interacting Boundaries . . . An Interview with Poet Thylias Moss." *Lily: A Monthly Online Literary Review* 1.7 (June 2004). http://freewebs.com/lilylitreview/1_7mossinterview.html (accessed March 11, 2010).

Silberman, Eve. "Thylias Moss: A Poet of Many Voices and a Spellbinding Delivery." *Michigan Today* 27.3 (October 1995). http://www.ns.umich.edu/ MT/95/Oct95/mt8095.html (accessed March 11, 2010).

Simeone, Michael. "On 'Crystals.'" Review of *Crystals,* by Thylias Moss. *Modern American Poetry* (2004). http://www.english.illinois.edu/maps/ poets/m_r/moss/crystals.html (accessed March 11, 2010).

Steinman, Lisa M. "Review: *Uses of Enchantment*." *The Women's Review of Books* 16.6 (1999): 16–17.

"Thylias Moss." In *Ecstatic Occasions, Expedient Forms: 85 Leading Contemporary Poets Select and Comment on Their Poems*, edited by David Lehman, 158–61. Ann Arbor: University of Michigan Press, 1996.

Waniek, Marilyn Nelson. "Review: A Multitude of Dreams." *The Kenyon Review* 13.4 (1991): 214–26.

Werner, Craig. *A Change is Gonna Come: Music, Race, and the Soul of America*. New York: Plume, 1998.

Winston, Jay. "The Trickster Metaphysics of Thylias Moss." In *Trickster Lives: Culture and Myth in American Fiction*, edited by Jeanne Campbell Reesman, 131–47. Athens and London: University of Georgia Press, 2001.

Cornelius Eady

hooks, bell. "Homeplace: A Site of Resistance." In *Yearning: Race, Gender, and Cultural Politics*, 41–49. Boston: South End Press, 1990.

Jones, Patricia Spears. "Cornelius Eady." *BOMB* 79 (Spring 2002). http://bombsite.com/issues/79/articles/2479 (accessed February 22, 2010).

Lorde, Audre. "The Master's Tools Will Never Dismantle the Master's House." In *Sister Outsider: Essays and Speeches*, 110–13. Freedom, Calif.: The Crossing Press, 1984.

———. "Poetry Is Not a Luxury." In *Sister Outsider: Essays and Speeches*, 36–44. Freedom, Calif.: The Crossing Press, 1984.

Peseroff, Joyce. Review of *The Gathering of My Name*, by Cornelius Eady. *Ploughshares* 17.2–3 (Fall 1991). http://www.pshares.org/issues/article-detail.cfm?intArticleID=3174 (accessed March 11, 2010).

Peters, Erskine. "Cornelius Eady's *You Don't Miss Your Water*: Its Womanist/Feminist Perspective." *Journal of African American Studies* 2.1 (1996): 15–31.

Pettis, Joyce. *African American Poets: Lives, Works and Sources*. Santa Barbara: Greenwood Press, 2002.

Rich, Adrienne. "Notes Toward a Politics of Location." In *Blood, Bread, and Poetry: Selected Prose 1979–1985*, 210–32. New York: W. W. Norton, 1986.

Trethewey, Natasha. "About Cornelius Eady." *Ploughshares* 28.1 (Spring 2002). http://www.pshares.org/issues/article-detail.cfm?intArticleID=7470 (accessed March 11, 2010).

Ullman, Leslie. "Review: To Speak on Behalf." *The Kenyon Review* 14.3 (1992): 174–87.

Wright, Carolyne. "Review: Five Short Reviews." *The Iowa Review* 27.1 (1997): 183–88.

Cyrus Cassells

Barber, Jennifer. Review of *Beautiful Signor*, by Cyrus Cassells. *Harvard Review* 14 (1998): 143–44.

Barrax, Gerald. "Review: Unfamiliar Territory." *Callaloo* 20 (1984): 141–47.

Furtado, K. "Poetry by: Cyrus Cassells, Mark Doty, and J. D. McClatchy." *Harvard Gay and Lesbian Review* 5 (1998): 50.

Jiménez, Mary Francis. "Interview with Cyrus Cassells." *African American Review* 43.1 (Spring 2010): 69–77.

Pereira, Malin. "An Interview with Cyrus Cassells." *Contemporary Literature* 44.3 (2003): 387–98.

———. " 'The Poet in the World, the World in the Poet': Cyrus Cassells's and Elizabeth Alexander's Versions of Post-Soul Cosmopolitanism." *African American Review* Special Issue on the Post-Soul Aesthetic 41.4 (Winter 2007): 709–25.

Purdy, Gilbert Wesley. Review of *More Than Peace and Cypresses*, by Cyrus Cassells. *Eclectica Magazine* 10.1 (January/February 2006). http://www .eclectica.org/v10n1/purdy_cassells.html (accessed February 22, 2010).

Waniek, Marilyn Nelson. "Review: *What the Soul Remembers*." *Callaloo* 20 (1984): 148–52.

Werner, Craig. *A Change Is Gonna Come: Music, Race, and the Soul of America*. New York: Plume, 1998.

Elizabeth Alexander

Alexander, Elizabeth. "The Negro Digs Up Her Past: *Amistad*." *South Atlantic Quarterly* 104.3 (Summer 2005): 463–80. http://saq.dukejournals.org/cgi/ reprint/104/3/463 (accessed March 11, 2010).

Brooks, Gwendolyn. *Blacks*. Chicago: The David Co., 1987.

Hong, Cathy. "Dream of Reason." *Voice Literary Supplement*, Oct 2001.

Jeffers, Honorée Fanonne. Review of *Antebellum Dream Book*, by Elizabeth Alexander. *Black Issue Book Review*, November/December 2001: 44.

Jones, Meta DuEwa. "Who is the Self Rooted in Language?: An Interview with Elizabeth Alexander." *The Writers Chronicle* 39.2 (October–November 2006): 28–36.

Keenan, Deborah, and Diane LeBlanc. "An Interview with Elizabeth Alexander." Graduate Liberal Studies Program at Hamline University on October 3, 2002.

Lynch, Doris. Review of *Antebellum Dream Book*, by Elizabeth Alexander. *Library Journal*, January 2002: 86.

McLane, Maureen. "Lives in Verse: Stark, Dreamy, and Cool." Review of

Antebellum Dream Book, by Elizabeth Alexander. *Chicago Tribune Book Review*, February 10, 2002.

Mullen, Harryette. "Reviews of *Arcade* by Erica Hunt and *Body of Life* by Elizabeth Alexander." *Antioch Review* 55.4 (1997): 500–1.

"Our Twenty-five Favorite Books of 2001." *The Village Voice*, December 4, 2001. http://www.villagevoice.com/2001-12-04/news/our-25-favorite-books-of-2001 (accessed March 11, 2010).

Pereira, Malin. " 'The Poet in the World, the World in the Poet': Cyrus Cassells's and Elizabeth Alexander's Versions of Post-Soul Cosmopolitanism." *African American Review* Special Issue on the Post-Soul Aesthetic 41.4 (Winter 2007): 709–25.

———. "Sister Seer and Scribe: Teaching Wanda Coleman's and Elizabeth Alexander's Poetic Responses to Sylvia Plath." *Plath Profiles* 1 (August 2008): 280–90. http://www.iun.edu/~plath/vol1/index.shtml.

Philip, Christine. "An Interview with Elizabeth Alexander." *Callaloo* 19.2 (1996): 493–507.

Philips, Robert. "O Lost!" Review of *Antebellum Dream Book*, by Elizabeth Alexander. *Hudson Review* 55.1 (2002): 156–52.

Review of *Antebellum Dream Book*, by Elizabeth Alexander. *Publishers Weekly*, July 23, 2001: 68.

Review of *Body of Life*, by Elizabeth Alexander. *Tribune Books*, April 1997: 3.

Review of *The Venus Hottentot*, by Elizabeth Alexander. *Poetry*, July 1991: 233.

Review of *The Venus Hottentot*, by Elizabeth Alexander. *Small Press Review*, October 1991: 10.

Review of *The Venus Hottentot*, by Elizabeth Alexander. *Voice Literary Supplement*, June 1990: 8.

INDEX

academe: black experience in, 220; influence of, 173–74, 232; teaching in, 156–57. *See also* education
Academy of American Poets, 10, 47, 71, 163, 244
acting, 201–202, 204–205
Africa, 29, 140, 150, 233–34, 236–38, 242
African American: creativity, 185; experience, 165, 169, 183, 185, 188, 194–95, 206–208, 210; groups, 179; literature, 175; poetry, 166–68, 170–78 passim, 189, 191, 203, 206, 210; students, 175–76. *See also* black Americans
African American Review, 108, 218
"African Beneath the American, The" (Coleman), 42
African heritage, influence of, 83, 88, 121, 141
African Sleeping Sickness (Coleman), 12, 13, 18, 20, 26, 35, 41
Ai, 42, 115, 119, 123, 134, 206
Akhmatova, Anna: "sistuhwomon," 18
Alexander, Elizabeth, 1–2, 4–6, 53, 57, 60, 67, 115, 119, 172, 216–42; *American Sublime*, 57, 217–18, 231–41 passim; *Amistad*, 57, 217, 231, 236–37, 239; *Antebellum Dream Book*, 1, 218, 221, 225–26, 228; art, 222–25, 228; Elizabeth Bishop, influence of, 217, 224; *The Black Interior*, 175, 218, 222; Covey, 237–

38; *Diva Girls*, 218; and Rita Dove, 219–20; fantasies and dreams, 228, 232; female agency, 221; female body, 220–22; grandmother, 223–24, 229, 242; home, 225, 229, 232–35, 240; identity, 217, 240–42; languages, 234–35; loss and trauma, 239; "Manhattan Elegy," 224; Middle Passage, 231, 236; and Toni Morrison, 217, 226–27, 237; mother, 217, 224, 226, 228–29, 234–36, 240–42; "Neonatology," 228, 237; and Sylvia Plath, 225–26; sexuality, 220–22; Anna Deavere Smith, influence of, 238–39; as teacher, 228, 230; travel, 224, 234–35; *The Venus Hottentot*, 216, 218–20, 222, 239; "Visitor," 224, 233
American Poet, 113–14
American Sonnets (Coleman), 10, 12, 19–20, 29
American Sublime (Alexander), 57, 217–18, 231–41 passim
Amistad (Alexander), 57, 217, 231, 236–37, 239
"Amnesia Fugue" (Coleman), 20
Angelou, Maya, 9; *A Song Flung Up to Heaven*, 9
"Annabelle Lee" (Poe), 56
Antebellum Dream Book (Alexander), 1, 218, 221, 225–26, 228
anti-ars poetica, 190
archetypes, use of, 58, 64, 198
Arizona State University, 69

LaVergne, TN USA
19 November 2010
205486LV00003B/7/P